A Commentary on
ACTS

UNLOCKING THE NEW TESTAMENT

A Commentary on
ACTS

David Pawson

Anchor Recordings

First published in Great Britain in 2014 by
Anchor Recordings Ltd
72 The Street, Kennington, Ashford TN24 9HS

**For more of David Pawson's teaching,
including MP3s, DVDs and CDs, go to
www.davidpawson.com
For further information,
email info@davidpawsonministry.com**

Map in Appendix:
Reprinted by permission of
HarperCollins Publishers Ltd ©2003

ISBN 978-1-909886-40-7

Printed by CreateSpace

Contents

This book is based on a series of talks. Originating as it does from the spoken word, its style will be found by many readers to be somewhat different from my usual written style. It is hoped that this will not detract from the substance of the biblical teaching found here.

As always, I ask the reader to compare everything I say or write with what is written in the Bible and, if at any point a conflict is found, always to rely upon the clear teaching of scripture.

David Pawson

INTRODUCTION

In this brief Introduction we will look at who the book is by, who the book is about, who the book is for, and why we should read it.

Acts was written by a doctor. We know very little about Luke, but we do know that he was a medical man and a scientist. It is rather wonderful that God chose a man with a scientific turn of mind to give us an account of the beginnings of the church, as if God wanted to make quite sure we got a careful, accurate, precise account of what actually happened. Details in the narrative are accurate. The description of Paul's shipwreck has been checked by naval historians and every little aspect is correct.

We know that Luke was a friend and companion of the great missionary Paul, and part of Acts is a personal diary. Again and again, the word, "they" changes to "we" and we are dealing with something very personal. But the most important thing we know about the writer of this book is that he is the only writer in the whole Bible who was not a Jew but a Gentile. It seems God wanted a Gentile to write the account of how the good news was taken from the sacred capital of the world, Jerusalem, to the secular capital of the world, Rome.

Who is it about? It is volume two of a two-volume history of the beginnings of Christianity. Volume one is the Gospel of Luke and that is about Jesus, but who is Acts about? I know that the title says "Acts of the Apostles", but it is the acts of a few – Peter and Paul in particular. The first half centres around Peter, the second around Paul, but I am not sure that "Acts of the Apostles" is the best title for this book. You could call it "The Acts of Jesus, Part Two", and indeed Luke begins by saying that he had written one volume already about all that Jesus began to do, and now we are shown that this is what he continued to do.

So it is still Jesus busy doing things, and as we go through this book we will notice a remarkable parallel between Luke and Acts. They both have Mary the mother of Jesus in the first chapter. They both move rapidly to the time when there is a baptism of the Holy Spirit. They both then move on to preaching, then to miracles of healing, then to growing opposition building into a crisis, and a trial. I am going to call this book "The acts of the Holy Spirit through the apostles". The Holy Spirit is mentioned forty times in the first twelve chapters alone.

Who is this book *for*? It is addressed to one man and his name is rather unusual: Theophilus. At the beginning of the Gospel of Luke he is called "Your Excellency" which suggests that he was a rather highly placed Roman official and that he was interested in Christianity, and that this medical doctor had the opportunity to present him with this account.

We can go a little further than that. One of the most speculative but intriguing suggestions that has been made is this: when Paul was finally on trial in Rome for his life, Luke wrote down for the Roman authorities a true account of Christianity so that Paul might not be misunderstood by Roman justice. That is speculation, but there is one very strong reason for making it: both the Gospel of Luke and Acts are at pains to show that the Roman authorities were not against Christianity, and that even though Jesus was crucified under a Roman order, it was acknowledged to be unjust; and, throughout both volumes, all the Romans are presented in a wonderful light. Have you ever noticed that? The centurions are always great fellows and very sympathetic to the Christian faith.

Time and again the Romans get Paul out of trouble, and it is as if Luke was saying to the Roman authorities: you have nothing to fear from this new religion; it is not anti-Roman, it is not subversive, not illegal, and even though you have heard that the Romans put its founder to death, it was really the Jews who were responsible. And it does seem that Luke is writing for a highly placed Roman official, but a man with that unusual name Theophilus (which may even be a nickname), meaning either "a man who loves God" or "a man who is loved by God". We are not quite sure which. We can sum it up by saying: a man who is friendly with God. It seems that Luke is writing to a man with some interest in God, who is seeking God and wants to love God with all his mind.

Luke was sending him Volume Two, explaining what Jesus continued to do with his other body. What Jesus did was change bodies. During the Gospel period he had his own body on earth. At the ascension he took that body to heaven. How could he continue acting on earth? The answer is: by using another body on earth; by using the eyes and the ears and the mouths of other people, and the church is his body that has continued his work.

How could *they* do what *he* did? The answer is very simple: he did what he did by the power of the Holy Spirit. All that was needed for his ministry to continue on earth was a new body given the same Holy Spirit whom he had received at his baptism, and that is the story of Acts in a nutshell. The whole meaning of Acts is this: when people on earth are filled with the same Holy Spirit that Jesus had, they can do the same things. They can continue his work on earth, and that is the thrilling reason for reading this.

Why should we read Acts? Three reasons: first for our *enlightenment* – there are many things you will not understand unless you study it. It is the link between the Gospels and the epistles, and you won't understand the epistles unless you read and study this link. It is the beginning of the church. Don't you want to know how it all began? Some people think it was a crazy idea to have a church. I have heard people say that if we could abolish the church we could have real Christianity. But whose idea was the church? Who started it in the first place? The answer is that Jesus did.

Secondly, we need to read it for our *encouragement*. The church started with twelve people, one of whom was a failure, reducing that bunch to eleven people for the whole world. And when they met on the day of Pentecost there were 120 – only one person for every thirty thousand Jews, to say nothing of the Gentiles. Yet within three hundred years, the whole Roman empire was officially Christian. If you want some encouragement, read this book. If you think that we are up against it and in difficult times, read this book. If you think that we are small and can do so little, read this book.

A third reason for reading it is for our *emulation*. I believe that in the Acts of the Apostles God has given us the pattern of church life that we need. I believe we see here what the church ought to be. If we could get back to the kind of church they were then, our communities would know about it. If we could discover their secret and discover how to be the kind of church they were, what could happen in your town?

1

Jesus Departed and Judas Replaced
Read Acts 1

Acts 1 is a prologue. It is the story so far, the introduction to all that is going to happen in the rest of the book. From one point of view, one would love to plunge in to chapter two, yet that would be a little too much for anybody, and it was too much for the disciples to plunge straight into Pentecost. They needed a breathing space after the cross and the resurrection, those wonderful six weeks when Jesus kept teaching them the Bible and eating with them. Now they were given ten days of quiet, earnest prayer and waiting, and that prepared them.

The contents of Volume One, the Gospel of Luke, are very briefly summarised in the first few verses of chapter one. But the chapter consists of two main sections: *the ministry of Jesus continued* and *the ministry of Judas continued*. In the case of Jesus, he changed bodies. In the case of Judas, he was replaced by someone else. But the work of God goes on and it did not stop when Jesus ascended to heaven.

You will never understand Christianity until you see that God is three persons in one. Every time a Christian prays, all three persons are involved: the believer is praying *to* the Father, *through* the Son, *in* the Spirit. If you are going to get anywhere in the Christian life, it will be as you learn to give each person of the godhead his rightful place, to see that God the Father, God the Son and God the Holy Spirit are all involved in your life and seeking to help you in different ways.

Luke now indicates that one of the greatest things Jesus ever did was to *teach*, which he began to do from the very beginning of his ministry, immediately he had been baptised and gone to Galilee. Luke says, "I've told you about all that he began to do and to teach", but you notice he says he did this *through the Holy Spirit*. The Holy Spirit was active in the teaching of Jesus. He was able to convince people of the truth because the Holy Spirit enabled him to do so, and if we are ever to convince anyone of the truth of the gospel, we shall have to do it the same way as Jesus did: through the Holy Spirit.

Jesus not only taught them until he died, he taught them during the vital six weeks between Easter and ascension. During that time he taught them more about the scriptures than during the previous three years. From the road to Emmaus onwards you find that Jesus was opening the Law, the Psalms, the Prophets, the whole Old Testament, until they could handle the scriptures properly. He told them everything in the Old Testament that referred to himself. Those must have been wonderful Bible studies! I would have given anything to have shared in those. Imagine having Jesus give you a Bible study!

After his resurrection he not only taught them things about the kingdom of God, as Luke says, he gave them many infallible proofs that he was alive. It was absolutely vital that the church start with a group of people who were utterly convinced so that they could never be unconvinced that Jesus had conquered death. There are those today who are saying, "It doesn't really matter whether Jesus rose from the dead or not, as long as we try to follow his teaching and try to live as he would have us live" – but it *does* matter. If Jesus didn't rise from the dead we might as well close our churches; I would be wasting my time preaching. It was vital that they should have infallible proofs, and our faith rests on proof – on evidence. It rests on fact. It is not a shaky faith, and it started with a group of people whom Jesus had taught before and after death, and who were convinced that he was alive.

I have heard many preachers say that the resurrection turned the frightened disciples into flaming apostles who went everywhere and preached. I want to qualify that. It was not the resurrection that did that, but Pentecost. They didn't go out and preach after the resurrection, however joyful they were. They could not have done. It is very important to realise that it is not just knowing that Jesus is alive that will help you to be a witness – you need much more, as they did. So, from speaking of the *teaching of Jesus*, Luke moves on to remind them of the *promise of the Father*. When was this promise made? Way back in the days of the first baptist, whose name was John.

John had plunged (immersed, baptised) people in water as a symbol of their repentance, their desire to wash away the past and to start clean. But that only dealt with their past. You need much more than that if you are going to be all that God wants you to be. You need to be plunged – immersed – right into the Holy Spirit. John said that he could not do that, but there was somebody coming after him who could. God had said to John: when you have baptised someone in water and you see the Holy Spirit come down on them, you will know that is the one who can plunge people in the Holy Spirit. We know that the day came when Jesus was baptised in the Jordan, and after his baptism he stood waiting and praying. John saw something white in the sky. It took the shape of a dove and it came right down on Jesus. John knew from that day that Jesus was the one who could take a human being and plunge him right into the Holy Spirit.

Jesus said that was a promise of God through John. Jesus had told them, and he told them again, that in a few days' time God would keep his word, and they would be plunged into the Holy Spirit as formerly they had been plunged into water by John the Baptist. In other words, what he is saying was that his followers needed two baptisms. There are those who are baptised in water and hope that this will bring them power. They are then disappointed to discover that it doesn't. It brings joy and it brings peace when you have done God's will. It also brings temptation, because Satan attacks those who are baptised, as he did Jesus, but that baptism in water cannot bring *power*. What the promise of the Father meant was that to the baptism in water would be added a baptism in Spirit that would bring real power.

Jesus said that this baptism would be theirs in a few days. So already, in just five verses, you have: Jesus, his teaching and his resurrection. God the Father and his Word and his promises, and now you have baptism in the Holy Spirit. All three persons of the Trinity involved, and the church would never have got going without all three. The church is not just a bunch of people who believe in God. If that were all it is, then it would be no different from any other religion in the world. The church is unique because it is the church of God the Father, the Son and the Holy Spirit. To put it another way: it is the family of the Father; the flock of the Son, and the fellowship of the Spirit and all through the New Testament the three persons are involved.

Now the disciples had to wait. That meant waiting *on* the Lord as well as *for* the Lord. The word "wait" in scripture is a wonderful word. It means positively *seeking* for it and *praying* for it to happen. "Those that wait on the Lord shall renew their power, their strength. They shall rise up with wings as eagles'." That doesn't just mean those who sit down in an armchair and wait. Mind you, that can renew your physical strength and a rest may be what you need from time to time, but the "waiting" here is not just sitting doing nothing. It is waiting earnestly, expectantly, with open hands, and we have a picture of 120 people who knew how to wait on God – they "waited" by praying together. Time and again, when you come to the word "wait" in scripture that is what it means – get together and ask him to do something about it.

The second section, vv. 6–11, which are primarily concerned with the ascension, could be labelled *the kingdom, the power, and the glory*, and you will see why in a moment. This section stretches our horizons in two directions: to the furthest end of the earth, and to the highest point in heaven. One of the temptations of the Christian is to become parochial – bound up within the four walls of his own little church – and to get a terribly small view. From our own church we should be able to see to the uttermost parts of the earth, and to the highest point in heaven, by faith. Our Lord was now going to teach them to get big views but, alas, what called forth his comments was the fact that they had such a narrow view. He had been speaking to them for six weeks about the kingdom of *God*, but they wanted to know when they were going to have the kingdom of *Israel*. Jesus did not say that he was never going to restore the kingdom to Israel, because that would not be true – he *is* going to do so. The Jews at that time wanted freedom. The disciples would be given power, but not power to get their little country free. Jesus was stretching their thinking. They would be plunged into the Holy Spirit and they would get power to go out to the whole world and witness to him.

The phrase "to be my witnesses" is very interesting. It means: *you will have the power to convince people about the truth of what you know of me*. That is a power that we need desperately. We talk to our neighbours; we try and talk to a group of people about Christ. We try to answer their questions, but we just cannot convince them of the truth, and Jesus is the truth. What do we need? We need *power* to do this. He would drop the power of the Holy Spirit into those disciples, and the ripples would spread out – Jerusalem, Judea, Samaria. "Samaria?" Jews were not on speaking terms with the people of Samaria! "And the uttermost parts of the earth." This is the pattern of the book of Acts. It begins in Jerusalem, it goes to Judea, it goes to Samaria, then it goes out into the then known world. This is the programme for the church today and it is still far from complete. Two thousand years later, Christ is still waiting for his church to do the one thing he told it to do the very moment he left the earth.

Out of some six thousand languages and dialects, there are still many in which there is no part of the Word of God. He is still waiting for us to do this, and even though the gospel has gone to many parts of the earth, there are still many people who have never heard about Jesus Christ. Why are we interested in missionary work? Is it because we are trying to civilise savages? No, it is because we are followers of the Lord Jesus and he told us to do this.

A Christian should always live on a world map. I heard of a lady in America who moved from a lovely home into a very poor basement to live so that she could support a missionary in the field herself. Somebody visiting that little basement said to her, "Oh, dear me, that beautiful home you had – don't you miss that lovely view?" because out of her main window she could only see a brick wall and then the pavement above. She said, "Do you know, from this window I can see the whole world?" That was the kind of vision Jesus was trying to give the apostles here: "the uttermost parts of the earth".

Now the *glory of heaven* – Jesus lifts their eyes up to the heights by going up himself.[1] No man has really been in space yet, except Jesus. Every astronaut who tries to go up there has to take enough of earth's atmosphere and food with them. Jesus is the Lord of the whole universe, and the very last words he uttered then were: "... the uttermost part of the earth." As their eyes looked out, they had to start looking up – because up he went, right into the clouds. I remember standing on the Mount of Olives once. It was a glorious, sunny day, but there were some lovely cumulus clouds coming, and the sun caught them. I stood up there and I remembered the words: "He is going to come back in the clouds in the same way in which he went." I could have said: "Come Lord, now, I'm ready for you." It was so wonderful to be there, in the very spot where they watched him go up.

Then Jesus disappeared. The angels were there when he first came to earth and when he went back to heaven. He was going back to highest heaven to sit on the throne. He was going to prepare a place for us, and he was going to pray for us. He was going home, having been away for thirty-three years. That is where he is, where his home really is – he was going home to his Father. So they were left gazing up. I don't know if they remembered the transfiguration when the cloud disappeared. I don't know if they expected him to come down again right then. I rather think they did, because there are the angels, who, funnily enough, say, "Don't look up into heaven because he's coming back again" – which sounds a bit contradictory at first, but what they are clearly implying is that there is going to be an interval. Their words mean: he has gone to heaven, now there is a job for you to get on with – back to Jerusalem, wait, pray and, when the power comes, get out to the uttermost parts of the earth. There are certain texts in scripture which suggest that the gospel must first be preached to all the nations before the end can come, and that by getting on with the task of spreading Christianity we are in fact hastening the day of his coming. The missionary task of the church is tied up with the end of history. The more we get on with that, the more sure we can be that his coming is near.

Now there is a glimpse of the kind of people who were the first 120 members. There were more followers of Jesus than this, but most of them would be back in Galilee by this time. There were at least five hundred who met him after the resurrection, but here we have 120, and that was what the church started with. The apostles are all there, bar one. Peter is already the pastor of the church. He is the leader, and I believe that when Jesus said "On this rock I will build my church" he was giving Peter a unique place (though I don't believe that Peter had any successors). When Jesus said to Peter "Feed my sheep" he was saying that he was making him the first pastor of the church. Sure enough, Peter is the pastor here and giving the lead, even before Pentecost. I notice that John is second, James third—the three in a circle of Jesus. Five of the eleven were probably physical relatives of Jesus. It is wonderful that Jesus started his church with so many of his own relatives. Consider the women —the other religions of the world first gathered a group of men. Now Christianity certainly began with men and it should continue with men, but from the very beginning women were vitally part of the fellowship. Among them was Mary, not at the front to be worshipped but sitting among the congregation, praying, like everybody else. The last glimpse we have of her in scripture is sitting in a meeting with the other believers. That is where we ought to place her in our thinking – as one of those who prayed, and as one of those who was filled with the Holy Spirit on the day of Pentecost, and she entered a new ministry. The Holy Spirit had come on her body thirty-three years previously. Now the Holy Spirit filled her again and she was to become a witness to her own son. Did you ever think of Mary doing this? Mary the mother, and his brethren – what a lovely touch.

There had been a time, only three years earlier, when his own brothers came to take Jesus home and lock him up, because they said he was beside himself, that there was something wrong with him – thinking he was the great "I am". Now here were his own brothers saying that the person they had lived with, who helped them as children, who ate and slept on the same floor and the same mattress – this person is God. Of the 120, quite a large proportion, perhaps ten percent of the early church, were the physical relatives of Jesus, and I find that marvellous, showing the effect of his life on his own family – and they were waiting, praying. Jesus had said to them years before: "If you know how to give good gifts to your children, how much more will your heavenly Father give the Holy Spirit to those who go on asking him." So the 120 met every day and prayed. I hope that you will meet and wait on God and say: "God, you have promised to give us power – we need power; will you do it?"

The second half of the chapter is much more briefly dealt with. It is the ministry of Judas continued. No-one could have invented this strange story. Peter is taking the role of pastor, but you will notice that he now calls all the 120 "brethren". We ought to use that term. We are brothers and sisters in Christ. People ought to see this in our behaviour toward one another and in our conversation. Peter stood up with all the brethren and told them that they ought to be replacing Judas.

Notice that he was not suggesting this simply because Judas was dead, otherwise when James died they would have replaced him and we would still have had twelve apostles. But there is no apostolic succession. There cannot be. They were unique, but Judas had lost his place and had forfeited his right, and they did not even expect him now to be among the twelve in heaven. So they had to replace him. Why did there have to be twelve? Two reasons, and this is where we get our guidance. Firstly, it was clearly the intention and desire of the Lord Jesus to have twelve, and it is clear why. He was building a new people of God to be his missionaries. Israel was made up of twelve sons, men who became the twelve tribes. He was going to start all over again with twelve new men. There was another reason. Peter was now beginning to get his orders from the scriptures he had been studying, which not only said that Judas was going to betray our Lord, but also that they should give his office to another. This is the beginning of Christian guidance: discover what the Lord intends and what his Word says. That is the general principle established, now comes the problem of *particular* guidance. Which one? This little section is a wonderful picture of how to find the will of God. You start by asking: "What is the desire of the Lord Jesus?" Then you ask, "Is there anything in scripture that bears directly on this situation?" and you will usually find some general principle stated there that helps you. Then comes the problem of how to apply it in your particular situation, and you now go to two more things. The thing many people then omit is to consult the church. Many get into problems with guidance because they will use the phrase "I feel led" and then act on it, but a good way to check guidance is to ask the advice of experienced Christians. How much heartache would be saved if we went to the church and discussed it – with all the sanctified commonsense God gives us!

So, having established the general principle that the Lord wanted twelve, and the scriptures told them to replace Judas, Peter now goes to the church and they discuss it very sensibly. They knew there were certain qualifications needed. It ought to be someone who had known Jesus as long as Judas had. It should be someone who had known Jesus before his death and after his resurrection, and then he could become a witness with them.

Now it is patently obvious that we cannot have apostles of this kind today. There can be no "successors" for very soon all would be dead who knew Jesus during his earthly life and in his resurrection. But after discussing things reasonably and sensibly they boiled it down to two possible replacements who were qualified, so now they come to the final stage. How did they find out which of these two should be chosen? In some churches today, the way deacons and officers of the church are selected is like this. You start from the understanding that it is the intention of the Lord to have certain people. You seek the guidance of the scripture as to what kind of job it is and how they are to act, then you go to the church and say: you study and look out those men whom you feel are qualified for this – and then still there is choice. How do you go to the next step? Here comes the surprise: they cast lots—they probably put the names on stones into a bag, then drew one out. Now this seems a surprising way. Is it an appeal to chance? No! They are doing this for two very good reasons: firstly, casting lots puts the decision out of human hands; but, secondly, they believed that God is almighty and that he can control lots. They were creating a situation in which God could exercise his control. All the way through the Old Testament this was how they chose the rota of priests.

So should we have dice every time at our church meetings? No! This is the very last occasion on which lots were cast. Why? Because from the day of Pentecost there was a more direct way of finding out what God wanted. When people are inhabited by the Holy Spirit, he can bring the answer into their minds – directly, without any lots. So a church can pray and know what to do. Of course, we need to be filled with the Spirit and sensitive to his guidance, or else our own ideas start creeping in.

After the day of Pentecost they chose by voting with their hands instead of lots, and they sought the direct guidance of the Holy Spirit. The whole principle is that for office in the church, it must be God's choice, not the church's. He must have the last word on whom he wants, and then and only then can we be sure that he is going to bless.

Though two of those disciples, Matthias and Barsabbas, were perfectly well qualified, one was God's choice. We never hear of either of them again, nor do we hear more about at least half a dozen of the apostles.

I have the picture here of a church that has so much and yet not enough: a church that is studying the Bible; a church that believes in Jesus and knows that he is alive; a church filled with joy, and filled with faith; a church that has seen the death and resurrection of Jesus and understands the meaning of those events; a church of 120 men and women who are eager to do everything that God wants them to do, but they are not doing it. What is missing?

You will never turn the world upside-down until you turn the church inside-out! How do you do this? How do you get a church praying? How do you get a church reaching out? How do you get a church that is on fire for the Lord and wants to bring all its neighbours to a love of the Lord Jesus? Bible study will be part of it. Believing in Jesus will be part of it. Joy and faith will be part of it. The death and resurrection of Christ will be at the centre of it. But there may still be something missing. The answer is to be found, very simply, in the third person of the Holy Trinity. It is only when a church begins to understand what it is to be filled with the Holy Spirit that it gets "inside out" and reaches out in power and effectiveness. God is the same today, and we need this power if we are going to witness effectively.

Note

[1] For a detailed study of the ascension, see the author's book *Where is Jesus Now – and what is he doing?*

2

The First Pentecostal Outpouring
Read 2:1–21

What does the "day of Pentecost" mean? The word means "fiftieth" and it was the fiftieth day after the Passover Feast. This day was special and had a double significance. It was a "harvest festival" when the first loaves of bread made from the barley harvest were offered to God — the first fruits. How very significant that the very first fruits of Christian mission should come on that day. Secondly, Pentecost commemorated the day when God gave the Ten Commandments to Moses on Mount Sinai. But within a very short time that Law had been broken and 3,000 people lost their lives. It is a remarkable contrast that when God gave the Spirit, 3,000 people were saved. It is as if God was going to tell us in a new way that what you need is not a list of commandments to keep – you need the Spirit within you. So this was the time, and it was nine o'clock on a Sunday morning in the year AD 29.

Where were they gathered? Now many people think that Pentecost happened in the upper room. There is nothing in the Bible to suggest this, and when we study the evidence it is quite clear that it happened in the temple. The evidence for this is as follows. First of all, they were in a very public place. Secondly, it was nine o'clock in the morning on a feast day, and every devout person would be in the temple at that time. Thirdly, we are told that the early Christians met every day in the temple at the time of the prayers, and the first prayers were at nine o'clock in the morning. Fourthly, in spite of the idea that they all went rushing out of the upper room into the streets, not one of those 120 people moved an inch. The 3,000 came to them. Did you ever notice that? You couldn't get that many into the upper room. In fact it says all they did was to stand up. It was the multitude that came running, so it must have been a huge place where thousands could gather. The only place that fits is the temple, and if somebody points out that it is called a "house" you will find in Acts 7 that the temple is also called a "house" there. Imagine 120 people in one of the porches of the temple, that magnificent building, at the time of Pentecost when there were a large number of visitors to the city camping on the hills all around and coming in each day. Here is a crowded city, a most critical time, a wonderful place, and now we come to the most important part – the heart of it. If somebody cut out Acts 2, we would not understand the rest of this book. It would not make any sense unless we knew what happened on this day.

Now we look at three things: the *experience* they had; the *excitement* it caused; and the *explanation* that Peter gave. First: what was the experience? I have studied so many books on this, but if I went on reading more I should get thoroughly confused! Once, at Cambridge, I was given by my tutor the task of writing about what happened on the day of Pentecost. I looked up the opinions of some forty scholars. After reading them all I was more confused than ever, and I came to the conclusion that very few of them had any experience themselves of what this was all about, but when we look at the Bible it is such a simple, lovely, and meaningful experience that I wonder why I was puzzled.

Let us look at what the Bible actually says happened. It is better to stick to the one book. Here were 120 people waiting. Their minds were filled with knowledge of the scriptures, their hearts full of prayer and love for each other – 120 people waiting for something to happen, and it was nine o'clock in the morning. It may seem a funny time of day for God to choose. Some people think that most moving experiences take place in the evening, but this was in the hard, cold light of morning – they were not meeting in misty shadows for some mystical experience. In their country it was rather like our Monday morning. So what do you think can happen to you at nine o'clock on a Monday morning? It is not the time we go in for deep spiritual experiences, but this is what happened here. We can divide this into what they *heard*, what they *saw* and what they *did*.

What did they hear? The answer is that *within* the building – not outside it or up in the sky but within the walls of the porch where they were sitting – they heard a gale. It blew all around them and they heard it quite distinctly. It was the beginning of something unusual because you don't normally hear that inside a building, you hear it outside.

You don't know what gales are until you have lived somewhere like the Shetland Islands! I have seen graveyards there where they lay the stones flat because if they put them upright they will be flat very quickly. A postman was battered to death by the winds while I was there. One of my neighbours went down to the beach in a gale to pull his little rowing boat further up the beach, and neither boat nor neighbour were seen again. I remember sitting at my study window and watching my dustbin cross the road without touching the ground. This speaks of mighty invisible power that can move things. A gale is frightening, and fishermen I knew treated the wind with great respect. They listened to what number gale force it would be. It was a matter of life and death – invisible power. The interesting thing is that the very word for "spirit" in the Old Testament means "gale force breath of God". There are two words for breathing in Hebrew. One is for the quiet breathing which you can't hear, and the other is for heavy breathing like that made by someone who is having difficulty in expelling air, making a noise. Interestingly, whenever the Bible speaks of the breath *of God* it uses the strong, heavy word *ruach*, meaning loud breathing you can hear. This is a sound of air moving forcefully. What some of us need is a howling gale behind us before we will do what God wants us to do. They heard this gale in the house and knew that it was the breath of God. "O breath of God, breathe on us now" — when you sing that you are saying: blow me where you want me to go.

There are a number of things in the Bible that would spring to their minds immediately. There was Ezekiel who had a dream and saw a valley full of bones lying around. God had said, "Do you believe I can do anything with these bones?" Ezekiel said, "I don't know," and God took the bones and fitted them together so they were human frames. Then God said again, "Do you think I can do anything with these skeletons?" Ezekiel said, "I don't know; you know," and God said, "Call the wind to blow on them." Ezekiel prayed for God's wind, and God's gale blew down that valley, and those bones stood up a mighty army. God was saying to Ezekiel: this is what I can do for a dead situation; this is what I can do when it all seems hopeless, when it seems to have ended in the grave; this is what I can do when I blow – when my Spirit blows, dead people come to life, a dead situation becomes alive.

That was what was happening on the day of Pentecost. There is a reference in John 3. A religious teacher of Israel came and had a chat one night with Jesus. They sat on the flat open roof of the house under a cover of darkness because the man was afraid to be seen with our Lord, and there was a wind blowing, as it can up the valleys around Jerusalem. Nicodemus (for that was his name) was holding his coat, and our Lord was probably doing the same. Nicodemus did not understand talk of the Spirit. What did Jesus mean? Jesus talked about the wind. You don't know where it came from, you don't know where it is going to, but you know when it has hit you. It *is* like that with the Spirit of God. You cannot explain, you don't know how, but when he comes to you, you *know*. Nobody can be filled with the Spirit and not know it. Nobody can have the Spirit poured out on them and remain unconscious of this experience.

Billy Graham and his team were going to Glasgow. He was apprehensive about the Scots; he thought they were a tough lot, so he was praying, wondering how the "Tell Scotland" movement would go. Right there in the railway compartment, as they knelt to pray, they heard a gale within the compartment. They heard the wind blowing round the railway carriage and they knew that God was going to work.

What did the disciples *see* on that day of Pentecost? They saw fire. God has time and again through the ages demonstrated his presence in fire. There was the time when Moses saw a bush ablaze with fire and it was not even singed. He realised this was not earthly fire but supernatural fire, and God spoke to him out of that fire. All through the wilderness, for forty years, wherever they walked there was a pillar of fire in front of them as God led them. When Elijah wanted to prove the presence of God to thousands of unbelieving fellow countrymen, he called on him to send down fire from heaven to show them he was still alive.

So on the day of Pentecost when the fire came they knew that God was there. They knew what it meant. It was God's power, God's purity and God's passion coming down on people. The description Luke gives us is remarkable. Tongues of flame! And the flames were upside-down – starting as one flame from the top and coming down, then dividing into little tongues and touching them all on the tops of their heads. It was burning from heaven to earth, not from earth to heaven – burning down, and touching them on the head. That was what he was describing, and not a hair was singed. This was God's fire.

The third thing was what they *did* and this is the strangest of all to many people. Their *mouths* were affected. Now somebody has said that if you are filled to overflowing the main opening where the overflow can take place is the mouth, and I notice that pretty well every time people were filled with the Spirit in New Testament days, they overflowed there, though not always in the same manner. I think this overflow was a mark of being filled with the Spirit.

Let us see what exactly happened. *They opened their mouths and they spoke.* It is at this point that all the commentators get tied up. They speak of ecstatic gibberish. I can think of nothing less likely to come from God's good hand then ecstatic gibberish! Were they losing control of themselves and shrieking? That is the impression some people give and get from this passage. *But it states quite simply that when they opened their mouths they spoke coherent words in languages they had never learned.* It is as simple as that. I wish we could get rid of the word "tongues" because I think that misleads many. I wish we could translate it properly as "languages".

Notice that there is not a word in Acts 2 about their feelings. It is not their feelings that we are concerned with, it is the facts. They opened their mouths and they did something that humanly speaking is absolutely impossible. Supernaturally speaking it is possible because God knows all the languages! There are not only six thousand languages on earth, there are other languages in heaven – the tongues of men and of angels, he knows every one. The significant thing is that they were speaking languages they did not know, so we may now say that in fact God was by-passing their intellect. He was using their mouths, not their minds. Their minds knew one language probably, in the Galilean accent.

So he was enabling their mouths to say something that was not in their minds. That was a miracle, a supernatural event, something that proved God could use ordinary people to do extraordinary things.

I want to underline something even more important: they were not given these languages to speak to men; *they were given the languages to praise God.* These languages were not to make it easier for missionaries. Missionaries have had to slog away at learning the languages ever since. They were not given to preach, because they used them long before the crowd came. Who were they using them *to*? They were using them to God. Here is the crunch and the big question: why on earth should God by-pass a person's mind to give him words from his mouth to praise him? What an extraordinary thing to do! But I can think of a very good reason for it. Isn't your mind one of the biggest blockages in prayer and praise? Time and again, we want to be free to pray, and many of us find that our minds wander. More than that, sometimes we want to pray yet we don't know how to phrase it, our words won't come. We don't know how to keep going though we want to do so. God in his infinite mercy gave them a gift that by-passed the mind and enabled their spirit to address God with their mouths, and to extol and praise him for his mighty works, and 120 people started praising God as they had never praised him before.

We are still not at the heart of the experience. The heart of it is not even this wind or the fire or the languages but, simply, for the first time, God was right *inside* them and had complete control of them. That is the meaning. What can God not do if he fills a person and gets complete control of them? The tragedy is that most of us would have to admit that for most of our time God does not have all of us, only part, and that there are parts he doesn't control.

So the real meaning of Pentecost is this: they had now met

the third person of the godhead. They had always believed in God the Father. They had then met God the Son, and after three years they came to realise that this human being was divine. But the night before he died he said: "Don't worry I am not going to leave you alone, like orphans ... he will not only be *with* you but will be *in* you. They did not understand at the time. The Holy Spirit was not someone outside them whom they could touch. He was going to be someone right *inside them*; he was going to possess them, and control them, and enable them to speak as they had never spoken in their lives. That is what was happening, and the power had come, so these ordinary people could now do extraordinary things. To their heartfelt *prayer* of the previous six weeks was now added *praise*. I would say that this is the first mark of the Spirit-filled life – that they can praise God out of a full heart, they can say "Hallelujah" and mean it. By *nature* we cannot praise God. We can present our prayers, but not our praise. We can come with our shopping list, especially if we are in trouble, but to *praise* God – just to come and tell him how wonderful he is – that is something the Spirit inspires.

The miracle of the opened mouth! They were filled with the Spirit and began to speak. I have probably been as guilty as any other preacher of haranguing congregations and telling them they must witness for the Lord. You can preach that until you are blue in the face, but to the Great Commission of our Lord, "Go into all the world, preach the gospel to every creature", there must be added the *great compulsion* before someone will do it. The Great Commission was not enough to make the disciples open their mouths. They needed the great compulsion from within, and then they did. They were all filled with the Spirit and began to speak! When the great compulsion of the Holy Spirit is inside you, then you do it. That is why they had to wait until Pentecost. You cannot keep such a thing to yourself!

They were on fire for the Lord now, and notice that they didn't have to go out, the people came to them. Why? *Because something was happening.* You find that in churches where things happen, people come. As we have noted, one of the most striking features of Acts 2 is that there isn't a single word about the feelings of the disciples. Never judge spiritual things by your feelings, judge them by the facts, the fruit. But there is quite a lot about the feelings of everybody else, and this is where it gets very interesting. June was the best month of the year for travelling, so it was the best-attended feast of the three main feasts (Passover, Pentecost, and Tabernacles). Three million people came, so the place was crowded! You can imagine 120 people there, praising God at the tops of their voices. Others were not going to ignore that. They would come running: "What's happening?" So thousands came to watch. Three thousand of them were converted, so maybe ten or fifteen thousand came, or even more. Still the 120 went on praising God. Did Peter wonder why there were people watching? He heard what they were saying. Now look at these people – who were they, where had they come from, and what did they think about it all?

Who were they? They were what were called "the Dispersion." There were more Jews living outside the Holy Land than in it, as there still are. They were dispersed around the whole Mediterranean world. They were Jews who had been born Jews; and there were proselytes who had become Jews by being circumcised, baptised and then offering sacrifice; and there were devout men who tried to keep the Ten Commandments, who were not Jews by birth or baptism.

These various groups came to Jerusalem three times a year, and there they were. Furthermore, they had come from north, south, east, and west. The whole world had been concentrated at this time. I find this a most striking reversal of the Tower of Babel. There was a day when God came down in power and confused the languages of men so that they couldn't understand each other, and they scattered. Now God in his infinite mercy has reversed the process. He has come down in power and he has given languages again, but now they come together and understand. It is marvellous how God is able to put right what goes wrong. He is able to offer mercy where formerly he brought judgement. So it is a reversal of Babel, and Genesis 10 describes the places from which these people came in Acts 2.

What did they think of it all? At first they were just curious. If you see 120 people making a din in the streets or in a public building, you would be curious. Then as they came nearer they were surprised because they heard a lot of different languages in this tiny group, and as they came nearer one man from Cyrene said, "You know that's the language we speak back home." Others listened and were surprised to hear their own local languages being uttered.

They would have looked at these people and said: "Galileans!" What they meant was: they have such a strong dialect! Were not all these men Galileans who couldn't even speak Hebrew properly? "Your speech betrays you," said somebody to Peter because he opened his mouth. He was from the north, and they could tell where a person came from. Galileans were speaking many languages! It was a miracle. As they got closer, people heard that they were speaking about God. Then they began to be afraid and perplexed. What did it all mean? They had begun to sense the supernatural, and when people sense the supernatural they don't come closer, they begin to pull back a bit. One lady once said to me, "I hope nothing supernatural ever happens in our church." Considering the reason we come to church, that's a priceless remark. We come to meet the supernatural, to meet God. We come to have things happen to us that nobody else can do for us on earth. We come to have a supernatural touch upon us.

Now at a point like this, when God is very near and supernatural things are happening, you will always get the honest person who will come along and explain it all in a thoroughly earthly manner. "They are drunk, you know." There is always somebody to give you a natural explanation for a supernatural miracle. But I have never known alcohol give anybody any fluency in a foreign language they have never learned!

So we come finally to the explanation Peter offered. Jesus had made him the first pastor, the leader of the church. Here was Peter who had been a reed, but he was now the rock,[1] filled with the Holy Spirit. He stood up to lead the church and he *preached*. I love the way he began. By the way, notice the eleven stood up with him. They didn't take a single step, they stood up where they were, and presumably the other 108 stayed praying and went on praising God in tongues. Peter saw the crowd that had come, he saw them running away a bit, and he saw his opportunity. "Listen! Men of Judea and Jerusalem, come here. Pay attention to me. I'll tell you what it is." He seized the opportunity.

He began in such a delightful way. With almost a touch of humour he was telling them: the bars aren't open yet; it's only nine o'clock in the morning and people don't get drunk at this time; you're quite wrong, they are filled with Spirit, but capital 'S', not small 's'; they're intoxicated with God. There is a remarkable parallel between being drunk and being filled with the Spirit. In both cases you overcome your self-consciousness and talk more freely than you otherwise would. In both cases you are able to establish relationships with others (that is why so many have to have a drinks party before they can talk to their neighbours). The Holy Spirit will make us want to tell others about Jesus and what he has done.

Peter shows that the natural explanation is thoroughly unreasonable, and now his message is this: you are Jews, you have come to this place; you know your scriptures well; this is something that God promised centuries ago and now it has happened. You can almost see Peter pointing to the 108 still praising God – this is that; you have been waiting centuries for this, well it has come.

Of course every Jew had been waiting. Let us go back to the very beginning. In the Old Testament, the Holy Spirit only came on a few people: as far as I can count them, only forty. He only came on them for short periods, not their life, but when he came they did extraordinary things, particularly with their mouths. They prophesied, they were able to speak things that were not in their minds. God's mind came straight through their mouth, and the prophets spoke: Isaiah, Jeremiah, Ezekiel, Amos, Hosea, Micah all spoke through the Spirit. Moses, who himself had prophesied and spoken in the Spirit, was told by a sneak, a telltale who came to him: "Moses, you're the prophet here, aren't you?" Moses said yes, and the man said, "Well, I've got news for you: there are two men the other side of camp, prophesying," and they thought that Moses would be terribly jealous. As if somebody came to me and said, "There are others in your congregation preaching," thinking I would be jealous.

Moses said, "Prophesying, Eldad and Medad"—those were their names. He said, " I would that all God's people were prophets. I wish everybody who belonged to God could be filled with the Spirit and speak." It was only a wish on Moses' lips, but centuries later the prophet Joel said, "God makes a promise to you that in the last days, the last period of human history, he will pour out his Spirit on everybody, on all his people, on all flesh. Regardless of gender, your sons and your daughters will prophesy. Regardless of age, your young men will see visions and your old men will dream dreams. Regardless of class, your menservants, your slaves, they can have it too." This was the great dream of the Old

Testament, a day when not just a few special prophets, but everybody who belonged to the people of God could be filled with the Spirit and open their mouths and have God fill their mouths with words. That promise began to be fulfilled on the day of Pentecost.

Peter pointed to what was happening. Look around. These 120 people—your sons, your daughters, old men, young men, maidservants, menservants—look at them; they are all prophesying. They are all having mouths filled with the Word of God. It is a wonderful moment. He continued: Joel said there's going to be a last period in human history, the last days. The beginning of it will be the Holy Spirit poured out in prophecy, and the end of it will be even the heavenly bodies – sun, moon and stars – changing.

That will be the last days, which means we are living in the last period of human history. The signs have come for the beginning of it. We are looking for the signs at the end of it. The moon is going to be blood-red one day, and the sun is going to be turned off and that will be the end of the last days. The last days will then give way to the great and terrible Day of the Lord, when the whole world must meet him, and when he is going to destroy this world which has been so spoiled, and so dirtied, and so stained with sin that he is going to make a new one all over again.

If this sounds gruesome and frightening, let me add, for Joel added it: during that period of the last days between Pentecost and the end of the world, *anybody* who calls on the name of the Lord can be saved. It is as if, having shown them history and even the end of the whole universe, he comes right down to the individual and says "whoever" – just one person. Now is the time to get ready and to call on the name of the Lord.

During these "last days" millions of people have called on the name of the Lord and have been saved. It all started on the day of Pentecost and it has been happening ever since.

Yet far too many Christians are living on the right side of Easter but the wrong side of Pentecost. They understand the death and resurrection of Christ, they know their Bibles, they pray, they are full of joy in believing in the Lord, but somehow they don't yet understand what it is to be filled with the Spirit to overflowing until your mouth becomes the channel of God's Word itself. I believe that the promise still holds, for Peter said, "The promise is to you and to your children, and to those who are afar off. As many as the Lord our God will call to him." That includes me and you, or else God's Word is not true. Those who say that Pentecost is only something of 2,000 years ago to remember yearly, like a centenary, have not read Acts chapter 2 properly, for the promise is to us today.

Note
[1] See the author's book: *Simon Peter – The Reed and the Rock*.

3

The First Sermon and its Fruit
Read 2:22–47

Taking up and applying a prediction given many centuries earlier, Peter preached about a name which – among all the names known on earth – was now the *only* name through which a man or woman could know salvation: *Jesus*.[1] It was a common name in those days. There are seven people called "Jesus" in the New Testament alone. So Peter had to begin by giving his address as well: Jesus *of Nazareth*.

One of the most striking things of all about the preaching of the New Testament is that they did not preach Christmas. I don't know if you have ever noticed this, because when you say "Jesus of Nazareth" or "Thomas of so and so" or "Judas of Kerioth" (that's what Judas Iscariot means), you actually gave the place of their birth, not where they lived. On my birth certificate is my name and where I was born. Now they used to say "Jesus of so and so," and you might think Peter would have said "Jesus of Bethlehem". This is very striking indeed. Why do I mention it? Because "Christmas" never saved anybody. It is interesting that the world perhaps thinks more about things that are in the Bible at Christmas than at any other time. Why is it that they don't get changed? Why is it that they don't get saved? Because the gospel is not the account of the nativity.

What *do* you need to know about Jesus Christ? *First, that he lived – he was a real man. He was in fact a carpenter of Nazareth. You need to know that he travelled around and that one of the main things that he did was to perform supernatural miracles for people.* You need to know that things happened in his life which are only to be explained by saying that God was in this man. He healed the sick, he made blind people see, he made deaf people hear and lame people walk. He even raised the dead to life. He changed water into wine at a wedding reception where they had run out. He stilled a storm at sea because people were in danger of drowning and were frightened. This man went about doing things that only God can do. "This Jesus of Nazareth, God worked through him signs and wonders and miracles...." Peter's hearers would have remembered these things happening. Now of course, we don't remember, we weren't there, but we need to know and believe these things.

Secondly, you need to know that Jesus died on a cross – and that that event at the age of thirty-three was no accident. Before the world began, God had arranged it in every detail. You need to know that among all the crosses of history, and among all the executions, there was one that God had planned for centuries before, and it was the cross of Jesus. You need to know that the Jews so worked things that they managed to get other people to do their dirty work for them, and they managed to get people outside their own law to put Jesus to death for something that was in their law and not in the Roman law. Peter says, "This Jesus, who by the determined plan and foreknowledge of God, was crucified ... you killed through the hands of lawless men." The Jews got the Romans to put Jesus on the cross, but if we ask who decided that he should die like that, the answer is: God.

Straight away, we are up against one of the great mysteries of the Bible. We are clearly shown that there is no contradiction between divine sovereignty and human responsibility. There is no contradiction between God's free will and man's free will, God doing something and man doing something. Both are true: God was responsible for the cross and so were men. The cross was a divine and a human event, when man was doing something evil and God was doing something good. That is why Christians ever since have called it Good Friday, not Bad Friday, because they have seen what God was doing.[2]

If you ask the important question "Why did the Jews want Jesus dead?" the answer is very simply because he said he was two things. It was because he said he was Christ their Saviour, their Messiah, the one they had awaited for a thousand years; and because he said he was Lord, which means he said he was God. Jews said that no man must say that he is God, that is blasphemy, he deserves to die. It was on the charge of blasphemy that they managed to engineer his death.

You need to know, thirdly, that God reversed the human verdict by raising him from the dead three days later.[3] Peter says: "God raised him from the dead, and we are personal witnesses. We met him, we spoke to him, we saw him, and we touched him. You need to know that God said you are wrong about this man, he is my Son. You said, 'He is too bad to live.' He said, 'He is too good to remain in the tomb.'"

At this point Peter went back to scripture. Peter was now a man of the Bible. He had been a fisherman, more at home with nets, when Jesus first met him.

Peter is pointing out that there are things said in the book of Psalms by David which couldn't possibly be true of David because they never happened to him. David was in fact predicting things that would happen in the future. He now quotes Psalm 16 where David ["he", using the personal pronoun] says: "You will not leave me in the grave". But in fact, David had been in his grave for a thousand years. David, in the Psalms said, "My flesh will not see corruption." Yet, in fact there was very little, if anything, left of his body in the grave. So Peter is explaining that David must have been talking about the *Son of David*, the Christ. It is very interesting that the Jews said (and still say) that corruption of the body begins on the fourth day. Lazarus had been in the tomb four days and his sister said, "Jesus, there will be a smell by now because he has been four days in the tomb." Therefore, David's prediction that God's Holy One would not see corruption demands that before the fourth day someone be brought out of their tomb. Peter also explains that they knew someone who was out of his tomb within three days, and that his name is Jesus. You need to know this if you are going to be saved.

The fourth thing you need to know about Jesus of Nazareth if you are going to be saved concerns where he is now. Bear in mind that Peter said this within a couple of hundred yards of the tomb in which Jesus had been buried. One of the proofs of the truth of the resurrection is that Peter would not have dared to say this within two months of the event when he knew perfectly well that all they would need to do to disprove it would be to go to the tomb and produce the corrupting remains of Jesus. No Jew could ever produce the dead body of Jesus, nor could any Roman. Now here is an interesting thought: the Jews and the Romans couldn't produce the dead body of Jesus, but the disciples couldn't produce the *live* body of Jesus. Did that ever strike you? The people could have said, "Well, we know the tomb's empty but you produce the live body, and we will believe you." They could not do so. Why not? Because Jesus was no longer on earth.

The fourth part of the gospel is this: Jesus, having lived on earth, performed miracles by God's power, having died on a cross by God's plan and man's evil action, having been raised from the dead the third day, went back to heaven and is there now at this very moment. We need to know this. Peter then proceeds to give proof of this fact of the ascension of Christ to his congregation. This is how he proves it: they always believed that when the Christ came, the promise that God had made through Joel would come true, and that when the Christ came, God would pour out his Spirit upon all flesh. Peter is saying that it has happened, and that proves not only that Jesus was the Christ, but that when he got back to heaven, the first thing he did was take this promise from the Father and pour the Spirit out upon us and prove he was the Christ. *The Spirit has come as proof.*

He quotes another psalm here, Psalm 110, the psalm most frequently quoted in the New Testament. Once again David sees a vision of somebody other than God whom he yet calls "Lord", sitting at the right hand of God, and all his enemies down below his feet. Peter is declaring that David, king of Israel says there is someone else up there, someone else he calls "Lord". "The Lord [God] said to my Lord, 'Sit at my right hand.'" Now who could David be talking about? Somebody else who is Lord of David, and the answer Peter gives is: "Jesus."

Now we have come to the crunch of the sermon, the statement that sums it all up. Peter says, "I want you, men of Israel, to know this: that the man Jesus whom you crucified, this one man, God has made him Lord and Christ." There are the two things that they didn't believe, the two things that they said were not true, the two things that made people say, "Crucify him." This, then, is the statement that Peter uses to clinch the sermon. They had crucified him because he said, "I am the Lord God", and they said that he wasn't. God had proved that they were all wrong, that this was the greatest crime that has ever been committed, that this is not only the murder of an innocent man but they lifted their hands against God when they lifted their hands against Jesus.

That is why when we talk of Jesus today, we don't talk of "Jesus of Nazareth", we speak of the "Lord Jesus Christ". That is the gospel. If I were to talk only of Jesus as Jesus of Nazareth, there would be no gospel for you. He could do nothing for you today except hold out before you the kind of life you can never live. There are people outside the church who believe in Jesus as a great man, a wonderful character, as perhaps the greatest man who has ever lived, but they have no gospel, no good news. Peter says, "the Lord Jesus Christ" – and that is great news. It means that Jesus is alive, that he is at the right hand of God the Father and he can do something for me.

Such was the heart of the marvellous sermon of an illiterate fisherman who had hardly been to school and couldn't speak his own language properly, and it is one of the finest sermons that has ever been preached. It is centred in the scriptures, it is centred in Jesus Christ—in his life, his death, his resurrection and ascension, which are the gospel. It is Trinitarian in that it speaks of the Father in heaven, Jesus the Son, and the Holy Spirit poured out. Where did a fisherman get to preach like that? Where did he learn this? The answer is that he had been with Jesus, and an ignorant and an unlearned man can preach like this when he has been with Jesus. There is no teacher like Jesus.

Now can you imagine someone coming to you and accusing you of murdering not just a great man but God's own Son? Can you imagine what you would feel like if you realised that it was true? Something would go through you like a knife. You would say, "What on earth can I do? There's nothing for me but the deepest hell if I've done that." Can you imagine how these people felt? Only seven weeks previously they had shouted, "Crucify him! Crucify him!" They had watched people spit on him, making jokes about him and saying, "If you are the Son of God, then save yourself; jump off the cross if you really can perform miracles." They laughed and they mocked, and they had all stood there and watched him stark naked as he died.

Well I think you might imagine how they felt if you begin to realise that your sins crucified Jesus Christ, that those people who jeered and mocked and shouted, "Crucify him!" were no worse than any of us, and that the sins which made them do it – cowardice, envy, other things are the sins that have been in your heart and mind, and therefore you were there when they crucified the Lord. So I say: this Jesus, whom you crucified, whom your sins nailed to the tree, God has made him Lord and Christ. This is God's opinion of Jesus; this is God's verdict on the trial of Jesus Christ. The lower courts said, "Blasphemy, away with him," but a higher court said, "Jesus is both Lord and Christ" (Messiah King).

So we come to the exhortation of Peter. It seems a hopeless situation. A man who realises he is guilty of murdering the Son of God might think that he had committed the unforgivable sin, but he hasn't. Remember that if people who murdered Christ can be forgiven, then you can be too. If there is mercy for those who killed the Son of God, there is mercy for you. A man who says, "Well, I could never be forgiven; I've done too many bad things; I'm beyond redemption" needs to read Acts 2 again, where the murderers of Christ were told how they could be saved. Even on the cross, as they gambled for Jesus' clothes at his feet, he had prayed, "Father, forgive them, for they know not what they do."

Peter gives a wonderful reply, full of hope, full of mercy. There is a complete answer to their crime. There are two things they need to do – *repent* and *be baptised*[4] – and if they do them, there are two things that God will do for them. Isn't that simple? He could have said (but didn't): "Well, do ten years' penance." He didn't say, "Come to church for ten years" or, "Well, try and live a decent life from now on, and try to put right what's wrong." But he didn't. He could have said, "Well, bring a lot of money for the work of the Lord," but he didn't. I can think of a hundred things that he might have said but didn't!

"Repent" —turn right away from your past. Literally the word "repent" in the Greek language means "afterthought" or "think again". Think again about all that you have done; disown it, turn away from it; turn your back on all that; turn right around and come to Jesus Christ, and then express the desire to be utterly cleansed of this thing by *having your whole body washed.* Be washed from head to toe, get it all cleaned up. Come to God and say, "God, I want to be clean." That's what baptism at first expresses. It means much more than that. It means a burial of all your sins, it means being identified *in Christ.* It means lining yourself up with Jesus because you are baptised into the name of Jesus Christ. It means so much.

I do not believe that baptism is an optional extra for any Christian. Peter said on the first day of Pentecost and I don't think the message has changed one bit, "Repent and be baptised, every one of you." This is the normal – indeed it is the *commanded* – way. It is the command of Jesus that this is how we express our coming to him. It is the way that Jesus commanded before he left them, and the way that Peter preached. It is a simple thing, over quickly – just a simple step, yet still people hesitate to be baptised into the name of Jesus Christ. Why? This is the ordained way to come. He didn't say, "Sign a decision card. Come to the front." He said, "Repent and be baptised." This is the way that Christ chose, and if he could go all the way to the cross for us, can we not go into the water for him? This was the way for them and it has been the way ever since.

Peter might have said, "Believe in the Lord Jesus," but they wouldn't have asked the question if they didn't believe already. *Faith alone is not the full response.* The full response in the Bible to the gospel is threefold: *repent, believe,* and *be baptised.* That response is how we are to accept the gospel of

Jesus. It is the total response of a simple believer. Peter knew they believed because they said, "What shall we do?" and a man doesn't say that unless he believes in Jesus. Then: repent and be baptised; complete your response; let there be an act of the will. You have understood with your mind, and you believe that Jesus is Lord and Christ. You have responded with your heart. You are therefore ready for the next two steps of the will: repent, turn away; be baptised, be washed.

"Then," says Peter, "God will do two things for you. *He will forgive your sins.*" Peter Forsyth, the great congregational preacher, once said, "Our churches are full of the nicest, kindest people who have never known the despair of guilt or the breathless wonder of forgiveness." This may be a reason why we don't love him as much as we should, because our love will vary in direct proportion to how much we have been forgiven. It may be that some of us have never been at the point where we see how much we need forgiving. I'll tell you this: those who have been forgiven much, love much.

Those people, then *we* have murdered the Son of God, and God is ready to forgive? He is ready to blot it out as if it had never been? I think one of the loveliest things about God is that he has a power to do something that I haven't the power to do: the power to forget the wrong things you have done. I will remember some of the things I have done to God and to other people until my dying day, as Paul remembered that he persecuted the church. Certain things you have done may come back to mind after twenty years, and you thought you had forgotten them. People have said to me, "Pastor, I can't forgive myself for doing this." The answer is, "Of course you can't, you never will. You can't forgive yourself because you can't forget." But it says in the scripture that God says, "When you are forgiven, I will remember your sins no more," and it means that one day when I meet God I'll say, "God, I really am sorry for doing that," and God will say, "Doing what?" "But Lord, you remember when I did so and so," and God will say, "I don't remember." To think that God can forget! That is what forgiving really is.

That deals with my past when I am forgiven, but I also have a future. What about my future when I am going to do these things again? The answer is, there is another gift. The gift of forgiveness for my past is matched with another gift for the future: *the gift of the Holy Spirit himself.* That deals with my future. Isn't God wonderful to think of everything? I constantly find myself amazed that I still haven't found any need that God hasn't thought about and provided for.

Peter is teaching the crowd that there is no limit to the promise of the Holy Spirit either in time or space: *the promise is to you and to your descendants and to those who are afar off, as many as the Lord our God shall call to him* – which, thank God, means me.

If I believed that Pentecost was over, I should be miserable. If I believed that the Holy Spirit couldn't be given today, I would wonder what on earth we could do about the Christian life – if we could just have forgiveness but not the power; if we could only have our past dealt with but the future remained still in the grip of our weakness. But thank God the promise is *still* to us. Peter went on counselling them with many words: remember this, if you're going to be saved, you'll have to step right out of this generation in which you live, the people around you, they are crooked. Their thinking is crooked; they behave in a crooked way. They are not upright. They have a crooked thinking about God. They have a crooked thinking about Jesus. They have a crooked thinking about right and wrong. Save yourselves from this crooked generation.

I heard a critic of the Christian faith say, "I think it's all wrong that Christians should get the idea that they are to save themselves, or that anybody should be given that idea. It is selfish." He said, "This is what Christians are: a lot of people who are saving *themselves*." My first question would be, "What's wrong with saving yourself?" Now that may sound extraordinary, but there is nothing wrong with it or Peter would never have told them to do it. It only becomes wrong if after saving yourself you don't seek to save others. If I were drowning in the sea, and a man in a boat trying to save people threw me a lifeline and said, "Grab this, quick!" I wouldn't say, "Now look here. This is not really a good motive for grabbing this. There may be others much more deserving than me." That would be foolish – I would grab it, since he was a man who had been helping to save me. But if when I got into his boat I said, "Now come on, let's get to the shore quickly," while there were others in the water, then that would be wrong. I am then in a position to double those who are throwing out the lifebelt. That's what would make it right.

There is nothing morally wrong in a preacher saying, "Save yourselves." Indeed, that's your first concern. You must render your account to God. He will deal with you as an individual. Save yourself from this crooked generation, but *then* seek to save others. Peter let them know that because they were being saved they would find themselves straight in a crooked world. They would be different – social misfits – and everybody needs to be told: "If you get saved you are going to find it difficult living in a crooked generation, but save yourselves rather than go down with the ship."

Now we come to the third and last section. Five verses at the end speak about the expression of this faith: the fellowship of the saints with 3000 converted and 120 Christians to deal with them! I have never seen a situation like that. One Christian to counsel and help 25 enquirers, can you imagine that? It would be wonderful if we each had one during twelve months. If each Christian in England won one other for Christ in twelve months, and those two won two more in the next twelve months, then in some five years England would be entirely Christian! This is the measure of our failure – it is at the moment taking 33 Christians twelve months to win one person for Christ.

Look at five things they *did*, and some things they *were* – a potted account of church membership as it ought to be. The five things they did: *baptism* for everybody as they came into the Christian faith and into the church. This was the way in; this was the normal, natural, right thing to do. The next thing they needed was *food* to grow; *they needed teaching and the apostles taught them*. We don't have the apostles, but we have got their writings, and so today *Bible study* is a must for a new convert. Thirdly, they had *fellowship*. This is something much deeper than friendship. It means not just doing things together but sharing the same thing. They *continued in fellowship*. Fourthly, *the breaking of bread*. That meant having a meal together. It meant sitting down around the meal table and eating as a family, and then at the end of the meal they would take the bread and wine.

Fifthly, they continued in *the prayers*, not just prayer. The prayers would be the Jewish prayers of the synagogue and the temple, prayers they had recited for years but had never truly understood. The prayers had been just words, parrot-fashion. Now they were real as well as read prayers – prayers become living and real after the Holy Spirit has come. Someone can go to church for years and have all the prayers out of the book. They can sing the hymns out of the book, and these are dead words recited. Then, one day, he or she comes to know God, and the Spirit enables them to sing the same words, go through the same prayers, and they are alive and real. They continued in *the prayers*.

Finally, some adjectives about this church. They were a *reverent* church – fear was upon them all. Why? Because supernatural things happened in that church; signs and wonders and mighty works were done. When that happens, people are afraid, and rightly so. God is in this place; it is none other than the house of God, the gate of heaven.

They were a *sharing* church. They even shared their money. It was not communism because it was voluntary. People were quite freely selling their property because some Christians are in need, and money must be given. That is real community, friendship, sharing.

They were a *consistent* church. Do you notice that they were just as happy in the temple and in their homes at their meals? They *praised* God in both. There was no hypocrisy here, it was a *sincere* church. Life was all of a piece. They were a *happy* church with glad and generous hearts.

Therefore, the last verse tells us they were a *growing* church, every single day. If your church continues in baptism, in teaching, in fellowship, in the breaking of bread, in the prayers – as a reverent church with the fear of the Lord in the members' hearts, a sharing church that cares in the name of the Lord, a happy, consistent church, in which we members are just as Christian at home as in meetings, then I believe yours will be a growing church. Notice that it was the Lord who grew the church. A minister and congregation can't make a church any bigger. You might get your name on a church roll, you might become a regular attender, but really the only way to get into the church is to be saved – and the Lord added to the church every single day those who were being saved. There has not been a single day for two thousand years when the Lord has not added to his church.

Notes

[1] In Hebrew the name is Yeshua (the "J" pronounced as "Y"). It is the same as "Joshua" and means: 'God saves" or "Saviour of God".

[2] Jesus probably died on a Wednesday. See Chapter 3 in the author's book: *The Seven Wonders of His Story.*

[3] See the author's book: *Explaining the Resurrection.*

[4] For a complete understanding of what has been called "the Peter principle", see the author's book: *The Normal Christian Birth.*

4

The First Healing and its Explanation
Read 3:1–26

Acts is the beginning that led ultimately to the churches in existence today. Look at how God did it! We can learn a great deal about how to grow churches from studying this book. People outside the church were attracted because so much happened inside it, because the people were so alive, so full of power, so dynamic, so able to do amazing things. Peter never needed to collect a congregation, he usually just preached to the people who came to see what was happening. The man who said that people will always come running when the house is on fire was describing what happened in Acts.

There are two parts to Acts 3, which I label "Healing the sick" and "Preaching the Saviour". Healing and preaching go together in perfect harmony in this chapter. We begin with the man who begged for alms and was given legs. This is one of the loveliest stories of the early church which highlights how alive the apostles were and how they behaved. Outside the temple you would find a group of beggars in need of aid, who had decided that was the best place to get it because they felt that people going to worship God were likely to have a quicker conscience about those in need. At the gate called "Beautiful" was a man who was not beautiful,who had been crippled from birth, who was carried there every day so he got some income. He may have been married, and this may have been the only support for his family. That would be a common pattern if it was the case. Peter and John came for the 3 p.m. prayers. It is very interesting that the apostles and the Christians kept up their Jewish prayers because now those prayers made sense, they were real and meaningful. The beggar saw the two apostles coming and thought he would touch them.

There are two things to say at the outset about the beggar. The first is that he got far more than he asked for. This is how God has dealt with me. Maybe you can say, "This is how God dealt with me, too; I asked him for this and he gave me far more; I asked him for a small blessing and he gave me a big one." Jesus once said that the way God gives to people is this: "Shaken together, pressed down and running over." His words mean that when he gives he fills the measure up with corn, then he shakes it to get it down, and then he presses it down, and then puts more in until it is running over, and then he says: "There it is." You always get more. I remember going to a sweet shop as a little boy where the man always got it up to the quarter pound and then threw an extra sweet in for us—that is how God gives. So the beggar asked for a little bit of money just to get a little bit of bread for another day, just to live a little bit longer, and he was given perfect health.

The second thing to note about the beggar is that he got the means to get what he asked for. He didn't get any money but he got the means to get money. It put him in a position to get employment – to go out and work in a vineyard or shop or something. Very often I have found in my life that when I have asked God for something he hasn't given me that, he has given me the means to get it, and this somehow alters the picture. It helps us to see that God answers prayer in different ways. We may say, "God, we need £20,000 and we are just going to go on praying." Maybe we will see a cheque float down from heaven, but God may answer our prayer by saying, "I'll give you the means to get it." This is another answer to prayer, and a more wonderful one. This man got indirect help. He would no longer be able to beg, he would no longer be able to scrounge. He would now have to work and earn, and it was a wonderful thing.

Look at the apostles. The thing that strikes me most about Peter and John was this: they had no human resources but all the divine resources. They were working men. They had nothing in their pockets to give. Peter said, "I've got something I can give you. Look me in the eyes, fasten your attention on me." Then he said something wonderful: "In the name of Jesus of Nazareth, get up." Do you realise the significance of that to the beggar? It was only two months since the whole of Jerusalem had been ringing with the words "Jesus of Nazareth". The words had been printed on a piece of board and nailed to a cross. Everybody knew he had been crucified – and this beggar would know it. It was the talk of the town. Here is a man two months later saying: "In the name of the man you heard was put on a cross, get up and walk." There is power in a name, depending on the position of the person whose name it is. Just occasionally someone might say to me, "If you want to go to such and such a place, use my name." I haven't found that works when the person is dead. It is a live person with authority and power whose name gets you places. Here is Peter saying, "In the name of Jesus of Nazareth get up and walk," and then Peter puts his hand out and says, "Come on, I'm going to lift you up." The man stands up and he tries a first step, and then a second, and the next minute he is leaping around. No wonder a crowd gathered. Especially when they recognised a man who had been like this forty years, since the day of his birth, and there he is running and jumping and praising.

We turn our attention now to the power that did this, and I want to define that power. Peter was always finding himself having to explain to the crowd what was going on. He was always having to tell them it wasn't what they thought it was but something else. He had earlier had to explain they were not drunk, but they had been affected by the Holy Spirit. On this occasion he is saying: you think we have some special power? You're staring at us as if we're different; we're just ordinary people; we don't have any magic secret, don't think that it is our piety.

Nowadays, certain people are canonised as saints, and it has to be proved that their piety has produced at least two miracles first. I don't know what Peter would have thought of that! I would point out that there was no medical means here, and it was a doctor recording the event. Here is a healing that is not medical and not magical. It is something else – miraculous – and Peter is letting the people know this: it's not we who have done this, it is the God you have worshipped, your God, the God of Abraham, Isaac and Jacob, the God you have said prayers to, the God you have sung hymns to; I want you to know that he has done it through Jesus; it is the name of Jesus that is the power we have got, and faith in Jesus' name that has brought this man perfect health.

Doctors have sometimes used a placebo, which simply means a substance which doesn't do patients any good at all but the patient thinks it does, and that can help. Such is the power of the mind over the matter of the human body that just to have faith in something like that may make a difference. There are different kinds of healing, but the healing here is *by faith in the name of Jesus*. It is not faith in Peter or John.

So we have to ask: *who* is this Jesus? This name must have power because he has position, and the higher the position the more the power. Jesus has the highest position in the universe and that is why the name of Jesus will get you further than any other name. Do you want to get to heaven? Use the name of Jesus. There is no other name will get you there. Do you want forgiveness from God? Use the name of Jesus. Jesus taught: when you pray, use my name and my Father will do it for you. Using the name of Jesus is a holy privilege and an awful responsibility because there are some prayers which would be such a contradiction of his nature that you could not use his name. You have got to be careful in using the name of Jesus that you use it for those things that *he* would use it for, and that may not be for the things that *we* would use it for. So Jesus' name is bound up in all this and it is no wonder that Peter goes straight on to a sermon about Jesus, to tell them about him.

We have already noted that the name "Jesus" was commonly used in that period, but this name for Christians has become unique. There is no other name anywhere near this. This is what we sing and what we believe. What does this name stand for? Not just for a man who lived, not just for a good man who went about helping people. Peter is saying that it stands for a man who died a most terrible death. This is Peter's second sermon and, a bit like other preachers, he sometimes repeats himself. So his sermon follows a very similar pattern to the sermon on the day of Pentecost. He begins with our Lord's passion and death. He left the people in no doubt that it was the most terrible crime that has ever been committed – that men should prefer a murderer to Jesus; that men, knowing that Pilate said he was innocent, should demand his execution. Jesus came to bring people life, and they murdered him at the age of thirty-three. The author of life and they killed him, and they did it in ignorance. Jesus prayed, "Father, forgive them for they know not what they do." Peter, in this sermon, says, "I know that you acted in ignorance as did your rulers. If you had known who you were handling like this you would never have done it." People are indifferent through ignorance.

If they had known that it was God's love they were throwing back in his face, they might not have done what they did. It was an ignoble, ignorant human act, but Peter says that it was God's act too. He knew it was coming. He told us that it was coming. He not only foreknew it, he foretold it through the prophets who told of the sufferings of Christ. So it was not a tragedy, it was something that God used, and God reversed the verdict. Peter is telling them: we are witnesses; we saw you put him to death; we saw God raise him to life; we saw you condemn him; we saw God acquit him; we saw you put him out of the world; we saw God put him back into it. We are witnesses against you.

So there is Jesus' *passion* and the next thing Peter talks about is his *person*. Jesus has some 250 names and titles but Peter gives six in this sermon. To the Jews they would mean a lot. He calls Jesus *God's servant*. Now that doesn't convey anything to us today, but Jews knew that seven hundred years earlier Isaiah had said, "There is going to come a man who is God's servant who will save people from their sins." One of the most wonderful chapters about that servant includes these words: "He was wounded for our transgressions, bruised for our iniquities, the chastisement of our peace was upon him, and with his stripes we are healed. A man of sorrows and acquainted with grief." Peter was saying he has come.

The second title does not mean much to us today: *the holy and righteous one*. It means someone who is perfect. Now you try saying, "I know a man who is perfect," and see what happens! But Peter is getting up and saying, "I know one who is perfect, utterly holy and utterly righteous and it is this person Jesus." But to the Jews this again would speak of the one who God promised to send. The "Prince of life" means, literally: "the trailblazer, the pioneer, the one who will open a way to eternal life". Peter is saying: you took the one who is to bring eternal life and you killed him, but he is still alive; you can't kill off the prince of life. He calls him *the Christ* and this means the one whom God has anointed to be King.

Peter calls him *the seed*. Way back in the beginning, God

said to Adam: "I will defeat Satan through the seed of the woman." To Abraham, God said: I will fulfil this promise through your *seed*. Christ is the fulfilment of the promises to Adam, to Abraham and to everybody else. What is Peter saying in all these titles, these names? He is saying that you can take all the threads of the Old Testament wherever they are, and they all lead to Jesus. The whole of the Old Testament, everything you read in those pages, is a thread that leads to Jesus if you follow it.

Peter finishes this magnificent sermon with the *purpose* of Jesus. What is Jesus doing? What has he come to do? Now it is quite obvious that there are many things that this promised Christ, our Saviour, was said to do in the Old Testament that didn't happen in the New; they didn't all come about when Jesus came. This was a perplexing thing to many disciples. The answer is so simple: Jesus is going to come twice. He came once for certain things and he is going to come again for others. On his first coming, says Peter, he came only to do two things: to get your sins wiped out, and to give you a refreshment of spirit. Thank God he accomplished those two things.

When I took weddings I used special record ink which has an acid in it which eats into the paper. It cannot be unwritten once it has been written. In ancient times they wrote on papyrus with ink that had no acid in it, so you could take a wet sponge and wipe it off, and nobody could tell what had been written. *Peter says that when Jesus came the first time it was that our sins might be wiped out.* Just think of the joy of knowing that things that I have done have been wiped out and nobody can ever see what was written – that is forgiveness. The refreshment of the spirit is that he has restored my soul and leads me in the paths of righteousness for his name's sake.

The *second* coming is the last thing Peter mentions and his message means: don't worry about all the other things that he didn't do – he is coming back; the heavens have received him until the time for the restoration of *all* things – a new heaven and a new earth. God is going to scrap this universe and start all over again. So a Christian is someone who looks back to the first coming and looks forward to the second.

Now comes the most serious word. Peter says: Moses told you that this man was coming. He told you to listen to everything he said, and that those who refused to listen would be destroyed from among the people. Now, he has come to you Jews first.

It is a wonderful thing to be a Jew. Some years ago a lady came to see me after a service and said, "I'm a Jewess," and I replied, "It's wonderful to meet you, someone who belongs to the people of God." She said, "Have you been trying to say in the pulpit that Jesus is the Messiah I'm waiting for?" I said, "Yes, that's what I believe." We looked together at one or two scriptures and her face lit up. She said, "You mean he's been." Within minutes she knew more about him than I did because it had been built into her history. To the Jew belongs all the history of God. They have got everything but Jesus, and that is why they only need to realise he is the Christ and then they are far ahead of any converted Gentile. That is why Saul of Tarsus was so dramatically changed when he realised Jesus was the Christ. That is the one key they need to unlock all their beliefs and all their history. So Peter can teach that this promised Christ was Jesus of Nazareth and he was given to you first – listen to what he has to say, repent and turn from your wickedness.

It is the name of Jesus that has power, so never use another name. Don't ever say, "Come and hear David Pawson." I'll tell you what will happen if you do, it will be one of my off days and the person will say, "Well I don't know what you get excited about." Don't say, "Come to the Baptists."

We don't do things in the name of the Baptists. People all through the ages have been tempted to use others' names and there isn't power in those names; they are just human names and nicknames. The only name that has this power is the name of Jesus. Why? Because Jesus was the one who came from highest heaven to lowest earth, all the way down to the bottom, was obedient even to death on a cross, and God has lifted him all the way back up again. This Jesus who has been all the way down and all the way up again is the Jesus who has complete authority all the way, at every level.

5

The First Arrest and Trial
Read 4:1–31

The proof that we live in an evil world is that anybody who goes about doing good will sooner or later get into serious trouble. The supreme example of this is the life of our Lord Jesus himself. He went about doing good and within weeks he was in serious trouble. It started when he healed a man with a withered hand. Early in Mark's Gospel we find opposition developing. Just as our Lord's ministry in his own body developed that way, one would expect his ministry in his next body, the church, to do the same thing. Therefore, very quickly in Acts, doing someone good leads the disciples into trouble.

Jesus had promised this to his followers. He never asked anybody to follow under false pretences. He said if you follow me you will be in trouble. If you follow me, the world will hate you as it hated me. If you follow me, you will be different. You will be social misfits and because of this you will be disliked. The other thing he said was: "When you get into trouble, don't worry. The Holy Spirit will tell you what to say, he will be your advocate and defend you, and he will tell you what to say in answer to the charges that will be made against you."

All that occurred very quickly and we are reading about it in Acts 4. It was the first time that Christians were ever charged with the crime of being Christians, and there has not been a single period of ten years ever since when Christians have not been charged with this. We live in a day when thousands upon thousands of Christians have been brought into court, thrown into prison, and executed for no other crime than the name of Jesus. So this is right up to date.

I have divided the chapter into four parts. First of all, there is the *arrest*. Why were they arrested and put into custody? I have tried to give three answers to this, and they are still the same answers as to why Christians are regarded as criminals, just as our Lord was regarded as a criminal. First of all, they *disturbed the peace*. I forget the circumstances, it was either a house to house visitation or I had gone in to a pub to talk to somebody about the Lord Jesus, and a man said, "Why can't you leave us alone in peace?" Christians have one rather nasty facet to their faith in the eyes of others and it is this: "I don't mind your holding this faith, but why do you have to think that I must hold it too? Why did you have to come and disturb us? You believe that, fine; I believe this. Let's leave each other alone; let's respect our privacy."

Now the captain of the temple guard had the job of keeping public order in the temple. Whenever a crowd got too big it was his job to break it up – particularly when Galileans led it, because they were notorious rebels. All the resistance movement to the Romans came from the north, in Galilee. So when the captain of the guard saw a large crowd gathering around some Galileans – disturbance of the peace! There was a danger here that the routine and order of this place was going to be disturbed, so he was party to the arrest of Peter and John. To this very day Christians will always be viewed with the suspicion that they might disturb the peace and order of life as it is. We deserve that reputation because wherever Christians have gone they have been a disturbing element.

The second reason comes from the priests, for they too were party to this. The reason why they supported the arrest was that the disciples were *disturbing their power*. They were the official teachers. They were in charge of the religious views of the people. They had been to theological college.

They had been specially trained, they had even inherited their position. The teaching of the people in religious matters was their monopoly and they were going to hang on to it. But here is a bigger congregation than any of them ever had, listening to some Galilean fisherman. So we are told the believers were arrested because they were teaching the people – in the priests' eyes they should not have been doing that.

The main reason why they were arrested came from the theologians, the Sadducees — wealthy, aristocratic, rationalists, who by collaborating with the enemy occupying powers now controlled the whole situation and the whole nation. The Sadducees did not believe in anything supernatural. They were the new theologians of their day. They could not believe in miracles, they even denied the possibility of resurrection from the dead. They controlled from the top, they were above the priests. The reason why they supported the arrest was that Peter and John were *disturbing their prejudice*. They had a prejudice against miracles; they had a prejudice against the supernatural. They were rationalists, and they didn't like the apostles teaching the resurrection of the dead, which cut right across their 'new' theology.

So I can see how the apostles got arrested. They disturbed the peace, they disturbed the power of the people — the monopolies, and they disturbed the prejudice of those who closed their minds to certain truths. The interesting thing is that the very next sentence after the arrest says that the church grew to five thousand men. Maybe one of the reasons why the church in England is not growing is that we are not arrested more often.

When I visited churches in West Berlin, and then went through and visited churches in communist East Berlin, I found there were more real Christians per head of population in East Berlin than in West, and we pitied them! But the church has always thrived under opposition. The blood of the martyrs has always been the seed of the church. Where the going is tough, Christians rise to the challenge. So they were arrested and the church grew. They were put in prison and multitudes believed. People could see that here were people ready to go to the utmost limit for their faith.

The church had five thousand men and you can add the women and children, and we come to a church of probably ten or twelve thousand within weeks of Jesus' death on the cross. It is magnificent to see how the church grew in those early days. Nothing can stop the gospel.

We come now to the trial, vv. 5–12. The first thing I notice is that this is the same court in which about three months previously Jesus had stood. There on the bench are the identical judges who cruelly and unjustly put him to death.

Both trials are similar. Both began without a real charge. In both cases, quite unjustly, the prisoners were asked a leading question, the answer to which would incriminate them from their own mouths. Annas and Caiaphas had not changed a bit, they were going to do it all over again. So the scene is set: imagine two fishermen, Peter and John, against the wealthiest, most educated, most influential people in the whole nation. They don't stand a chance. They are given no counsel for the defence, no advocate; they are on their own. Yet they are not on their own, they have the best advocate you can ever have – the Holy Spirit. If you have him you don't need to worry. Who is up against you? You are on the winning side.

So we now see what happened. Peter doesn't just defend himself, he is not even bothered about that now. He knows – or at least the Holy Spirit reveals to him – that the best form of defence is attack. The whole situation reverses until Peter and John become the judges and everybody else, all the seventy sitting in the Sanhedrin, are in the dock. It is a most amazing performance. In just ninety Greek words here, a minute or so of speech, he puts all the judges in the dock. He says first, "Are we charged with the crime of helping a cripple?" Now think of the effect of that on the court. Just one sentence: are we being examined because we helped a helpless man? Is that a crime – to help the helpless? Do you recall something about the early ministry of Jesus? The first time Jesus ran into trouble, when he healed the man with the withered hand, he said to his accusers: "Is it lawful to do good or evil? To save life or to kill?" In other words: is it a crime to help someone? Now that's the first thing that Peter said, and that alone would have been enough to throw the case out of court. Is it a crime to do good?

Secondly, his words meant this, and we might paraphrase the points he makes: If you want the one who did this, it's Jesus. I accuse you of murdering the Messiah, but you didn't succeed in getting rid of him because God raised him from the dead. We had no power to heal this man; it's not our name that we used, we used the name of Jesus. If he is dead this would not have happened because the name of a dead person has no power, only the name of someone who is alive.

So Peter completely turned the tables. Only the Holy Spirit can give a man such brilliant argument, such amazing, unanswerable logic. That was Peter's defence and I don't think anybody could have improved on it. I don't think the greatest lawyer in the land could have put up a better case.

It was at this point that Peter added two more things about his own faith in Jesus. He quoted Psalm 118:22 and the verse he quoted is a picture of a man building a large house. He is wanting the most important stone, which is the head of the corner – what we nowadays called a header. He looks for a large stone to put at the foundation of the corner of two walls on which the two walls may rest and be built – the key stone. In a sense if you pull that out then the whole building tumbles and becomes useless. It must be absolutely right, it must be square and firm, and then the building will stand. The builder will look at a block and say, "No, I can't use that," then throw that stone away and use another. Another man may come along and say, "Well, I think I could use that stone, and I will make it the head of the corner in my house," and he would use the stone and build on it. Psalm 118 says: "The stone which the builder rejected has become the head of the corner." That psalm is all about the Messiah who wasn't to come for a thousand years. Peter is saying: you could not fit Jesus into your religion, your system, he had too many awkward corners in your sight, so you said, "Crucify him, away with him." God took this Jesus and has built everything on him. He is building a new faith—and the foundation is Jesus. This is a very wonderful picture.

This is one of the problems that every missionary faces when they come up against another religion. We now come to the most exclusive verse in the whole of the New Testament. Christianity is an exclusive religion. What do I mean by that? It is *inclusive* in that, as Peter said on the day of Pentecost, whoever calls on the name of the Lord shall be saved. It is as inclusive as the "whosoever believes" of John 3. But the *exclusiveness* is this, "In no other name is there salvation." You cannot mix our faith with any other faith. There have been inter-faith events at which representatives of different religions all read little bits of their religious writings. Some have predicted that this is the new world faith that is coming. I believe that it is. I believe that one of the biggest dangers we are going to have to face is that there will be an ecumenical movement among all religions to come together into one religion. Christianity won't fit. They will have to reject Christ because that stone doesn't fit the building. Because he doesn't, it's either Christ or every other religion; it can't be both. So the same Peter who said, "Whoever calls on the name of the Lord shall be saved" said, "Listen, among all the names under heaven there is one, and only one, whereby a man can be saved."

A group of people from all world religions gathered together, including a Christian missionary. Each was asked, "What can your religion give us that no other religion in the world can give us?" The missionary said, "Forgiveness." That is a profound answer. I have spoken to Muslims and said, "Do you know that you are forgiven? Are you sure that you are on your way to heaven?" They are not, they hope so; they are trying hard.

It is not just other religions. There is a religion in this country called "Churchianity" and it uses the name of a church, and it seeks to save in the name of church. Talk to a "churchian", talk to someone who has gone through all the ritual, who goes to church and pays up regularly on the nail and supports the church, and ask them, "Do you know that your sins are forgiven? Is heaven yours? Have you the guarantee within your heart that you are saved?" You will find they don't know either. There is no other name given among men whereby we must be saved – *only* one.

Here is Peter speaking at his own trial, and he is preaching the gospel. He is more concerned about their salvation than his own safety. He is more concerned about their forgiveness than his own freedom, and this is how he talks now! At this point they decided to go into closed session – and no wonder! They looked at certain evidence which was incontrovertible. There is one surprising omission here, and it is so surprising that I must point it out. Why did they not produce the body of Jesus? His tomb was a few hundred yards away from this courtroom. Here the apostles are, saying, "He's alive, God raised him from the dead." Why did those Jews not just go up the road and open the tomb? The answer is that the tomb was empty. That is the evidence part of it – that Jesus was raised from the dead. No one was ever able to produce the body.

That was only negative evidence that Jesus is not in the grave. The positive evidence that he is alive is here: it is the evidence of changed lives. That is the one unanswerable argument. They had the proof: they looked at Peter and John, and they marvelled. They said, "Look at those men." They marvelled at their *boldness*. After all, would you dare to say to the murderers of your best friend, "You murdered him," knowing that they could well murder you? Would you dare to confront them with their crime if you were in the dock and they had the power to destroy you? The courage of these men! The judges could see that these were uneducated working men, country people, yet they marvelled because of their brilliant answers.

They recognised that the apostles had been with Jesus. This could mean one of several things. I will leave you to take your pick. It could mean quite simply that one of the judges said, "I recognise these two. Do you remember when we had the trial of Jesus? Both of them were in this building." We know from the Gospel account that Peter and John followed Jesus when the others fled; that John got right in and Peter got as far as the courtyard. I have no doubt that one of the judges said: "I recognise these men. They were with Jesus that night, remember?" Maybe they remembered the Peter who swore that he didn't know Jesus –the man who ran away as soon as he was asked, "Are you with Jesus?" Here is the same man now standing up and now he didn't mind being associated with Jesus. He didn't mind accusing them of his murder, but would tell them anything to their faces now. This is Peter!

Or it could mean that they were saying, "You know, they must have been well trained by Jesus to be able to talk like this. He must have really been able to teach them." Well, that was partly true, but it wasn't the reason for their boldness and their brilliance. The real reason was that the same Holy Spirit who had been in Jesus three months before in that courtroom was now in Peter and John. To put it in another way: the disciples were still with Jesus. It wasn't that they *had* been with him, they still were with him; his Spirit was in them, and therefore they could do what he did in that courtroom and confound his judges.

Well, they had the evidence of the changed apostles, but they had one other visible piece of evidence – a man standing beside them. Do you notice that phrase, "Standing beside them"? In the dock were three people: the two changed apostles and a man who had never stood on his own two feet in forty years. As the judges looked at these three they said, "We had better go into closed session. Close the court, empty the public gallery, get the prisoners out of here and we will decide what to do."

Then they began to discuss, "What on earth can we do about these men?" Now at this point those judges were right there at the fork of the road which most of us meet. They could have taken the right road and said: there must be something in this; call them back in, let's hear more about this Jesus – let us find out if he really did rise. They could have said as hundreds of Jews had said already: "What must we do to be saved?" It's right, he must be alive. They could have done that, but they didn't. What did they do?

They said: we can't deny the miracle but we can deny its cause, and we can deal with the effect. We will deny that it came from Jesus and we will stop any more of this. We will make a new law so that if they ever do this again they will be criminals. This is typical totalitarian government persecution: you arrest the Christians, you find out they are not criminals, so you pass a new edict that they must not do it again. Then, if they do, we can arrest them and put them in prison.

71

How human beings responsible for justice can so blind their minds to the truth that they do this kind of thing beats us until we find ourselves doing it. A man faced with the evidence of the changed life of Christians can turn away from the truth and think: I don't believe it, I can't accept it. I'm not going to believe the truth, I'll find some other explanation and stop them preaching to me. It may be his pride, it may be his envy, it may be all kinds of things, but he is shutting his mind to the truth.

They called the disciples back in and were telling them in effect: we have discussed your case and passed a new law that from now on it is a crime to do what you have done – we are going to let you go, but don't do it again or you will be criminals. What is Peter going to say about that? Peter's message now is this: We have made up our minds. We have decided before God we are going to do what he told us. We are refusing to suppress the truth. We will only speak publicly of what is true, what we have seen and heard. If you tell us to suppress the truth then you answer to God for it.

That really put them in a cleft stick, and they could do nothing at all except let them go. They tried the typical attitude of a bully, they threatened them, they said, "Now if you do, we'll get you." Now all they could do was open the door and let them out.

So the apostles went to the other Christians – they told the church. Now it was against the law to preach, to mention the name of Jesus publicly and to heal a cripple in his name. The church prayed. It is a glorious prayer which begins: "Sovereign Lord God, you are in charge, you're powerful; you're in control of everything. God, you made heaven and earth and sea and everything in it...." That put those little judges in context. The first thing to do when you are worried or afraid is to get a big view of God, and to realise that if you fear God you needn't fear anyone else. If you fear him, you will be cured of every other fear you have. They quote Psalm 2. How silly for the nations to lift themselves up against God and his anointed One. Pilate, Herod, Jews and Gentiles had lifted up their hands against the Messiah, but how silly of them because the Father only allowed to happen what he had planned, and he raised Jesus up. God is in charge. It is tremendous to look out at the world and, even as you hear the national and international news, with all the worry and chaos in it, still to declare: God, you are in charge. You allow things to happen that you plan, but you are in control.

Having a right view of God, they asked in their prayer for two things. What would you ask for if your life had been threatened and you knew that if you went on doing a certain thing you would almost certainly die? What would you ask for? Safety for yourself? Vengeance on your enemies? They never asked God whether they should stop preaching. They knew they were servants of the Lord, therefore there was no question as to what they were to do. The Lord had told them to preach, so they would go on preaching. They asked for *boldness, courage to preach, speaking God's word*, and they asked God to go on *performing the miracles*. They knew that humanly speaking they were weak, humanly speaking they could give in to this totalitarian persecution. They saw that the Lord doing the miracles drew the crowds, confirming the message, and convincing their hearers. So they were asking for the courage to go on.

This, then, is the ministry of the church. We are to ask God to give us the courage to preach, and for him to go on performing miracles, touching and changing lives for good. There was a most dramatic answer to their prayer: God joined in the prayer meeting! Why did he shake the building? He was letting them know that they were in his hand. History and nature – all is in his hand, and he was showing them what he can do. It was a tremendous moment.

God gave them another Pentecost. It happened again. They were all filled with the Spirit and once again the same thing happened: they began to *speak*. Invariably this is what happens with the filling of the Spirit. *They were filled with the Holy Spirit and they began to speak with boldness*. See those people now running out into the streets and preaching with courage – they got their answer.

The first big wave of opposition had hit the infant church. Their frail little craft, just ordinary people, came up over the wave of opposition and sailed on. We will see that the second wave was very close behind, but they sailed through that too. More and more people got on board and the church grew, and the more the authorities tried to stamp it out, the more it grew.

6

The First Discipline
Read 4:32–5:16

Perhaps we look for a church in the place where we live and wander around and hope that each one will be better than the last. Then you come to the conclusion there isn't a perfect one. Even if you found one, they might not be all that glad to have you. But if you don't find a perfect one in this age, you may begin to start looking for a perfect one in a past age. I am amazed how many people I meet who live in a past era, either among the Puritans or the early Methodists or the Reformers or some period of church history that they feel was really *it*. But you can't live in that era, it is *now* you have to live. I suppose the supreme example of this is those who think that the New Testament church was perfect, and if only we lived then, we would have been in a marvellous church. But if you read the New Testament carefully, you see that the church was full of imperfect people.

Thank God the Bible is transparently honest. Luke showed us the church as it was. When Oliver Cromwell had his portrait painted they brought the finished picture to show him and he saw that the artist had very tactfully omitted some rather disfiguring warts. He said, "Take it away and paint it again, warts and all" – a phrase that has gone down in history. In the New Testament you have a picture of the early church, warts and all – a mixture of people. If you ever think you have found the perfect church, sooner or later you will discover that it is made up of imperfect people, and it is a test of your loyalty when you discover this. As once appeared on a church notice board: *This church is full of sinners but there is always room for one more.* That is what the church is meant to be: a hospital for sin-sick people. It only worries me if they never get any better.

In Acts we are given an honest picture of people who were just like us, with all their faults and failings. If so far our studies in Acts have been rather wonderful and rather nice and almost an ideal picture, we are now going to come down to earth with a big bump. There was a couple in the early church called Ananias and Sapphira. We are going to see what they did and what happened to them because they did it. But before we come to that, we have to look at something good. Here is a profound lesson to be learned from the New Testament: if you are going to say something bad about someone, say something good first and then you are keeping a balanced picture. The Bible does this. Before looking at Ananias and Sapphira, you have to look at Barnabas, who was generous and unselfish, before you look at someone who was selfish and greedy.

You have to look at the church as a whole, so there are four layers to the "sandwich". Layer number one is bread, if you like – the bread of the church. Layer number two is rather a nice filling – Barnabas. Layer number three, not so nice – Ananias and Sapphira. Then layer number four, back to the church again. I can distinguish between the first and the bottom layer this way: in the first section we are shown the church and its relationships between the members *in private*; in the last layer we are shown the church and its relationships with people out *in public*.

We begin with the private life of the church, and the word "great" keeps coming up and, like so many words, it is being devalued, to signify nowadays: "a little better than usual". But in those days there really were great things happening. Here are some of them: with *great power* the apostles witnessed to the resurrection, which means they convinced hundreds of people that Jesus was alive. Then *great grace* was upon them all. "Grace" is the loveliest word: G-R-A-C-E, "God's Riches At Christ's Expense". It means the things you get that are free, the things you get that you don't have to pay for or earn. Grace is what God pours out upon you – lovely surprises of things you had never dreamt you would have. Great grace was upon them all. He was always giving them things they didn't deserve.

When you receive great grace, it produces *great gratitude*. When you have great gratitude, it produces *great generosity* and that is the kind of pattern that I notice again and again. The more grace someone receives, the more grateful they are and the more generous they become. If I am niggardly in my giving, and if I tend to hang on to things rather than let them go, it must surely be because I know so little of grace. The more grace I know, the more grateful I am, and generosity is directly related to your gratitude. If you are a thankful person, I will guarantee that you are a generous person. If you are a greedy and a covetous person, I will guarantee that you are a complaining, grumbling person, not a grateful person.

The result of the great grace was that they began to share their goods at a practical level – they each put their hand in their pocket and gave money to someone else in the church. This is a thing that perhaps has never been practised so fully and so freely since those days, which is a great pity. As soon as a need was known, it was met by other Christians. Furthermore, if they hadn't the money to give, they would go and sell something to give it. If they had a bit of property they would realise their capital. Today it would be that they would go and sell their stocks and shares rather than see another Christian go without.

Some have made the mistake of thinking that this was communism but, as we have already noticed, it was nothing like it. Here are a few of the differences. *Christians were of one heart*. Nobody had to force anybody else to accept this. They loved each other first. Their sharing was on a spiritual basis. *They were of one soul*, whereas communism is utterly atheistic and has no spiritual basis. For the Christians, *giving was spontaneous*. Nobody made them do it, they wanted to do it. There was no need to liquidate the capitalist. There was no need to get rid of this person and that person who didn't fit the system. Property was under no-one's control but their own; they didn't abolish private property and put it all in the state's hands or the church's hands. Peter says to Ananias, "While it was in your hands, you could do with it what you liked." There was no control of private property. Something happened that no communist state in the world has yet achieved – *everyone being helped according to their need*. Therefore, I would say the sharing of the early Christians leaves communism way behind.

I once read *The Jesus Family in Communist China*. It was a book about a group of Chinese Christians who, when the communists came and made all the farms collective, asked for permission to have a Christian collective farm and they were allowed to do so. They had their farm and they had no police, no inspectors, no big whip, no pressure, and their farm produced two to three times as much as the other collective farms! The communists sent inspectors to find out how this collective farm was doing so much better than the others, and they just found love. They found people who enjoyed sharing, and a farm that gave according to need.

One of the people who practised Christian sharing was Barnabas. As soon as I get to heaven I am going to ask for Barnabas – I want to meet him! There is something about him that draws me. Two people in the New Testament are called "good". One is Joseph of Arimathea and the other is Joseph called Barnabas, and they both did the same thing.

One had a garden and the other had a field, and they both said, "Lord, you can have it." The word "good" in scripture means someone who is generous – who has received so much he gives out.

Barnabas was a man whose attitude was: I have a field – if he wants to use it, he can have it. He sold the field and he brought the money because there was need in the church. Why was there so much need in the Jerusalem church? Because thousands had become Christians and were losing their jobs. So this good man brought it. Others did this, so why are we told about Barnabas? The answer is very simple. We are told to look at a good man before we look at a bad man—that's all. We are told to look at Barnabas, the son of encouragement. It is lovely when a person can encourage another. I get a very mixed bag of post, as you might imagine, and receive all sorts of comments, questions and criticisms. I thank God for it. I do welcome letters of criticism. I learn probably more about myself and my need of more grace from those than from letters of the other kind. I have noticed over the years that every time I receive a critical letter in the post, there is in the same post an encouraging letter. Isn't it kind of God to arrange that? So I am able to take the criticism and to ask God, "Is there truth in this? If so, I bring it to you now. You tell me." Just to keep me from being too far down, he puts another letter in the post too. I thank God for those who through my ministry have at the right time sent a little word that encouraged and lifted up. I am sure you thank God for those too. You have maybe felt a little down. Maybe you felt that your work wasn't noticed or appreciated. You have maybe felt that you weren't achieving much for the Lord. Somebody came along and said, "Thank you for doing that." Barnabas was the son of encouragement. They gave him that nickname. Barnabas means, "Somebody who picks others up." I have a feeling that when Barnabas brought that money and laid it at the apostles' feet, he was the one who did so first. He was the one who encouraged others to do it.

Alas, we have to look at the other side. In the book of Joshua the walls of Jericho tumbled down. They were victorious *but* there was Achan who looted for himself. Here in the church there is Ananias, and we have to look at this man. Some people get terribly upset by this incident. Some people object to it morally and say, "What a terrible punishment for just that little sin. Anybody could have done that; and to kill the poor man...." Others have had intellectual problems with it and ask, "How did death occur?" But let's start at the right place.

For the first time in Acts the word "church" is used. *You will never understand this event unless you get a right view of the church and a right view of God. The church is not a human construction. The word means, literally: "the people that God has called out to him."* When you get a view of the church like that, you begin to see something very important. If the church is the people of God, the family of God, the flock of Christ, the fellowship of the Spirit, what you do to the church is done to God the Holy Father, the Holy Son, and the Holy Spirit. If you laugh at the church, you are laughing at God. If you stay away from church, you are staying away from Christ. If you deceive the church, you are lying to the Holy Spirit. Whatever you do to the church, you do to him. So what Ananias did, he didn't do to the people, he did to the Holy Spirit, and that is serious.

The other thing is this: *we need a high view of God.* The world laughs at the supposed cleverness of a thing like the sin of Ananias. Or the world would excuse it. But in God's sight it was the most enormous crime. It was the worst thing in Jesus' eyes. Do you know what Jesus condemned more than anything else? *Hypocrisy.* Do you know what the word means? Originally the word in Greek meant "actor". The actors in the Greek theatre used to come on to the stage holding masks in front of their faces instead of using make-up. The mask was called "a hypocrite". It means showing a different face to somebody else, letting them think you are something other than what you really are.

Our Lord was tender with a woman taken in adultery but he blazed against hypocrisy. He said, "Whitewashed tombs, that's all you are." I have the feeling that the church has somewhat reversed our Lord's ideas. We tend to regard sexual aberration as about the worst there is and we let hypocrisy go by, but our Lord had hypocrisy at the top of the list.

Let us look at what Ananias and Sapphira really did. They sold some land, so the money was theirs and they could do with it what they wanted. The wife and husband talked it over and decided to keep some for themselves and give some to the church for the relief of the poor and needy. They had seen Barnabas come forward and give all his money, and they came forward and gave part of the sale proceeds. Everybody looked at Ananias and Sapphira and thought they were as generous as Barnabas was – and they were not.

The sin was not that they held money back. They were perfectly entitled to divide the money according to their own decision. *The sin was that they wanted to be thought to be better than they were. They wanted to be thought to be more generous than they were. They wanted to be higher in other people's estimation than they had a right to be.*

There may have been greed in it, and there may have been a bit of pride. There may have been compromise, in that they wanted the best of both worlds. I remember a minister saying to me: "I'd love to be an ex-missionary. You know, you've been through all those dangers and you've been out in the jungle!" He was joking of course, but have you not sometimes found this in your own heart?

Ananias and Sapphira wanted people to think very highly of them, more highly than they ought to be thought of. Why did Peter take this so seriously? Because this sin was exactly the same to the church as the sin of Achan had been to Israel. *Peter knew that, if it had been allowed to go unchecked, this sin of hypocrisy would wreck the early church.* If this thing crept in it would become a cancer that would spread to the whole body and would wreck the witness of that church. There is nothing that wrecks a church's reputation more quickly than a bit of hypocrisy in the members.

The Holy Spirit gave Peter supernatural knowledge and there was a terrible moment. I don't know whether Ananias died of the shock of being discovered, or whether this was a case of the kind of thing that Paul mentions of a man who is delivered to Satan for the destruction of the flesh, that his spirit might be saved in the last day. But I know that he died.

Years ago I heard about a man who was wrecking a church. At every church meeting he was saying things that spoiled the fellowship. One night the minister and his wife were going home after another meeting ruined by that man, and the wife said to the minister, "You know, if we were living in the days of the New Testament, that man wouldn't be allowed to live." That night, the man's soul was required of him and a phone call in the early hours of the morning told them that the Lord had taken him.

It was vital that the early church should advance and not be damaged at this crucial, critical stage. So Peter also asked Sapphira how much the land was sold for, then again there was the deception, and she died too.

What I want to affirm now is a most serious thing. *The church has far more to fear from corruption within than from opposition without. They could go to prison, they could face martyrdom, and the church would go on growing, but a bit of hypocrisy inside and the church would be finished.* That is why Peter took it so seriously; that was why Joshua took Achan so seriously. I find this the most challenging part of Acts because it comes home in a very direct way to all of us. Is there anything in my life that could be doing just this kind of thing to the church of which I am a member? Could I be letting people think that I am better than I am? Could I be wanting them to think I am better? Could I be making them think that I am better? Could I be saying things about myself that are not true? It is a sobering and solemn thought.

The result of this event was that great *fear* came upon the whole church. Twice it is mentioned. A church full of the right kind of fear will not be a hypocritical church. No wonder great fear came upon the church! What effect did it have on the church in its public relations? You might have thought this would have finished them off all together. No, it didn't. I come to the last bit of bread in the sandwich. We go back now to the whole church, and we have a final picture of the church in its external relations. They didn't have a building in which they could hide themselves from the public gaze. There were about 5,000 men, and the women and children. They had to meet publicly in Solomon's Portico. Everybody could see the church in full view. If they had a church meeting, the crowd was there to listen. Everything they did, people came and watched. I wonder how we would stand up to such a searching gaze. They literally lived in a shop window, but there is one word that sums up that church – *it was a supernatural church*.

Look at six things in the next few verses, not one of which can be done with natural gifts and energy. First: signs and wonders. The gospel was visible. People could see as well as hear what the power of Christ could do. Second: there was a complete unity in the church and the crowd could see that they were of one accord in Solomon's Portico. Third: there was a clear boundary between believers and unbelievers.

There was a very clear boundary between church and world. There was no blurring of that. It didn't damage their evangelism, many people crossed the boundary but the boundary was clear. You could tell who was a Christian and who wasn't in those days; there were no kinds of greys in between. You were either a saint or a sinner. You either belonged to Jesus or you didn't. Fourth: their evangelism was as effective among the men as it was among the women. Fifth: sickness was healed so much so that the people even brought the sick into the street so that the shadow of the preacher might fall across them, just as a woman had come touching the hem of Jesus' garment. Sixth: people with unclean spirits possessed by demons came to that church and the demons were cast out.

None of those six things can be organised by any committee or any human being. This was the church where God was busy. This was a church where things happened that had no human explanation. You can't explain sickness being healed. You can't explain men being converted as well as women. You can't explain demon-possessed people becoming sane and whole again, and you can't explain that unity. The early church was supernatural. No wonder the people joined them.

You notice that the people who believed were not added to the church, they were added to the Lord. They didn't join the membership roll, they joined Jesus Christ; it was him they came to.

The question I found myself asking as I read that passage was: "Do I really want to belong to a church like this? I would love to see crowds coming in the numbers that came then. I would love to see as much happening now as then. I would love to see all of us sharing our possessions so that none of us says, "That's mine", and we all say "It's his, therefore it's yours." I would love to see the unity and fellowship that they had, but would I really love to see some of the other things? Would I really love to be in a church where sin is publicly exposed and hypocrisy is exposed? Would I love to be in a church where people with unclean spirits came and disturbed the worship? Would I love to be in a church where great fear was upon them all? Would I love to be in a church in which God might say my property is needed for someone else? That is the question. It is all very well studying the book of Acts and saying "What a wonderful church!" but the question really is: do I want that kind of church?

I have sat among scholars and Bible students who have argued the question: "Can we ever have a church like this?" They have come to the conclusion that we can't, and that it was all locked up in the New Testament. I believe that is the biggest lie. God hasn't changed. Jesus is the same yesterday, today, and forever. The Holy Spirit was poured out for the last days. Therefore, how dare we say that these things are not for today? I believe the question is not, "*Can there be* such a church today?" but, "*Do I really want* such a church today?" If I am honest, my question might be answered, "Lord, I'd like some of it, but not the rest." I would like the Holy Spirit but not the unclean spirits. I would like the generosity but I am not sure I would like to let my property go. I would like to see people being healed, but not sure that I would like to see my favourite seat in the church filled so I can't get it.

We must come to God and say: "God, you have shown us in the book of Acts what your church can be: imperfect people, yes, but what a picture of fellowship filled with the Holy Spirit. They were sharing everything, witnessing with power to the fact that Jesus is alive."

7

The Second Arrest and Release
Read 5:17–42

Our Lord's prediction that the world will hate the church is true. The nearer you live to Christ, the more likely you are to upset people and become unpopular. Persecution is the lot of the Christian church and has been for two thousand years. Now in Acts we see how the persecution became more and more fierce and how these sufferings they were called upon to go through became worse. Here is a picture of the Christian life, because there is a kind of honeymoon period when you become a Christian when life is wonderful, when you are walking on the mountaintops and you think, "Isn't it going to be great if it's like this for the rest of my life!"

Then your first problem comes, your first opposition, your first battle and you discover everybody else isn't quite as thrilled that you are a Christian as you are. In fact, you discover that some people are not at all pleased. You are now going to be the odd one out, the misfit, the one who doesn't like those office jokes.

Let us see what was going to happen to the apostles now. For the second time they are going to be thrown into prison for no other crime than that they preached Jesus. Whenever we meet together in the liberty we enjoy, we need to remember that today there are many people in prison for preaching, and for believing in Jesus. Some of them are being tortured and some of them have not seen loved ones for years. The contrast I want to draw is between, on the one hand, the Christians, with their reckless boldness which scorns safety; and, on the other hand, a man who was tolerant, cautious, careful, and whose commonsense would appeal tremendously to the world – but whose commonsense was as far removed from the Christian outlook as the east is from the west.

First of all, the Christians. There were four points at which commonsense would have said stop the fight, and at which they could have got out of the problem. They had four opportunities to run away and be safe, and they did not take any of them.

Firstly, they had already been warned that if they preached in the name of Jesus once more they would be arrested. Did that stop them? On the contrary, they just went out into the streets and preached Jesus.

It seemed to spark them off, not to stop them. This was their opportunity. They could have migrated; they could have left Jerusalem and gone somewhere else. They had been told they must not preach in that city any more about the new belief in the resurrection and in Jesus Christ, but they just went on. It was absolutely inevitable that they would get into trouble for doing so. It didn't make any difference to them at all.

One of the reasons why it was inevitable that they would get into trouble was because the authorities were jealous. Jealousy makes people do terrible things. It makes people cruel, unjust and unfair; it will make people do and say things which are just not right. Why would they be jealous? Simply because the authorities were the official religious leaders of the whole nation and here were a bunch of ignorant fishermen who could draw ten times the number of people. These amateurs walked straight into their temple and all the people flocked to listen to them. No wonder they tried to stop it. Envy was responsible for the *first* murder in history – Cain killed Abel for envy; and envy was responsible for the *worst* murder in history. That was why Pilate saw that

Annas and Caiaphas wanted Jesus dead – for envy they delivered him up.

So now the authorities arrested the apostles, who had missed opportunity number one to be safe. Now they were going to have another opportunity to be safe. An angel of the Lord came and let them out of prison. It is amazing that the angel shut the door behind him and locked it again. That was a delightful touch. I don't know what the angel did to the guards – put them to sleep in some way maybe. But the angel got through the locked doors and got those twelve men out. All the apostles were in this time, not just two of them. He got them out and brought them through the prison doors, past the guards. They must have looked at those sleeping guards and thought, "We're free, we're free!" They dashed out into the streets, and the angel told them to go and stand in the temple and speak to the people "all the words of this life". When the angel got them out of prison they were free; the chains had fallen off. They could have run away then. They could have got out of trouble. Did they take their opportunity? They went straight back into the temple and, as soon as the people arrived in the morning, they were preaching again! You can't stop this, nothing can stop the gospel. For two thousand years people have tried to stop the truth getting out in one way and another.

Notice the angel said that they were to go and speak all the words of this *life*. Christianity is not a religion. I keep trying to tell people this. It is not just *a* way of life, it is *the way to life*. In fact it is Jesus who said, "I am the way, the truth and the life." We can witness like those apostles today: don't tell people about your religion, your theology, your church – but *all the words of this life* that started when Jesus burst out of the tomb.

So the apostles had missed their second opportunity. Now we see the irony. The court assembles. We can picture the scene: "Call the prisoners" – down the corridor the shout would go. "They're not here." Those guards would be in for trouble. Do you realise that it probably cost them their lives? They had let prisoners get out, but then the padlocks were still fastened and the chains were still there. You can imagine the consternation in court. Then somebody walks in and says, they are preaching in the temple – the very thing they had been doing when they were arrested!

It was a few years later that the great missionary Paul, lying in a dungeon in Rome and chained to a Roman soldier, wrote these words: *the Word of God is not bound.* Even though he was in chains, the gospel was getting right into Caesar's palace from that prisoner in chains.

The third opportunity for escape came when the soldiers tried to arrest them for the second time, because it is quite clear that an angry murmur ran through the crowd then. If the apostles had lifted one finger, there would have been such a riot that every temple guard would have been murdered on the spot. There is no doubt about it that the apostles were in a strong position. The crowd was with them and completely outnumbered the soldiers. But the apostles did not resist. They quietly submitted to be led into the court. The angel had led them out of prison but they walked freely into court the following morning. When a man does that kind of thing, something happens.

The apostles had missed their third opportunity to escape and be safe. Now they are in the court and they are charged with two things. The first was disobeying a court order. The order was that they must not teach in the name of Jesus, and they had done so. Secondly, and this showed the judge was more than partial, he accused them of intending to "bring this Man's blood on us" – to pin the murder of Jesus on them.

Peter then states a principle which applies to all situations, all times, all divided loyalties: *we must obey God rather than men*. Fortunately, in most of our lives and most of the decisions we have to take, we can obey both. When children are called upon to obey their parents, they can obey God in obeying their parents because God said, "Honour your father and mother." When the boss says, "Do this," and you do it for the boss, you can obey God, because God said, "Obey the boss." You can read all about it in Ephesians 5.

There are many occasions we can obey God and men, but in every single one of our lives there will come a point – maybe in a little thing, maybe a bigger – when you have to stand like Peter and say: God has told me to do this and if you tell me not to do it, it's against God. God has told me to be straight and if you're telling me to be crooked, I can't do it. God has told me to be pure, and if you're telling me to be impure, I must obey God rather than men. This fundamental principle is at the heart of Christian living. Christians are those who take their orders from higher up. This is why a Christian basically fears no man because he fears God more.

This makes for true freedom because a man is never so free as when he says, "God has told me to do it, therefore I must do it." Then Peter goads them further, almost as if he did not like them talking of "this man" when they referred to Jesus. Peter is saying of Jesus, whom they had murdered by hanging him on a tree, that "the God of our fathers", the God of Abraham and Isaac and Jacob, had raised this Jesus up, and had exalted him to his right hand, to be Prince and Saviour, and to give repentance and forgiveness of sins. They were the witnesses, and so was the Holy Spirit, whom God gave to those who obey him.

Here then is the double evidence for the fact that Jesus is alive: the evidence of the mouths of those who know he is alive, and the evidence of the Holy Spirit who confirms that this is true. This is unshakeable evidence and testimony. No wonder Peter really had them tied up in knots again, but this time, the literal Greek says: "They were so sawn through"– a most telling phrase. They looked as if somebody was literally sawing them in half. We would say in modern language that they looked very cut up about it. They were enraged, and decided to try to kill these men. The apostles could have escaped even at this late hour by saying, "We're sorry, we promise not to teach in the name of Jesus. We have been wrong in the evidence. He's not alive." They could have escaped again. Their fourth opportunity – they could have recanted but they didn't. Time and again, Christians have had the opportunity to be safe by recanting, by saying they are wrong, by denying the faith, and they have not taken it.

Normal wisdom would say, "Peter, James, John, you are being foolish, gluttons for punishment heading for trouble. Go on like this and you'll be dead." You would have been speaking the sober truth, for within a very short time these apostles were dead – all but one who survived and died of old age, so far as we know – the apostle John. The others all died violent deaths at the hands of their persecutors.

In contrast to all that, here now is a man who is typically worldly-wise, sensible, tolerant and cautious – Gamaliel. I hope I am not going to upset you with this, but I am going to say that I believe Gamaliel was a bad man, not a good man. I believe that his example is bad, not good; that his tolerance was a bad thing, not a good thing; that his caution was a bad thing, not a good thing. Gamaliel is often held up as a great man and in one sense he was. He was very popular, greatly respected, a peacemaker, tolerant of different points of view. He had a liberal theology and a wide circle of friends. Unlike the others, he was a Pharisee, which meant he believed in the resurrection from the dead. He took his religion seriously as the Sadducees didn't – they just played about with religion. Now Gamaliel spoke to the Sanhedrin – the prisoners were moved out and his approach was: "Be very careful what you do with these men. If the movement they have started is a human thing, it will die out. It will get into trouble sooner or later. The Romans will do our dirty work for us. Remember Theudas? He tried this and they killed him. Remember Judas? He tried this and they killed him. All we need to do is leave this movement alone." He knew there was just a possibility that it was of God. If it was a divine movement they would never blot it out. He never spoke a truer word in his life. Two thousand years later and we belong to this same church and it has not been blotted out. You wait until you get to heaven and see how many members there are! The church is a divine movement.

What were Gamaliel's motives in saying, "Be careful, let's wait and see; let's give it time, let's be cautious." His motive was that he was afraid to take sides. Gamaliel was typical of the tolerant, cautious man who says, "Well I'm not going to make up my mind now. I'd rather wait and see if it's good or bad – of God or of men." He was unwilling to take a stand either for or against this movement because he was just a little bit afraid that God might be in it. No wonder, because he believed in resurrection and they were claiming that it had happened. He took his religion seriously and obviously these fishermen did too. The tragedy was that he never made his mind up. You might ask: but, surely, wasn't he wise? Wasn't he good, wasn't he being tolerant, cautious and sensible in saying wait and see? Let me put it this way: you never hear any more about Gamaliel. He vanishes from the picture. We know that the day he died, which was many years later, he still had not made up his mind whether it was of God or of men. He was the man who was apparently very wise and very tolerant but was over-cautious, afraid to commit.

Someone like that you never hear of again. They may come to church, hear the gospel of Jesus Christ and say, "Well there might be something in it. I'm not against going to church mind you, and not against this. I don't want you to think I'm against you," but such are not *for* either. They go away, they are going to give it time; they are just going to be tolerant.

Gamaliel was a theological professor who lectured to students about faith in God. Sitting in the front row of one of his lecture rooms was a young man who was keen on theology and desperate to be a great religious man – his name was Saul and he came from Tarsus. When Saul heard about this new religion he was against it. He intended to fight that religion and wipe it out. That is why you hear of Saul again. I would much rather people fought against Christianity instead of saying "Let's wait and see." I would rather see Saul's attitude than Gamaliel's. Give me a man who will go to Damascus as a missionary to kill the church. Then Christ can get hold of that man, turn him right round and say, "Carry on, but only build up the church now." Give me the person who is interested enough to be antagonistic.

One of the reasons why we have so great a difficulty in spreading the gospel in England today is that many people are like Gamaliel. "Well, there might be something in it. Yes I'm not against it. No, I don't want to risk being against it. I might just be against God and I wouldn't like that on my conscience..." – but they sit on the fence.

It is true that Gamaliel got safety for the Christians, but was safety what they needed? Safety never helped the church. It is persecution under which it seems to thrive. They were beaten. I don't know if you can realise what that means. It just states it in three words: they were beaten and then let go. That was illegal. It meant the twelve apostles were lined up and thirty-nine times each of them was struck until their bare backs were raw and bleeding. This was the first time Christians had suffered in the body for Jesus. What was their reaction? Did they curse? Did they swear? Did they struggle? No, they rejoiced that they were worthy to suffer. Can you imagine that?

Some years ago, seven people were thrown into prison in Nepal and their crime was that one man had been baptising the other six, and the other six had been baptised by him. Word reached an Indian church that these people were in prison, and they gathered to have a special prayer meeting because the man who had done the baptising had been sent as a missionary to Nepal. They gathered together in that meeting and began to pray. One prayed, "Lord bring them out of that prison." Another prayed, "Lord, keep them safe." "Lord, keep them from being tortured." "Lord, keep them from harm." Round the circle the prayers went until an elderly Indian woman prayed: "Lord, why did you give them the privilege of suffering, and not us? Lord why should they be able to suffer for your name and not us? Lord, why didn't you give us the honour? Aren't we worth the honour?" She went on praying like this. It transformed the prayer meeting. They began to look at suffering in quite a different light.

In Germany in the 1930s, Paul Schneider boldly condemned the sins of the Nazis from his pulpit. His members came to him and said, "Dr Schneider if you go on preaching like this, they will kill you." The mayor of the town came and said, "Pastor Schneider, we don't want to lose you from this town. You're a great influence here. Don't go on preaching like this." But he said, "It's wrong, and I must." The day came when Paul Schneider was driven away in the Gestapo lorry and said goodbye to his wife and four children and unborn child. He went away in the lorries smiling. I have some of the letters he wrote to his wife from Buchenwald concentration camp. The word that occurs more often than any other in those letters is the word "joy". He was finally flogged to death after being starved for months – joy.

The apostles have been scarred in the body for this, so they rejoiced. What did they do next? Catch the first bus out of Jerusalem? No, they ceased not to teach and to preach, both in the temple and in their homes, that Jesus was the Christ. There is one difference between being a Jew and being a Christian: we believe that Jesus is the Christ. This was the one thing that those Jewish fishermen believed now that meant *life* for them. So they ceased not to teach and to preach. They were just asking for more trouble, but they counted undergoing such trouble to be the mark of a true Christian.

8

The First Deacons and Stephen's Arrest
Read Acts 6

Has it ever struck you as strange that Christianity is no longer a Jewish religion – considering that the founder of our faith, the Saviour himself, was born a Jew and died a Jew; considering every author of the books of the Bible except Luke was a Jew, the twelve were Jews, the first few thousand members of the church were Jews, and that everything Jesus did and said was in that little part of the world we call the Holy Land? Considering all that, isn't it the strangest thing that Christianity became a world faith? It might never have happened, except of course that God intended it to, and what he wills must happen.

Humanly speaking, it might never have happened but for one man whose name was Stephen, who was one of the first deacons of the church. We are going to see what he did to drive a wedge between the Jewish religion, which we call Judaism, and Christianity – a wedge which was to break them from one another so that Christianity was able to sail free of the Jews into the Gentile world and become a universal religion. Otherwise it would be one of the most exclusive religions in the world, whereas it is the most inclusive there has ever been.

It happened almost accidentally because a group of church members grumbled. Now that doesn't justify grumbling in a church. God is able to make all things work together for good, and simply because he made this work for good doesn't justify you having a grumble. But that's how it began, a group within the first church in Jerusalem began to complain about some of the others and about the leaders. Out of that grumble came the first step towards this division between the Jewish and the Christian faiths, which has meant so much liberty for us. You are not bound now by the Jewish law. You are not bound now to go to the temple to offer sacrifice. You are not bound now with the heavy burdens which the Pharisees placed upon the Jewish people if they were ever going to get to heaven. We are free of all that as Gentiles. Let's see how it happened: how did such an exclusive race as the Jews ever begin to open up to others? Two things they did even before Christ came helped to accomplish this.

The first is that from that little nationalist land, similar in size to Wales, the Jews began to spread out in all directions. They were good businessmen, they travelled and spread right round the Mediterranean, around the Roman empire. They were known as the Diaspora, the dispersed Jews who had gone to the uttermost parts of the then-known world to live. These Jews gradually forgot the language of their fathers, so there were Jews all around the Mediterranean who could not speak a word of Hebrew. They spoke Greek like everybody else, but they were Jews and proud of it. The two groups of Jews with the two languages were called Hebrews if they spoke Hebrew, or Hellenist if they spoke Greek. That explains the two labels in the first verse of chapter 6. The Hebrews were Hebrew-speaking Jews in the land of their fathers. The Hellenists were Greek-speaking Jews who visited the land of their fathers but couldn't speak the language. Therefore when they went to worship in Jerusalem, they had to go to special places of worship. So in Jerusalem you had Hebrew synagogues which worshipped in Hebrew, and Hellenist synagogues which worshipped in Greek.

The second thing which began to open up chinks in the Jewish armour to the Gentile world was this: they began to allow other people who were not Jews to come to their synagogues. I want you to imagine that in a synagogue they kept three lists. There were, first of all, the Jewish members themselves, who had been born Jews. That was the top list to be on. The next list down was a list of people called "proselytes", who had been born Gentiles but had become Jews. They had been converted to the religion, they had been circumcised and baptised and they now kept the law; they were Jews in all but their birth. This was a new step and it happened before Jesus came.

The third circle consisted of those who liked worshipping in the synagogue but did not want to get too involved. There is a circle like that in most churches too. This outer circle, this last list, was called the "God-fearers". Usually you find this translated in our Bible as "those who feared God". They didn't become Jews, they didn't get baptised or circumcised, but they were on the fringe. They attended the services and they liked what the Jews believed about God and thought they were right. So the Jews had already begun to open up a bit. When Christianity began, it grew rapidly at first, by the thousand. Every day there were converts, but for the first year or so, every convert was a Jew. You can imagine that as they grew to a church of some thousands in Jerusalem, they began to have problems. There are problems with a big church. Mind you, I would rather have those problems than the problems of a small church.

The problems of a big church include people beginning to form groups of those who have something in common before they get into the church. This is what happened in the synagogues and in the church. Gradually they developed two groups of Christians in the one church. Some of them were Hellenist Jews and spoke Greek; some of them were Hebrew Jews and spoke Hebrew, and you had a bilingual church. For the first time, the church was facing the problem of two quite different culture groups meeting within one fellowship. That is a problem which occurs whenever you get a church that mixes different cultural groups – not necessarily different races but different languages, different backgrounds, homes, education and so on. Thank God when you get the mixture, but it produces problems.

Every day in this church, the widows came along for a cooked meal. Widows in those days got no pension. A widow might have no support at all, no-one to look after her, and the church looked after its widows. Those who spoke Greek sat at one table and those who spoke Hebrew sat at another. You can understand that – they wanted to talk together while they ate, so naturally they gravitated to the group of their language. One group thought that the other group got a bit more food. One group thought that the other was served first while it was still hot, and they began to complain. I am putting it like this to show you the early church was a human church made up of ordinary folk who were subject to all the frailties, weaknesses and temptations of ordinary human nature. They told the leaders, the apostles Peter, John and James, and it was that simple little grumble that started something off, and Christianity would split from Judaism. Jesus himself had seen it coming. He said, "If you pour new wine into an old wineskin it will crack and burst. If you sew a patch of new cloth onto an old garment, it will shrink and pull the cloth and rip it." Jesus was saying that you cannot pin Christianity on to Judaism. You cannot take what he teaches and fit it into your religion. It is something so new, so fresh and so lively that it is going to burst out of these religious traditions.

Peter, James, and John dealt with the complaint quickly, wisely and effectively, and stopped it from causing festering division. The one thing that might have come from that grumble, and it would have been a bad thing, would have been a split in the church and two denominations – the

Hellenist church at one end of the road and the Hebrew church down at the other – but that split never occurred. Grumbles need not cause splits if they are handled wisely, straight away.

What did Peter and John do? Four principles stand out in the developing organisation of the church. The greater the numbers coming into the church, the more you have to structure it. It needn't become an institution, but it ought to be ordered. They called a church meeting and there are four basic principles they laid down which still apply to every problem that a growing church has today.

There is first what I call *the principle of suitable management*. What do I mean by that? I mean they chose a structure, an organisation, that matched the need. They did not start with fixed ideas as to how a church ought to be run. They were concerned with what the need is and how best they could meet it.

The second principle is this: *the principle of separate ministries*. There is no church that God intends to have one minister. A one-minister church is not a church. The trouble is that many churches look for and expect to find a minister with all the gifts, but they never will. They think they have found such a one for the first six months of the new ministry, then they realise he hasn't, and hope the next one will have. But this is not God's pattern. You will never find a minister with all the gifts because God doesn't give any man all the gifts. The principle is shared ministry. So the apostles said: It is not right that we should leave our task and start on this. We have been called to pray and to preach the Word and this is our ministry and we have got to get on with it. We must have somebody else to do this and look into this. So you look out seven good men and we will establish another sort of ministry to look after this side of the church's work.

Happy is that church where the ministry is shared out.

Every Christian is a minister, and every minister is a member. This is the way to think of the church, but it doesn't mean you do without pastors or deacons. The early church had a pastor, Peter. The early church had deacons as we are seeing now, but that's a difference of ministry. It is not one minister and a committee, it is different ministries. The principle is: here is a need, find the right men to minister to that need. The word "minister" means "servant, helper."

The third principle is *the principle of saintly men*. If you are going to have a man to lay tables, you need a man full of the Holy Spirit. Now I am sure you would never think that unless you read the Bible. You might have thought: men are not much good at serving tables anyway, you need a ladies' committee for that, but they chose men, no doubt to supervise it and act in an advisory capacity! We are very good at that while the ladies actually do the work! But they chose seven men and they said that to serve tables they must be qualified in three directions. In relation to others, they must be men of good repute. In relation to God, they must be full of the Holy Spirit; in relation to themselves each must be wise, which is different from being clever. A wise man is not necessarily the one who has encyclopaedic knowledge in his head, but one who knows what is the right thing to do. I have noticed that education and wisdom are not necessarily the same thing. You can have a very clever person who is also very silly. You can have an uneducated person who is very wise. So he said, "Look out saintly men who are highly thought of, men whom God has filled with his Spirit, men who are wise, and put them in charge of serving tables, and they will sort these widows out." So it turns out that we hear no more grumbles, no more problems. These saintly men took the situation over and they soon had it under control.

The fourth principle is the *principle of the selective method*. The leaders of the church said to the whole church:

"*You* find the men and *we* will appoint them. You select them, we will commission them. You select seven men, bring them to us, and then we lay hands on them and pray that God will use them in this work." That is the principle which the church at its best has followed ever since. We say to the members, "These are the qualifications that we need under God for this job. You select them and we will set them apart for this task."

When we read the list of the seven men they chose, there are two very interesting things. This is where this apparently trivial incident became something highly significant. Every one of these seven men had a Greek name, not one of them had a Hebrew name. Not even a name like the apostles John, James, Peter. Just look at them – Stephen, Philip, Procorus, Nicanor, Timon, Parmenas, Nicolas – these are Greek names. The only person in the Gospel we know of called Philip was a man to whom the Greeks used to come, so presumably he had Greek connections. Was it not wise of the church of Jesus Christ in those early days to say that if it is the Greek-speaking widows who are grumbling, we will give them Greek-speaking men to help them? If only the church had followed this principle. It was only gradually realised in the West in the twentieth century that indigenous ministries are needed. What the Chinese needed was not more and more English and American missionaries in China but more and more Chinese pastors and preachers who could go on after the missionaries had gone, and the same applies of course worldwide.[1]

Now we see that from the very beginning this principle is clear. By the same token, if you are going to win teenagers, give them some teenage Christians. If you are going to win the elderly, send some Christian senior citizens out after them! This is the principle: matching the people to the need, and it is written into this simple little incident.

There is another interesting thing about this list: one of these seven had not been born a Jew – a proselyte called Nicolas, a Gentile from the city which had the most evil reputation in the Roman empire. He had become a Jew and was now a Christian. So we are beginning to see a breaking out of the Jewish circle. The church is starting to break into the Gentile world, making a group of Greek-speaking men responsible for service in the church.

There was a man to watch whose career was terribly short, and had probably only been a Christian leader for six months at the most, who paid for it with his life, and became the first man to shed his blood for Jesus: Stephen, a man to whom, under God, we owe the apostle Paul. Reading the scriptures, *Stephen saw that Christianity meant the end of the temple and the end of the law, and he began to speak about this.*

"The word of God increased and multiplied." Isn't this summary statement lovely? Every so often in Acts you get this. In 6:1, "Now in these days when the disciples were increasing in number." At 6:7, "And the word of God increased and the number of the disciples multiplied greatly." What a wonderful progress report! Again and again it comes up in Acts – there is never a decrease, the church goes on growing.

I like the fact that v. 7 follows v. 6. They set apart these "deacons" – and that is actually the word "serving". These deacons were servants of the church, and because the grumbling was stopped and it was all sorted out, the word of God increased and the disciples multiplied. I tell you this: if you have a church where grumbling goes on and is not put right, that church will decrease. But if you have a church where if complaining starts it is dealt with promptly and lovingly, and put right so that the cause for complaint is removed, that church is likely to grow and the word of God will increase. People will see love.

Three things now caused division between Jews and Christians. The first was that priests began to get converted. As soon as a Jewish priest is converted, you are faced with this question: what is he to do now? Now that he believes that Jesus is the Lamb of God slain from the foundation of the world, and that there is no other sacrifice for sin, must he go on cutting the throats of lambs and goats on his altar? Has he to resign the priesthood? Supposing a pagan priest was converted and became a Christian and said, "Well, I get my living from being a priest, what must I do?" I think you would say straight away, "Well, I'm sorry you can't go on being a priest. You will have to leave that religion." It was not quite as clear with a Jewish priest who worshipped the same God.

Stephen was allowed still to go to Greek-speaking synagogues in Jerusalem, and he was preaching two things: that *Christ is the end of the temple* – you can come to God anywhere now, any time, without a sacrifice; and that *Christ is the end of the law* — you no longer need to keep the Ten Commandments to get to heaven.

That can be misunderstood, but it is what he was preaching. The law is no longer the way to heaven, and what a relief that is. The Christian is not under the Sabbath or tithing laws for example, and that is far-reaching in its implications. We are no longer under the laws of the Jews, we are under the grace of Christ. That does not mean we can do wrong. It does not mean we can do what we like, but we are living in the liberty of the law of Christ which is the law of love.

Stephen went around and he preached this, and they argued with him and they never won an argument. When they lost their argument, they resorted to force. They began to bring in false witnesses who accused Stephen of doing exactly what they accused Jesus of doing. So we now have the opposition of the Jews to Stephen. They began to see that if Stephen was right, they were wrong; that if what he said about Jesus was true, the Jewish religion was obsolete and finished, and was not worth anything.

Years later, the man who was led to the Lord by Stephen's example was a man called Saul. Saul said, "I was born a Jew, the smallest tribe of Benjamin. I was named after the first king of Israel, Saul. I was a Pharisee, I was a Hebrew of the Hebrews." What he meant was: I didn't speak Greek. I wasn't even a Greek-speaking Jew. I was the Hebrew of Hebrews. I was as much in the Jewish race and exclusivism as I could possibly be; as touching the Law, blameless – a real Jew. When I came to know Jesus Christ, I looked back over all that I had done and I saw that it was rubbish, dirty dung to be thrown out. That was what he thought about his Jewish religion when he came to see Jesus, but in the early days of the church nobody had seen this and they had all stayed on as Jews.

When you know Christ, all your religion, all your good deeds, are dung compared with his grace. All that you have tried to do for yourself to lift yourself by pulling on your own bootlaces is dung. The Jewish religion in Christian eyes was dung. Again and again this comes out in the gospel message.

It took some months before they began to realise in the early church that you cannot mix Christianity and any other religion including the Jewish religion. It was Stephen who saw it – Stephen, who finished up facing the same court that Jesus faced, the same judges who crucified Christ, on the same false charge of blasphemy. Stephen knew in his heart that at the end of this trial he would be stoned to death. He could see it in their faces. They had done his Lord to death and he was now going to follow him. He looked up to heaven, and he was already there. The judge said, "Have you anything to say to this charge?"

For a moment he didn't speak – they looked at his face

and it was like the face of an angel. I wonder what they saw. Was it shining? Was it radiant? I would say it was unearthly. They saw in Stephen the face of a man who didn't live here but already had one foot in heaven, in glory. I have seen that look on faces of the dying. What a privilege it is to see it. I have gone into a sickroom and seen the face of an angel in the bed – a face of someone who is already in glory even though their body has not quite caught up with them. Stephen was like that, a man who knew he was about to die, a man who was looking death in the face at an early age. The first Christian martyr, he had no inspiration or example but Jesus to follow. When he began to speak, he knew it was to be his last sermon.

Once you have Christ, you don't need a temple, you don't need the Ten Commandments, you have everything you need because you have the Holy Spirit. If you have "religion" you tend to resist the Holy Spirit. You tend to turn away from Christ.

Stephen testified that he saw Jesus standing in the place of honour at God's right hand. In uttering these words of his speech, Stephen had signed his own death warrant.

Note

[1] See the books by Roland Allen, including *Missionary Methods – St. Paul's or Ours?* An ex-missionary in China, he was Anglican Vicar of Chalfont St. Peter, Buckinghamshire, where I was later a Baptist pastor. He had to retire because of his rigorist attitude to infant baptism and from Kenya exercised the role of a mission statesman, advocating "The Ministry of the Spirit".

9

The First Martyr
Read Acts 7:1–8:3

There is one moment I will never forget as long as I live. I was in Berlin and I was invited to shake hands with a man I knew to be a murderer. I remember taking his right hand in mine and thinking, "That was the hand that murdered some young men who tried to take the gospel of Jesus Christ into a place where he had never been heard of." For the man I was shaking hands with was an Auca Indian and he was the man who killed the pilots who went into that jungle area in Ecuador, seeking to reach that tribe with the gospel, and in 1952 paid for that venture with their lives.

I shook the hands of this murderer and again, as I looked into the face which was now like the face of an angel I remembered that there has not been a period of ten years since the death of Jesus on the cross when there have not been Christian martyrs. From the records we have, to say nothing of the hundreds of whom we have never heard, there is a continual line of men and women who have died for Jesus Christ.

We now consider in greater depth the very first martyr. I don't know if you have ever wondered what it would be like if suddenly in England we woke up one morning to find that being a Christian was a criminal offence, punishable by death. I have often wondered whether I would have grace to be a martyr – or would I run? I will never forget discussing this with another Christian who said something that I thought was very wise: "David, you can only be faithful in such circumstances if you have been faithful in the lesser trials that you have had already" – in other words, in the little irritations and social embarrassments and lesser persecutions. A person can lose his job for being a Christian in this country. If we have already trusted Christ for grace to be firm, straight and true to him, then, when the big crisis comes, the same Lord who gave us grace in the lesser crisis will give us the greater grace. That stopped me thinking, "Could I be a martyr?" and started me thinking, "Could he help me to be one?"

I don't know if in my lifetime I will ever have to face such a decision, but if so then I do think I will go straight back to this account of Stephen, a young man who knew that if he said what he ought to say at this moment he would sign his own death warrant. At last the authorities had a Christian on definite charges, and the charges were blasphemy against the temple and the law. These were the two pillars of the Jewish religion. The high priest, who was also the main judge, said, "Stephen, is this so?" What follows is rather surprising. It seems almost like a lecture from an Old Testament tutor. It seems irrelevant to the question. Stephen asked for a hearing and then began on a kind of balloon trip through Old Testament history. It seems to us to be an extraordinary speech to make when you are on trial for your life.

Why did he go back to the earliest days of the Jewish faith and give them a resumé of the vital chunk of their history from Abraham to Solomon? At first sight it looks as if he is playing for time. It looks as if he is just saying things they know already, but when you begin to read this chapter again and again (and you have got to do that with every chapter if you are going to understand it) you will begin to see what he was getting at, and that this was the most brilliant speech he had ever made. What was said of Stephen in chapter 6 was so true – that he spoke with such wisdom that nobody could withstand it. You begin to see that the same thing happened here, and he managed to speak for about thirty minutes perhaps before they shut their ears and refused to listen to any more.

They must have wondered what he was getting at, and then, as they listened, the message began to get through. He was accusing them and putting them in the dock just as Peter had done a few months earlier. He did not try to defend himself; he did not try to defend Christianity. He attacked their understanding of their religion. He was communicating this: I am a Jew, I know the Bible, I know your religion and I accuse you of twisting it. I accuse you of doing two things. The first thing I accuse you of doing is restricting God's dwelling. You've got God locked up in your nice little temple; you've got God just where you want him in that lovely building, but God is bigger than that.

He made two points. The first was that almost every time God spoke to one of our Jewish forefathers he spoke outside the Holy Land, never mind a temple. Did they think they had got God in that stone box there? Where did he speak to Abraham? Mesopotamia; Ur of the Chaldees. Where did he speak to all the others? He spoke to them in Egypt; he spoke to Moses in Sinai, in Midian. He spoke to the Jews in the wilderness. Did they think they have God locked up there in a little dwelling place? God is bigger than your ideas; you are restricting God's dwelling. God spoke in many countries before this ever became the Holy Land.

Everywhere God speaks is holy land. "Put off your shoes, Moses." In the Sinai peninsula, it is holy ground. You can't limit God. The little girl who said her prayers the night before going on holiday and said, "Well, goodbye, Lord. We're off to Blackpool tomorrow morning," was making the fundamental mistake that so many people make – thinking that God is locked up and just lives here. Never call a church building the "house of God" because you will get mistaken ideas if you do. Said a lady to me, "I can't pray unless I can get inside a church." I wonder if she was praying when she did get inside, if her praying were so dependent on a place.

God is everywhere and, once we begin to realise that, then our daily life is affected. If you "keep God in the temple" you can do all sorts of things "outside the temple" and imagine that he doesn't notice.

Stephen points out that God preferred to live in a tent rather than in a temple. Why? Because he was a God who walked in front of the people. God was on the move, and God's symbol, the symbol of the meeting place between God and man, was a tent – in biblical language a "tabernacle" which was prefabricated and portable and could be taken down and moved on because God moved on. The building had to catch up with him.

So God didn't ask for the temple – he wanted a tent. David sought a habitation for him, but Solomon built a house. Notice that "but". Stephen uses every word carefully, "But Solomon built him a house" – got him nicely settled down in the suburbs of Jerusalem. Here was God, down to earth, where you could manage him. The prophet had to come to Solomon, and Stephen quotes him. The prophet had to say, "Heaven is my throne and earth my footstool. What house will you build for me?" Stephen makes his first charge in such a subtle and clever way that they didn't realise what he was saying until he neared the end.

Secondly, he accuses them of thinking they have the law of Moses but not keeping it. From the very first day that Moses gave the law, they and their fathers had refused to obey him. From the very beginning they wanted a golden calf. They wanted something they could see in their worship; they wanted an image, an idol. They got sick of Moses staying up the mountain with God, and said to Aaron, "Build us a golden calf." They brought their earrings and rings and all the gold they could, to make this golden calf. In the wilderness they were worshipping the stars. When the prophets came to tell them the right way, to call them back to the law, they stoned the prophets and killed them.

You can see where all this is heading. Stephen points out that they claimed to have the law. Why did they betray and murder the greatest Prophet of them all, predicted by Moses, the holy and righteous one – Jesus? *Must you forever resist the Holy Spirit?*

Jesus said, "Men can be forgiven for what they say against me, but the man who blasphemes against the Holy Spirit cannot be forgiven." Why? Because there is no-one left to help him if he resists and blasphemes against the Holy Spirit. Stephen told them that was what they were doing. They were going to kill him because they killed Jesus.

So Stephen was accusing them of persistent wilfulness against the will of God, and of pagan worship all through their history. They were so angry they didn't even bother this time to go and get Pontius Pilate's signature. After all, he had gone back to Caesarea and he might never hear about it if they got on with it quickly – no appeal, no trial.

There is an extraordinary parallel between Stephen's trial and the trial of Jesus. There was no counsel for the defence. The judges were probably led by Caiaphas, the same high priest who condemned Jesus. The false charge was blasphemy against the temple – the same charge. The counter-charge, that they had rejected the prophets, came from Jesus and Stephen. Stephen said something almost identical with Jesus at this point.

Stephen's accusers were so angry, but there was such a contrast between their contorted faces and blazing eyes, and the face like that of an angel looking up to heaven. Stephen said, "I can see something. Wait," he said, "I can see." Beyond all the angry faces of the judges, he could see Jesus, and he said, "I can see the Son of Man at the right hand of God in glory." Jesus at his trial had said, "You will see the Son of Man coming in clouds of glory," and now Stephen echoes his words.

The judges were now so angry that they closed their ears; they wouldn't listen to another word and they rushed on him. What a scene – this wasn't an execution, it was a lynching. How utterly foolish men are to think that they can kill the truth by killing those who hold it. How foolish men are who think they can blot out an idea by obliterating those who believe it. They rushed on this man and lynched him. I don't think you would like to see a stoning. They would take a man to a hillside. They would throw him down and then they would drop boulders on him until he died – a horrible death and a very painful one. They threw him over and they started dropping the boulders, but he wasn't finished yet – he prayed.

Do you remember when Jesus was dying and he prayed, "Father, into your hands I commit my spirit"? Stephen, like his Lord, said, "Lord Jesus, receive my spirit." They could do what they liked with his body, but his spirit is safe. It is a moving moment. It would have been a fitting climax to this young man's saintly life, but it wasn't the climax. There was something even more wonderful that showed how Christ-like he was. He prayed, "Lord Jesus, do not hold this sin against them."

I remember visiting Kenya and seeing some of the Kikuyu Christians. I was told about a prayer meeting in an African church one day when a few faithful Kikuyu Christians were meeting in the little mud wall chapel and praying. The doors burst open and in came the Mau Mau terrorists, brandishing weapons and shouting, "Stop praying or we'll kill you!" The African pastor at the front went on praying, and one of the terrorists, with a terrible blow, severed one of his arms. The man sank to the ground, dying. But as he sank he prayed, "Father, forgive them for they know not what they do." Within minutes, those terrorists were on their knees begging for mercy. Not from the pastor, for he was dead. Not from the Christians, but from Christ because they met Christ in that simple African pastor. I met some of those terrorists with the scars of their fighting still on their faces, but now they had the faces of angels and they were preachers and Sunday school teachers.

Stephen would not like in the great day of judgement to feel that they were being condemned because of what they did to him. He was an amazing pray-er.

Though it was absolutely forbidden to bury a man who was stoned, devout Jews came, just as Joseph of Arimathea had done, and begged for the body and buried him with great lamentation.

There was a young man watching everything that went on – a young theological student, a student of Gamaliel. Where was Gamaliel in all this? We don't hear a word from that tolerant man now. But Saul was looking after the jackets of those who said, "Here, hold my jacket. I want to drop a stone on this blasphemer" and he watched Stephen die.

Saul had built his religion on the temple and the law, devoting his life to being a Pharisee, a Hebrew of the Hebrews. Saul had banked on all this to get him to heaven and he looked down and saw Stephen, and saw something in Stephen's face that shook him to the depths of his being. He knew in his heart that they both could not be right. He vowed that he would wipe out every Christian. That young man went into homes and he dragged out men, women, and children and threw them into prison. Christians had to flee for their lives from Saul. They fled to an alien country they would never have gone to if they had not been persecuted. Isn't it interesting that this is often how God works? People would never have gone to a certain place unless they had been in trouble and persecuted, and the gospel is spread.

I would love to go on and on with this account because that young man became the greatest Christian missionary there has ever been because he kicked against the goads. You can't blot out the truth. You may kill every Christian there is, but the truth is still true. What church history has proved again and again is this: the blood of the martyrs is the seed of the church.

10

The First Persecution and Philip's Mission
Read Acts 8:4–40

Acts 8 tells us how surprisingly quickly the gospel of Jesus spread. It was jumping over man-made barriers very quickly. It not only spread from one country to another but also from one race to another, within months of the first sermon being preached.

In this chapter we find the gospel not only going to the Samaritans, those half-caste people very disliked by the true Jews, we also have the first mention of the gospel of Jesus going to Africa. This Ethiopian lived in what is now the Sudan, not quite modern Ethiopia which is a little further to the south and higher up in the mountains. It is quite clear that the people are related because the Ethiopians of the Bible are described, and that physical appearance suits the modern Ethiopians, so they must have migrated up the hills.

The amazing thing is that the programme for Christianity, which was a world programme, was not promoted by any society or committee, nor even any individual. Jesus gave them the programme when he said, "You shall be my witnesses in Jerusalem, Judea, Samaria and to the uttermost parts of the earth" – but you almost feel that Christianity spread because what moved it first from the Jewish nation to the Samaritans was persecution.

In fact, Saul was promoting the spread of Christianity long before he became a Christian! We are told that they were running away from Saul when they went to Samaria. Here was Saul, who was fighting to stamp out Christianity, and the more he fought the further he spread it. It shows again, that God can so use the wrath of men to praise himself, that he can use you to spread the gospel of Christ even before you are converted. God has the power to overrule the malice of people to accomplish his own purpose.

In the old Anglo-Saxon Bible (I have only once seen a copy), it says in v. 4, "And everywhere they went, they gossiped the word." These were not professional preachers but ordinary men and women like ourselves. They just talked about it at the shop, in the backyard, down the street, in the fields, at the well. No wonder it spread. We must bear in mind that there was a real tension between Jew and Samaritan. It was partly to do with racial purity, but it was more than that. It was due to many factors, but they hated the sight of each other and they didn't talk to each other.

There is a remarkable story in the Gospel of Luke where Jesus and his disciples go to a Samaritan village and they are thrown out forcibly. John the disciple, who was still a son of thunder (Jesus' nickname for him), said, "Shall we call down fire from heaven on these Samaritans because they won't have us in their village?" Jesus said no – John didn't know how to act yet. Yet John was going to come back to the city of Samaria and lay hands on these people and call down the fire of the Holy Spirit from heaven. Such was the change in John.

Philip was the man who started it all. He was a deacon who had been put in charge of the serving of the tables in the church. He was one of those who ran for his life to Samaria, and when he ran he preached. When he got there he preached with such effect that he got huge crowds listening, and they listened because they saw. When you see as well as hear, then you learn and you are interested. It is this double testimony of hearing and seeing which God is longing for the church to give. When people can see things happening and lives being transformed dramatically, then they are ready to hear the gospel and they will say, "What is it that you have to say?" Philip had a great time. Many of them were set free from demon possession, which is not the same as mental illness. Many of them had diseases cured. They were baptised in the name of the Lord. It says, "There was much joy in that city." It is not usual that a city is very happy to receive alien immigrants, displaced persons, refugees. This city was thrilled to see them because they brought an answer to so many problems, and they welcomed them with open arms even though they were Jews and came from a hated nation.

There was a man called Simon and we are introduced to him with the word "but". It is one of the saddest words in the Bible. It usually comes after a description of something wonderful. Then there comes "but" and something is then said that spoils it. So frail and weak are we in our human nature that we invariably spoil a work of God. There is always somebody around to be the "but", who comes into the situation to ruin it. There was a man there who was a magician. He was the equivalent of what you may find in villages in parts of Africa – the witch doctor. He was the man who dabbled in religious magic, the man who claimed to have the power of the great God, the man who was looked up to, feared and held in awe, who had prestige as well as power, and this man admitted that he was beaten by Philip. He had never seen things happen in his own power like this.

While it is true that the devil, through magic, can give people amazing powers, those powers cannot reach the power of God. Do you remember when Moses turned his stick into a snake in front of Pharaoh? Pharaoh called his magicians and said, "Can you do that?" They said, "We think we can," and they did it by magic. It looked as if their magic was as strong as Moses' miracle until Moses told his snake to swallow up theirs. It is a wonderful account and I love it. I think of one slithering the other one down its throat, and that was the end of the magic.

There is something in magic. Never laugh at it. Take it desperately seriously and never dabble in it. That is why a missionary does well to respect the witch doctor for the power he can have from Satan – it is more than natural power. But let the missionary also be quite sure the power of Jesus is greater. The missionary's snake can swallow up the other one.

Now Simon admitted he was beaten and he believed, and asked to be baptised. They welcomed him. I have no doubt if it happened today, he would be on the Christian circuit very quickly. "Come and hear the converted witch doctor." He would be talking all around the place and crowds would be flocking to hear this dramatic conversion story. That is sometimes the mistake we make when there is a dramatic conversion. We sometimes too early assume that it is genuine. We will see why it is introduced with the word "but" in a moment.

Here was this great revival – people were coming, hearing the gospel, seeing, believing, getting baptised, and they were filled with joy. But there was one thing missing. They had not yet received the power which Philip had. Now I suppose if they had asked some people today, they would have been told not to want it. They would have been told: "Well, if God gives power to Philip, you don't need it." Some would have said to them: "Well, you received the Holy Spirit when you believed, you don't need anything more." They would have been told all kinds of things, but in those days they didn't talk like that. There has been much speculation as to why the Holy Spirit had not come on them in power at first. One reason given by some is that you have got to have an apostle around before this can happen. I don't believe that, because in the next chapter Ananias, who was certainly not an apostle, was able to help Paul to receive this gift. Others say, "Well, some Christians have a ministry of helping others into this power and some do not." There may be an element of truth in this. I think God held back this power in this case because he didn't want a Samaritan church separated from the Jewish church. So he made them wait until they had got Jewish Christians with them from Jerusalem before the Holy Spirit was poured out. In this way there would never be a division.

Peter and John came down. Here is the John who had earlier said, "Lord, shall we call down fire from heaven and destroy them?" It takes faith to talk like that, but it is faith without love. When John came back the next time, in this chapter, to this very same place, he had love as well as faith. He wanted fire from heaven, but now not to destroy them but to fill them with power.

So they prayed. The literal translation of the next verse would be: "As they laid hands on them, they received one by one the Holy Spirit." Down the line they went, and Simon's eyes were almost popping out of his head. Now I don't know what he saw and heard, but he saw and heard *something*. Simon wouldn't have been willing to offer a penny if nothing had happened, but it was precisely because when the Holy Spirit is poured out that things happen to the person on whom he comes, that Simon reached for his money. Simon wanted to buy that power, and revealed incidentally exactly how he had got many of his tricks for his magic – by buying them. He saw Peter just touching people and things happening to them. Could I have that power? I'll give you a cheque for your cause. I'll give you a handsome donation if you'll give me the power to lay hands on people.

Now Simon was a man whose heart had two things in it which a person's heart should not have and will not have if they have truly repented and believed in the Lord Jesus. First, he had a *boasting* heart. Second, he had a *bargaining* heart.

If you have really come to the Lord Jesus, those are the two things that vanish. Here was a man who was still concerned about his own prestige and still wanted to be looked up to by everybody else, a man who still wanted powers that other people didn't have and who wanted to be top dog. Here was a man who thought that you can *buy* from God the gifts that God is willing to *give*.

A boastful, bargaining heart reveals straightaway that a man is not truly converted, because if you have really repented and known the grace of our Lord Jesus Christ, which is a free gift, you never again try to buy things from God. You can't – you receive it all as a gift. You can't bargain with God after he has forgiven you, a sinner. The effect of being forgiven freely through the blood of Jesus is precisely that you will not bargain with God from then on. You will not say, "God, if I give you money, will you do this?" You would not hear a new convert trying to get prestige above everybody else by buying some power. This told Peter something terrible about this man.

Here was a man who had professed faith and been baptised but had not been converted. It is comforting and challenging that the New Testament is honest enough to say that even Peter and John could make mistakes, and Philip. No-one claims that the church today is any less fallible than this. It is terribly possible from time to time to make a mistake and to baptise someone on profession of faith whose heart is not right with God. Fortunately it is rare, but when it occurs it needs to be dealt with straightaway or that person will be left in a position of false security and think that they are alright.

Peter says: to hell with you and your money. You think you can buy the gift of God? You think you can have prestige above everybody else? Repent of this quickly before God punishes you for this false profession you have made. "Simony", so named after this Simon, refers to the attitude of those who think they can buy something from God by giving a handsome donation. When we give our money to a church, we are not buying anything.

Peter and John went back to Jerusalem. They didn't waste their journey, they preached all the way. There is a stark contrast between the fertile valleys of Samaria and the desert of Gaza. There is a great contrast, too, between the multitudes listening in Samaria and a congregation of one in the Gaza desert strip – but God wants Philip to minister to both. It is vital that a man should have as much time for the one as for the many, and should go to preach the gospel to one if the Holy Spirit directs – and should go to a place that is uncongenial as well as those that are congenial. (I can say that some of the happiest services I have ever had were with a congregation of one.)

Philip was told to leave the fertile valleys and the multitudes and the revival going on in Samaria, and to go into the middle of the desert to find one man who was an extraordinary person, one who was disqualified on a number of counts from worshipping in the temple at Jerusalem, yet he had been up to stand outside and pray to the God of the Jews. He could not enter the courts of the Lord because he was an Ethiopian. That kept him out of the court of the Jews; he would for that reason only have been allowed into the court of the Gentiles, but a man who was also a eunuch, whether by accident or deliberately or by birth, was forbidden by the law of Moses even to go into the court of the Gentiles.

This man was in charge of the treasure of Queen Candace, yet, because he was seeking God and reality, he was humble enough to go to a foreign land where he knew he would not be allowed to enter the temple. In his own country, people worshipped the sun, and they prostrated themselves before it because they thought it was alive. He wasn't satisfied with that. I have a great respect for this very humble, modest man who was determined to find the truth even if he had to stand outside the temple to find it. Somebody had given him a scroll of a portion of Isaiah. He was on his way back, with all his retinue walking in front and behind. He was in his carriage and he was reading this scroll, and he had never read anything like it. It was the best bit of the scriptures they could have given him, considering they only had the Old Testament. It was the book Isaiah, but he was finding it heavy going. Most people who read the Bible before they know Jesus find it very heavy going. He got to chapter 53 by this time, and he couldn't have got stuck in a better place. Then Philip came up to the chariot. Here was Philip, a very ordinary man, and there was this Chancellor of the Exchequer in his carriage. The Holy Spirit said, "Go near and overtake this chariot." Holy boldness was needed.

A preacher near where I lived said to his congregation, "If you have an impulse to speak to somebody about Jesus, follow that impulse, no matter who it is." A dear lady sitting, listening to him thought of George Brown, the then Foreign Secretary, and thought, "I wonder if anybody's told him about the Lord Jesus." She reflected, "Well that's a silly idea," and put it out of her head, but it came back again, "George Brown, George Brown." She thought, "Well, the minister said you must talk to whoever you get an impulse to talk to." So she looked out for George Brown. Now she did have a job in high circles, and she thought it was a chance that she might meet him. So she looked out for him for months. Finally she got on her knees and prayed, "Lord, if you've told me to speak to him about you then you'll have to bring him to me." She decided to write a letter to him, which she did, and she thought, "Well, that will be the end of that. He must get loads of letters." Two days later, she went into a shop in London and there was George Brown standing at the counter! She went up to him and spoke to him. He said,

"Are you the lady that sent me that letter?" She said, "Yes," and he later promised to go with her to a church.

I mention that because I think it is an example of what happened here. God has no respect for persons. He might send you to anyone at the top of the social ladder or at the bottom – there are "up and outs" as well as "down and outs" and he may send you to either! When the Holy Spirit tells you to go and join a person you must go to them. Philip went and jumped up into the chariot with that Chancellor of the Exchequer and said, "What are you reading? Do you understand all that?" The man said, "Well, no; I need someone to tell me," So Philip talked to him.

When D. L. Moody came to this country as an evangelist, he was under some suspicion from ministers of churches. He met a number of them and they said, "Mr Moody, would you please write out what you believe so that we may examine it to see if it's sound and to see if it's orthodox?" They didn't know anything about this young American evangelist. So he said, "Well, actually it is in print." So they said, "Well, where can we get a copy of it so that we can study it?" He said, "Well, you've probably got a copy of it on your shelves." They said, "Well, what is it then?" He said, "It is Isaiah chapter fifty-three. So the only thing I'll preach while I'm here is, 'He was wounded for our transgressions. He was bruised for our iniquities. The chastisement of our peace was upon him and with his stripes, we are healed. All we, like sheep have gone astray and the Lord laid on him the iniquity of us all.'"

That is the very chapter this Ethiopian was reading. He didn't understand. Is Isaiah talking about himself? Or who is this person who can take your sins onto himself and take them off you?

A good translation would be: "Then Philip, beginning with this scripture preached," Not just spoke to him or told him, but preached. We must get away from the idea that preaching is from a pulpit and a crowd in front sitting passively. Preaching can be just talking to someone on the bus. Preaching is telling anyone about Jesus. Beginning at the same scripture, *Philip preached Jesus*. We are not offering a system; we are not offering a church, a denomination, an organisation, a philosophy – we are offering Jesus. Only he can satisfy and meet the needs of people.

So Philip talked to the eunuch about Jesus, and then the Ethiopian exclaimed, "Look, here is water. What hinders me to be baptised?" You can see the glory of that question: he couldn't get into the Jewish religion; he was a eunuch, he was an Ethiopian, but if you repent toward God and believe in Jesus you can come right in. So they went down into the water and, in front of all his servants, the man was humbled, being dipped in the water and baptised. The highest in his land next to the queen – and here he is being brought to the level of every other sinner seeking the grace of Christ.

Immediately afterwards, Philip vanished. Clearly, the language implies a supernatural transportation of this man of God to one of the Philistine cities. He went on preaching his way all up the coast to Caesarea, and the Ethiopian never saw him again. You would have thought that would have made him sad – so many questions he wanted to ask. All he had to take back with him into Africa was one book of the Old Testament, a baptism and faith in Jesus – nothing more.

I want to span the centuries now and tell you something else. I have been to Ethiopia, talked to Christians there and heard something of what followed. Why did this Ethiopian come to Jerusalem? Did you know that when Solomon had a visit from the queen of Sheba, she lived just over the sea from Ethiopia? There were close relations between Ethiopia and what is now the Yemen, which was then Sheba. There is a clear link going back as far as that. It is almost certain that we can trace back Jewish influence in Ethiopia to the time of Solomon. That may be how the Ethiopian came to Jerusalem.

Remarkably, in the great continent of Africa with its teeming people there is only one area that has remained Christian from the earliest days of Christianity, and it is Ethiopia. All the other lands lost Christianity, if ever they had it. Christian churches along the North African coast were obliterated by Islam. Many Africans elsewhere in that continent remained for centuries in their primitive and superstitious animism.

So Philip had gone out of his way to speak to one man. You will never know what could happen as a result of speaking to one person about Jesus.

11

Saul Meets Jesus
Read Acts 9:1–9

The conversion of Saul of Tarsus is the most famous conversion in all history. The greatest enemy of the Christian faith became the greatest friend; the greatest opponent became the greatest advocate. Not only is this the most famous conversion in history, it is also the most important, because it is through this man that we Gentiles got the gospel of our Lord Jesus and around half the New Testament.

Though we have the facts of our Lord's life, death, and resurrection in Matthew, Mark, Luke and John, it is from Paul that we get the gospel. He was the first and indeed the only writer in the Bible to state the gospel in a straightforward way. His letter to the Romans has been more influential in Christian history (and even in secular history) than any other writing. It was the discovery of the meaning of the third chapter of that letter that changed Augustine's life. It was the discovery of the meaning of the fifth chapter of that letter that changed Martin Luther's life. It was the discovery of the meaning of the eighth chapter that changed John Wesley's life, and so I could go on. It all began on the road to Damascus.

Two warnings are to be given at the outset. The first is that *this is not a typical conversion*. I mention this because many have felt that they must go through this kind of experience to become a Christian. I do not know of anyone else who has been converted in just this way. There are features of his conversion which have not occurred in anyone else's. If we think that we must expect a lightning flash from heaven before we can become a Christian then we have made the mistake of taking one person's experience as the pattern for everybody's. I didn't have a very dramatic conversion myself, though I do remember the date I became a Christian. There were many things Paul experienced that I didn't, and there were one or two things that I experienced that I don't think he did on the road to Damascus. But the important thing is we both knew Christ. Whether you had a dramatic, sudden conversion or a gradual, quiet one, the vital thing is this: are you converted? Have you met Jesus Christ? We must not be depressed or discouraged if we didn't have a conversion like that of someone else.

Paul himself said he was the last to meet Jesus in this particular way. He said that Jesus had appeared to Peter, to John, to the others, to the twelve, to five hundred at once, and last of all he appeared to him, Saul. So he had a unique meeting with Jesus not a "typical" conversion.

Secondly, *this is not a sudden conversion*. It all *seems* to happen so quickly – there he is walking along a road and minutes later he is a Christian. Yet it is not sudden, because one of the things that Jesus said to him was, "It is hard for you to kick against the goads" – which means that there had been a considerable process of preparation within his mind and heart long before this dramatic crisis. If you have a dramatic crisis at your conversion, if you look back you may realise that God had been stepping into your life for a long time before – preparing you, speaking to you, bringing you to this crisis. So it is not a sudden conversion in the sense of a conversion out of the blue. We will see soon what led up to it.

Consider Saul—a man who literally had everything but Christ. Materially, mentally, morally, he had everything but Christ, and therefore his life was a waste of time. When you meet Jesus, you can look back over your former life and say,

"What a waste! What rubbish! It's just so much to throw away now – all that I've tried to do." That's how you think when you meet Jesus. You can have everything but him and when you meet him you realise you had nothing. The Bible states quite simply that he who has the Son of God has life; he that has not the Son does not have life. That was the one thing this man didn't have.

What did he have? He was an educated man of culture who had been brought up in the Greek city of Tarsus, where education was second to none. There was a university there and much cultural activity – music, art, and drama. He had all that and he was a Roman citizen, which means that he was a man of some wealth and position. It means he had certain privileges which very few others had.

Above all, he was a man with a really deep religion. He had taken it in with his mother's milk. He was a man who had come from a long ancestry of Hebraic Jews. He could trace his line right back to king Saul. He could go right back to the tribe of Benjamin. He had known the scriptures from his earliest days. He was religious to his fingertips. Here was a man who had everything but Jesus. That was the man who met Jesus on the Damascus road.

What of his temperament – because that comes into your conversion and into your Christian life? He was a man with ambition, drive, determination – a single-minded man who would set himself a high goal and go all out for it. It is a temperament that can take you a long way, and this marked this young man out as one so full of promise that his teachers and his elders saw in him one of the future leaders of the nation of Israel. He went to university in Jerusalem as well as Tarsus. He studied under Gamaliel.

Everybody marked this young man out for a great career – a man with everything at his feet. But he wasn't at anybody else's feet, and that is what was wrong. He was a man who would do no good until he became someone's slave. That is one of the dangers of this temperament. The other danger is that while you are very determined to get to your goal, you will ride ruthlessly over anyone who stands between you and it. Some of the world's greatest criminals and dictators have had that kind of temperament. Paul might have been a dictator, and he nearly was a religious dictator. "Pharisee of the Pharisees" – and his religion could be summed up in one sentence: he was determined to get to heaven under his own steam.

Why was he so violently anti-Christian? If he was so determined to be a good Jew, why did he run around and drag men and women out of their homes and fling them into prison? There are two reasons that I think lay behind this fanatical cruelty. You almost see Hitler's attitude to the Jews in Saul's attitude to the Christians. The other side of anti-Semitism, the Gentile's reaction to the Jew, was the Jew's reaction to the Christian, which was just as strong and just as malicious and deadly. Paul was as anti-Christian as many with his temperament have been anti-Jewish. Why? For two reasons. First of all, he saw that Christianity could be a rival to his own religion. A man like this cannot abide any rivalry, he must obliterate any it; he must stamp on any threat to what he stands for. He realised, quite simply, that Christianity and the Jewish religion don't mix. Not the kind of Jewish religion that Paul had, which was a "do-it-yourself" salvation. He saw perfectly well that there are only two kinds of religion in the world: his was one kind, and the religion of Jesus was the other. Hence, Jesus and the Pharisees were at complete loggerheads.

I have met many who are living in Paul's kind of religion, which is that you must do your best in order to get to heaven. Whether you spend eternity with God or not depends on how well you do on earth, how well you live, how many kind deeds you do to others, how far you can manage to be worthy of God's standards and to merit his salvation. In other words, that way to heaven is the way of justice – I want to be good enough so that God must justly give me heaven. I want to deserve to get there so that he will have to take me in because I deserve it!

The other kind of religion, which Jesus came to teach, is a religion of mercy that gets a man to heaven the moment he says, "God be merciful to me, a sinner. I don't deserve it and I never will." This is basically the difference between Christianity and every other religion in the world, including Judaism. Every other religion says: "justice"; "deserve"; "do your best"; "be good enough", and Christianity says you never will get there because you will never be good enough—*what you need is not justice, it is mercy*. When you realise that you will never get there under your own steam and you come to God and say, "God, be merciful to me a sinner," instead of having to batter at the gates of heaven, then they are flung wide open. In other words, the only people who will ever get to heaven are beggars who beg for mercy.

Paul realised that these two religions would never mix. Jesus said it is like new wine in an old wineskin. The religion of the Pharisees won't mix with that of Jesus. Jesus' religion is free grace and favour, the mercy of God. The other is justice – and you will never make it.

Paul fought the Christians because he saw that there wasn't room in the world for Judaism and Christianity. He had sold himself to Judaism, giving his whole life to it and he could not stand a rival. That is the first reason he was so fanatically anti-Christian and became the first anti-Christian missionary, the first man to leave his home and his land and to go into other countries to stop the gospel.

We live in a day in which there is an increase in anti-Christian missionaries who are prepared to travel to stop the gospel. But Paul was the first missionary against Christ, a man prepared to go out and fight these Christians.

There must be more explanation than I have given, though, for his fanatical cruelty – dragging men and women off to prison until he had a prison full, then hunting them into the next country. Mind you, it must have maddened him to realise that the more he persecuted them, and the more they ran, the more the gospel spread. It seemed as if he couldn't keep up and he didn't know which direction to run after them, and finally he decided on Damascus.

Here is the second reason. He not only saw Christianity as a possible rival, he had a horrible suspicion that Christianity was right. When a man gets that psychologically he will fight harder than ever, which is why I am encouraged when someone fights Christianity rather than just being indifferent to it. It means that he is beginning to think it might be right. If you have a suspicion you are wrong you will fight harder, becoming even more vehement in your denials.

If the Christians were right, then everything Saul had done was wrong. Everything he had hoped in was wrong. Everything he had tried to do, as he later said himself, was dung, refuse, waste to be thrown out. He didn't want to face that, and nor does anybody else. His own lecturer, Gamaliel, had said: "Beware what you do about these Christians. You might just be fighting against God."

In London one day, I sat on the grass in Hyde Park and talked to a Jew from Toronto, Canada about the Lord Jesus. The visitor was educated and could really speak logically, clearly, with great breadth of knowledge and grasp of things. He could argue about philosophers and Christian theologians. He believed in God, and he believed that there must be a God and that we must be rightly related to him. So much that we believe, he believed too. But when I said that Jesus was the Son of God he looked at me and said,

"Heresy." That was his reaction. He would lose everything if he believed that, and Paul was like this young man – educated, cultured, *everything but Jesus*.

What had caused Paul to begin to think that Christians might be right? Jesus was going to be telling him as he travelled that road, "Paul, you're like an animal whom a driver is driving in a particular direction with a pointed stick" (which was to goad an animal, to steer it). A ploughman would use this from behind, to keep an animal straight if it strayed, and it would get back in line.

Look again at Saul's life. It may be that Paul had seen Jesus in the flesh. It is quite possible – he was a student in Jerusalem at the time of our Lord's crucifixion and resurrection. In one of his letters Paul wrote: "Some of us have known Jesus after the flesh, though we don't know him like this any more." It may be that he was referring to someone he once saw hanging on a cross when he was a young student. I don't know if that was one of the goads against which he was kicking or not. That is speculation.

He had certainly seen the early disciples – he had a prison full of them. They were absolutely convinced that Jesus was alive, and therefore prison seemed to have no terror for them. With holy boldness they would get up in court and twist their judge's arguments into knots, and charge their judges with murder. He had never before met people like this – ordinary people, illiterate fishermen. Their arguments were better than his and he had been educated in logic, in how to talk, how to argue about matters of the law.

That must have been one of the goads, but the biggest one was the death of Stephen. Saul could not get over that. This young man had appeared before the Jewish Sanhedrin, had taken his judges through the Old Testament and had been saying: from your own scriptures I show you that you can't lock God up in your temple and in your Holy Land; every time he appeared to Abraham, to Moses, it was outside your Holy Land. Saul was given the jackets to hold while the men rolled up their sleeves and threw the boulders down on Stephen. He had never seen a man die like that before. Here was a man who died in hope, who was just going to Jesus, convinced that Jesus had risen from the dead, therefore he would be alive beyond the grave. Here was a man who looked up as he died and could say that he could see Jesus; Jesus was waiting to receive him. Lord Jesus, here's my spirit. This was life: a man being stoned to death and he was alive and had peace with God. As Saul stood there holding the jackets that day, he must have thought it cannot be true, Jesus is dead, he was put on a cross, and he was buried – he is not alive, the man's deluded. But a little doubt in his mind said he was not deluded; Jesus is alive and this man has real life; he has found the way to heaven, and it is not the way of trying to do good, it is the *Way*, believing in Jesus.

Imagine the journey Paul made to Damascus – 150 miles. I have been part of that way myself. It would have taken about seven days, striding ahead – the Pharisee would not even mix with his attendants – this young man was on the way to murder men and women or drag them to jail. So determined is he to get there to kill and to imprison that he is travelling in the midday sun, a thing nobody does unless they are on urgent business. Then he comes within sight of Damascus, in what is now Syria.

I think it is most significant that he met Jesus within sight of Damascus. Do you realise the significance of that? Of course it was before he got near any Christians so it was before he could do them harm, but that is not the significance. The significance was that this Jew of Jews, Hebrew of the Hebrews, Pharisee of the Pharisees didn't meet Jesus till he stepped out of the Holy Land, until he was off Jewish soil and on unclean territory that he would have said is not God's land at all. The lesson he had to learn was that you have got to get out of your own prejudice, out of man-made religion if you are going to meet Jesus the Saviour.

Remember again: this man had everything *but* Jesus and therefore had nothing. It was not lightning and thunder, as some of his attendants thought; it was *like* that. Suddenly at midday there was a light in the sky brighter than the midday sun. In those days there was no light as bright as that. There is one light now as bright as that, which we know. I remember reading the terrible story of Hiroshima. I remember reading the account of one man who was in that city when the atom bomb dropped and he said, "A light came that was brighter than the midday sun." But this happened in the days before atom bombs and was not a destructive light. This light brighter than the midday sun flashed from heaven and Paul fell on the ground.

Then came the voice – it was in his own language and it was someone who knew his own name. When you meet Jesus you get the sense "he knows me". You might be in the middle of a congregation, you might be in the middle of a crowd of thousands, and suddenly you feel: Jesus is speaking to *me*, personally. It is the most amazing thing that Jesus knows every one of us by name. Jesus said, "Saul, Saul." What do you think is the most important word in the question that he asked, "Why are you persecuting me?" The "why" challenges this young man to think through what he is doing and produce a justification for his persecution, but the really important word in this is the word "me". It was the word that Paul fastened on immediately: "me". Who is "me"? – and who is this talking to me? But he didn't just say that, he said, "Lord".

Here is the dilemma in Paul's mind – let me try and shape it for you. This light is the light of the glory of God. There is only one light brighter than the sun, and that is the glory of God. It must be God—Lord God. Yet it can't be God because I've been following God all my life. I'm not against God, I'm against these Christians. I'm not against God, I believe in God.

So many people say to me, "I'm not against the church; I'm not against these things. I believe in God." Ah, but Jesus says, "You're against me."

Then comes the most amazing statement: "I am Jesus." Which do you think is the most important word there? I'll tell you, two words: "I am". You know what those words are, don't you? That is the name of God, the name by which Moses knew God, the name that Paul dare not pronounce. No Jew pronounced that name for fear of being struck dead – it was too holy a name, too revered. God is the great "I am", and the voice said, "I am Jesus." The name which Paul had known all his life as the name of God became the name of Jesus that moment. "Jesus"? Then he was alive; then he *was* the Son of God. Then he, Saul, was wrong and Stephen was right. This Jesus was the Son of God, not just a great man, not just even the greatest man; this Jesus was God Yahweh, the Son of God, the eternal God, and the Son of the eternal Father – Jesus. "I am Jesus."

Saul now saw something else too: that your attitude toward Christians is your attitude to Christ; that if you laugh at Christians, you are laughing at Christ; if you criticise Christians, you are criticising Christ; if you attack Christians, you are attacking Christ; if you persecute Christians, you are persecuting Christ. If you put Christians in prison, you are putting Christ in prison. For inasmuch as you do it to the least of these, his brethren, you do it to him. Paul, in that terrible moment, realised that he was guilty of attacking the Son of God himself. It is a terrible thing to realise that the person you have really been hurting is Jesus.

Do you know what the worst sin in the Bible is? It is the

sin of not believing in Jesus. Again and again we are told this. If you have heard about Jesus and you have heard that he is the Son of God and your Saviour, that he died that you might be forgiven, that he died to make you good, that you might go at last to heaven saved by his precious blood – if you have heard that and not believed it for yourself, that is the worst thing you could have done. There may come a day when you realise that you did this to Jesus – and that God loved the world and gave his only Son. The biggest present you ever got and you threw it back in his face and said, "I can manage. I'll get to heaven, I'm good enough. I can make my own way there, thank you, I don't need help." It really is the worst thing you can do. Saul realised that he had been fighting against God.

What did he expect to happen next? If you had been Saul what would you have expected? To be incinerated on the spot by another flash of lightning? That would have been justice. To have been put in prison yourself? That would have been justice. To have been tortured, put to death? That would have been just. I am quite sure if that had happened to Saul he would have said, "It's only what I deserve." But the voice said, "Get up. Go into the city and you will be told what to do." Isn't that amazing? Not a single rebuke, not a single bit of punishment. Nothing, just "Go and wait and I will tell you what to do next" – which brings me to the next thing I want to say about Jesus.

Jesus challenged him but the second thing was that he commanded him.

The biggest surprise of Saul's life was to meet Jesus and know that he was alive. The second biggest surprise of his life was that instead of wondering what Jesus was going to do to him, Jesus told him that he would learn what he was to do. The message meant this: you have been fighting *against me*, now you are going to fight *for me*.

Two things come out of this: the *mercy* of Jesus and the *majesty* of Jesus. No conversion, I think, is complete unless it experiences both. The mercy of Jesus is that when you meet him and realise how you have treated him and refused him all these years, that you find he doesn't punish you for it, he doesn't rebuke you for it. He wants to start from that moment and make you a new life. In the same moment you meet the majesty of Jesus. The majesty of Jesus is that you have met the King of kings and the Lord of lords, and that from now on *he commands*.

In other words, when you come to Jesus you are not doing him a favour, he is doing you a favour. You are not coming in a patronising way and saying, "Well, Jesus if you'd like to come into my life – poor old thing standing outside the door and knocking, come on in." You're not doing that at all. That famous text about standing at the door and knocking is not a text for people who are not Christians. It was addressed to Christians. It is not a conversion text at all. This isn't the picture; it's not that Jesus is pleading to come in. Jesus confronts us. He is the King of kings and the Lord of lords and he steps right into your life and he says, "Now I'm going to tell you what to do." So Jesus commands Paul.

For ever afterwards Paul always called himself two things: an "apostle" – because he had been *sent* by the Lord Jesus, and a "slave of Jesus Christ". He always called himself that, "Paul, a bond slave of Jesus." From his conversion onwards he was a slave, and that is just what his temperament needed. He would achieve great things, provided somebody else bossed him. If he had made his own career, he would have wrecked his own life and others'. He needed someone to rule him if he was going to make the most of his gifts, his experience, his education, his culture, and all the other things. Only if God was in control of his life would these things be useful. It was a total surrender that day he got up.

He was blinded. He got up and he opened those eyes and he couldn't see a thing. The friends rushed up to him and helped him to his feet, unsure what had happened. They heard the voice and they heard him talking. They looked into those blank eyes and they realised he was sightless. This great tough man who had been striding on ahead of them in the midday sun, eager to get hold of those Christians and drag them into prison – this man had to be led like a little child by the hand into Damascus. Can you see him? Stumbling over every pebble, a man whom God has broken.

I don't think you ever get anywhere in the Christian life until God has taken your life and smashed it; until he has broken you so that you come as a little child and put your hand out. The song goes: "Break me, melt me, mould me, fill me...." How can you hope to be filled? How can you hope to be moulded? How can you hope to be God's man or woman until you have got to the point where you are broken? This poor little Jew, walking along the road now. This man with a career set ahead of him, here he is stumbling in, "Will you help me? Where's the door...." And in he comes. He sat there for three solid days. He didn't eat, he didn't drink, and he couldn't see to feed himself. He didn't want to. He sat there for three days thinking....

Why did God blind Saul? I think to help him to see. There was a flash of light from heaven so bright that it blinded those eyes, but it illuminated his whole being. I am quite sure he was saying to himself through those three days: I have been so blind but now I can see. I was blind to Jesus. I thought he was a criminal. Now I see he is the Son of God. I thought he deserved to die, and now I see it was the worst thing we ever did. I thought he was dead and gone, and now I see that he is alive. *Now Saul saw.* This man was to become one of the greatest missionaries who has ever lived. I love his writings. It all began on that day on the road to Damascus.

I think of an Arab called Nammour. He had once given lectures against Christianity and to do so he had read a bit of the Bible, including the Sermon on the Mount, but that was all he knew of Christianity. He had never been to church, never met a missionary. Part of his ambition was to have a wife and a family. He married a beautiful girl. Then they had a little baby daughter and his cup of joy was complete and he thought he had got everything: high in political circles, wife and a little girl, but she was born a "blue baby" and she died. He was so cut up about it that he had a heart attack and was rushed into a Jerusalem hospital. While he lay there, his wife came to see him. There was one phrase going through his mind again and again, and he couldn't get rid of it: "Where your treasure is, there your heart will be also." He thought, "Where have I seen that? Where have I read it? My little baby girl was my treasure and she's dead and my heart has had this attack because it followed my baby girl – she's my treasure and my heart's dead now."

Then, as his wife sat by the bedside, he looked down to the foot of the bed. There was nobody there, but he started talking to someone. His wife thought he was delirious, but he wasn't. He said to her afterwards, "Do you know who has just spoken to me?" She said, "No, who?" He said, "Jesus – And he said to me 'three days'. I don't know what it means. It is either that I will be better and out of hospital in three days or else I'll be dead in three days."

Three days later, though the doctor said he would be months in that hospital, he walked out of there a fit man. As soon as he got out he began to preach about Jesus. He soon had led a number of Arabs to the Lord, and he started a little church. On the rooftop of his house there was a room which he made into a meeting room, and here he met with sixty converted Arabs. Still he had not met a missionary and still he hadn't been to another church. The only thing he had was a Bible in Arabic. One Easter Sunday morning, when a group of us were out in Jerusalem, there had been a riot two days before, so we were under curfew. The streets were deserted, but we got permission to go out. We had set out to look for a place to worship and there was nobody to be seen, just an odd soldier at a street corner. Then we saw this man leaning over a rooftop and he was saying, "Come up!" When we went up, we said, "Who are you, and why did you say come up?" He said, "I have a little church here but none of my people can come to it this morning and it's Easter Sunday. I have prepared a sermon on the resurrection. I've got to preach it to somebody, and I knew that nobody could come because of the curfew and I've been praying for two hours that God would give me a congregation to preach to. When I looked over the roof and saw you coming I knew that God had answered my prayer." We went up into that little room and Nammour told us the story of his conversion. A man who had preached against Christ, a man who stirred up trouble, a man of ambition, a man who was really going to the top – a modern man. Then he met Jesus and his life was changed. I don't know where he is today, or even whether he is alive or dead. Whichever, he is living because he knows Jesus.

Here is why I have recounted this: *You can meet Jesus Christ today. You may have everything but Jesus, and if you have, you've got nothing. You may have nothing but Jesus, but if you have him you've got everything.*

12

Ananias Baptises Saul
Read Acts 9:10–31

It is fascinating to listen to the testimonies of other Christians as to how they came to know the Lord. The part I am always most interested in is not the most spectacular or sensational, but what happens after they are converted. Far too many testimonies stop maybe five, ten or twenty years ago, as though nothing has happened since conversion. I don't care if you have moving experiences – I am really interested in where they move you *to*. The real question about a conversion is not, "How did it happen? How spectacular was it? How unexpected was it?" The real question is: "Did it last? What difference did it make? What did it lead to?"

In studying Paul's testimony in Acts 9, we have passed the most spectacular part. But we are just coming to the most interesting part, because we are going to see what happened afterwards. Did it last? It lasted nearly forty years with him and it is still lasting! We left Saul of Tarsus sitting in the corner of a dark little room in a street called "Straight" which you can still visit in Damascus today. We left a man about whom two things could truly be said. First, he could see nothing. Second, he could see everything. He could see nothing because his eyes were sightless. He couldn't see to do a thing for himself; he neither ate nor drank. There he was – sitting in darkness.

Did you ever wonder why he was blind? The answer is, he had met the risen Jesus. But just a moment – Peter met the risen Jesus and he wasn't blinded; John met him, the eleven disciples met him, five hundred people at one time met him, and none of them were blinded. Why was Saul the only one to be blinded when he met the risen Jesus? Because he was the only one to meet the risen Jesus *after* he had ascended into the glory that he had with his Father before the world began. The glory of Jesus is too bright for you to look at. These physical eyes of ours could not take a glimpse of the glory of Jesus – we would be blinded.

So Paul, the last of the apostles, was the only one to see Jesus risen, ascended and glorified, and it was just too bright. Thank God we see through a glass darkly. If you go out and stare at the sun it will damage the retina of your eye, and the glory of Jesus is brighter than the noonday sun. One day we will see him face to face, but we will need new eyes to do it and we will have new eyes.

But it was also true of this man sitting in the corner of the room that he could now see everything. He knew the scriptures back to front. He had attended the synagogue every day. He had lived a good life; he had observed the law. He had been *there* – except that until then he had been spiritually blind; he had not seen the truth that Jesus was the Son of God. But *now* he could see everything. He could see that fifteen hundred years of his own history pointed to Jesus; that all the threads of Jewish law pointed to Jesus; that all the sacrifices of the temple pointed to Jesus; that everything he had been taught as a child and as a student pointed to Jesus, and that in Jesus everything was fulfilled. Whilst physically he could see nothing, spiritually he could see everything.

What happened after that conversion is the important thing. It could have frittered away into nothing or it might have been a moving experience which he would then forget. But, instead, it went on into a fruitful obedient life of service. I confess that in the whole of Paul's conversion my favourite part is what happened next. Paul could not remain very long in this lonely experience. He needed Christian friends. One of the first things you need after you become a Christian is a Christian friend. Somehow the Lord has a wonderful way of sending just the person you need to help you to learn what it was all about – to take the next step. Ananias was the man.

These two men were half a mile apart and they would never have come closer to each other than that if God hadn't told them to. There are people I know and count among my closest friends whom I would never have met if the Lord hadn't brought us together. Our paths would never have crossed, our interests would have never coincided, but God can bring people together. Ananias was sitting in his room and Saul was sitting in another room and they both had a vision. Saul had a vision about Ananias and Ananias had a vision about Saul. God spoke to them both simultaneously and he got them both on the line – God can do this!

I remember a dear lady who was in deep trouble one Monday morning. She tried to phone me again and again and couldn't get through because there was something wrong with the line. She was desperate, and so finally she just sat by the telephone and said, "Lord, get me through to Mr. Pawson." I was sitting at my desk in the study preparing a sermon and I reached out and picked up the phone and I dialled this woman's number. I hadn't called her in a couple of months or more. When I got through she said, "Oh, Mr. Pawson what do you want?" I said, "I don't know. I just had to ring you up." She said, 'Do you know I've been trying to get you for half an hour and it took the Lord thirty seconds to get us through.'" This is how he does it.

God has such a wonderful communications system! He told Saul: there's a man called Ananias and he can help you. And he informed Ananias: there's a man called Saul who needs your help. So he got them together. But not very easily because Ananias started telling God what sort of a person

147

Saul was – as if the Lord didn't know!

I think that was fear or bewilderment. Ananias couldn't understand the Lord helping a man like that. He should have known better, he should have known that God knew all about Saul and could change such a man. Above all, he should have known that the Lord had the right to order him to do anything – even for his worst enemy.

The Lord was wonderfully patient. He let Ananias know that Saul was no longer under the orders of the chief priests, but was the Lord's chosen instrument. Saul was going to be imprisoned, starved, beaten and shipwrecked. He was going to suffer – not for his sins, but for the name of Jesus. Ananias was told that Saul would bear the Lord's name to Gentiles, kings and people of Israel.

So Ananias went. He entered the house where Saul was, and one word he said was I think the most wonderful in this whole account: "Brother...." This to Saul, a man who had come threatening murder, and would have thrown Ananias in prison and dragged his wife off to a cell and put her in chains. The whole of Christianity is in that phrase: "Brother Saul". Nobody can achieve the "brotherhood of man" because until you are children of the same father you can't be brothers. Until you are sons of God through the Lord Jesus how can you call your worst enemy your brother?

Then Ananias set about consecrating Saul for his task. The believer had the job of helping this young Christian, a spiritual baby, telling him what to do next. Ananias laid his hands on Saul and spoke of the Lord who had appeared to Saul on the road having sent him, so that Paul would receive his sight and be filled with the Holy Spirit. It is interesting the man who wrote this, Luke the physician, used medical terms – "something like scales" fell from Saul's eyes. It is a doctor describing this miracle.

Saul had been converted and he believed. You need to be

filled with the Holy Spirit, and Saul had his Pentecost three days after his conversion. He was filled with the Holy Spirit. I don't know what happened. Did he speak in tongues as the other apostles had done? I think he may well have done because he said some years later, "I thank God I speak in tongues more than you all." If you despise that gift you are despising Paul. He said, "I want you all to have the same gift." He said that it was a precious gift to him. But I don't know if he had this straight away. Having been filled with the Spirit, he now had been given power and gifts and lovely things from on high to do his ministry.

The next thing he needed was to be baptised in water. It was never known in the New Testament for a Christian to say: I am converted and I believe in Christ so I don't need to be baptised. It was never an optional extra. To obey his command to be baptised was the way to seal your faith, to accept Christ as Lord as well as Saviour. It is still the next step once you have come to know the Lord. Alas, I was fourteen years a Christian before I was baptised. I am sorry that it never came to my attention before. When it did, I had to think about it and pray about it, and the devil said, "It's fourteen years, leave it now. It's too late." It's not too late at all. Better late than never. I baptise people of seventy and eighty.

What did Paul do when he was baptised? He called on Jesus to wash away his sins. He tells us that later when he recounts his testimony.

That was the first part of the "afterlife" for Paul. Now the second: straight away, he started talking to others about his faith. Now the easiest time of all to confess the Saviour is just after you are converted. It is how you feel when your first child is born. You feel so full of it. That is how it is when you have been born again. You wonder why everybody doesn't ask you about it, so you tell them – not always wisely, not always tactfully. Sometimes you have to learn that with those you live nearest to, maybe preaching isn't quite the best way of sharing the Lord with them but you are bursting!

Saul confessed publicly in the most difficult place of all that he now believed in Jesus. Where was the most difficult place? It was surely the synagogues expecting him to come and preach *against* Christ. Now he might have said, "Let's be discreet about this. I'll go somewhere else and start being a missionary." It is always much easier to think that if only you were somewhere else you could witness for the Lord. But Paul must have thought: I'm going to go to the very synagogues where I have got letters of introduction to get me into their pulpits, and they are expecting me, so I'll go.

He got into their pulpits and instead of saying, "Christ Jesus was not the Christ. He's not the Son of God and we must stamp out this thing" he got up and he told them that since leaving Jerusalem he had changed his mind – Jesus *is* the Son of God. Then he proved it to them from the scriptures. Could you prove from the Old Testament that Jesus is the Son of God? It is an interesting exercise, but he could. He didn't have a New Testament, he hadn't written it yet! So he had to use the Old Testament and he proved from their scriptures that Jesus was the Christ.

This amazed them because it was the exact opposite of what they expected – and because of his courage saying it there! One of the best bits of advice I can give to a young Christian is: where would be the most difficult place for you to say that you are now a Christian? Then go and tell them. It sounds hard advice, but that is the place to begin – not the easiest, the most difficult. That will strengthen you very quickly. They obviously recovered from their amazement rapidly, and started arguing. They didn't like him because every argument they used he just flattened. Remember he was trained in law and he knew how to present a case. Now all these gifts were available to the Lord, and when they argued with Saul he just argued them out. He *proved* that Jesus was the Christ. This is the only difference between a Jew and a Christian. A Jew believes in Christ but he doesn't know who it is; he doesn't know the name of the Messiah. The Christian says Jesus is the Christ so you now believe in Jesus Christ. Every Jew believes in the Christ, only the Christian believes that Jesus is the Christ and this is what makes all the difference. The Jew is looking for the Saviour. The Jew is hoping that one day God will send a divine person to help them.

A taxi driver was taking me around the shores of Galilee. We were discussing the Six Day War, which was only a fortnight old. He said to me, "I don't know what you think sir, but I think our Messiah is coming soon. I said, "I agree with you, but I think he's been once already. Jesus is the Christ." All the Jewish hopes of centuries are summed up in him. Well, that was Paul's confession. We are told to confess our sins and to confess our Saviour. Every Christian should confess. I remember a priest once saying to me, "You don't believe in confession in your church, do you?" I said, "We certainly do!" I continued, "If you came along to one of our fellowship meetings you would hear more confession than you hear on a Saturday evening." He argued about this. But, I went on: "There's something more than confessing sins – we don't confess to a priest; we do confess our sins to one another." We did in that fellowship; we were close enough to do so. We prayed for one another. There was a lot of confession. We are supposed to confess our sins, but we are *also* told to confess the Saviour. To confess your sins means to bring them out and tell someone else you have sinned. To confess your Saviour is to bring him out and tell someone else you belong to him.

Jesus said, "...whoever is ashamed of me and my words

in this adulterous and sinful generation, of him the Son of Man will also be ashamed when he comes in the glory of his Father with the holy angels."

Now comes the next stage: very soon Paul was in real trouble. The man who had hunted others had his own life put in danger. First of all, he was deeply resented by the Jews in Damascus. They couldn't beat him in arguments so they resorted to physical violence. How often a man who loses the argument intellectually will put his fists up and use the physical argument. That is what their reaction was. They wanted to kill him.

The contrast is amazing: Saul had meant to march out of that city a proud conqueror with a string of prisoners in chains behind him, but instead the Christians let him down in a basket by night – how humiliating. They did it because it was not yet God's time for him to die. He wasn't running away. He was simply recognising that he had something to do before he died. Just as Jesus had his life threatened at least five times before the cross, and each time he deliberately escaped to continue his work, Saul was going to do the same thing. It is foolhardy to rush into being a martyr. You need to do it at the right time in the right place when God has decided you should die.

Now came the hardest test. He came back to the church in Jerusalem, and the Christians who knew his past were too suspicious of him. I think the hardest test for someone who has had a dramatic conversion is to find that Christians do not readily accept him if they know his past. It is a hard test for them too. We can understand them wondering whether it was real. How could they know he was not a spy planted to find out the names of those who came to meetings? He tried to join them but they wouldn't have him. They were afraid. He had been a violent man who attacked them, so no wonder they were afraid. Their own relatives were in prison because of him. How would you accept a man into your fellowship who was responsible for your wife and children being in jail? Could you? Let's just be realistic and human about this. We would be just as afraid as they were.

But there was one man, Barnabas, who believed Saul had been converted, for two reasons. Firstly, because Saul had *met the Lord*. Secondly, as proof of that, he was now *preaching for the Lord*. Barnabas was not a sentimentalist. He wanted evidence that there really was a changed life, but when he got the evidence he was prepared to believe it. Barnabas was the second Christian friend, who introduced Saul to the fellowship – and he came in.

Now Saul did a very wonderful thing. He disputed with the Hellenists. Do you get excited about that? Does it stir your heart? It does for me, because he was taking up the work of Stephen. The last time you heard that phrase, "disputing with the Hellenists" was in Acts 6, and it had been Stephen who had been killed for it. Paul took up what Stephen had begun. That is real evidence of a converted man who has been changed completely by the Lord. He is taking up a most difficult task, and he knows perfectly well he runs the risk of losing his own life if he does so, because he saw Stephen die for doing that very thing. So he disputed with the Hellenists and they decided to kill him too.

He told the Christians and they didn't think it was right for him to die then – if he has called you to be a missionary to the Gentiles, off you go. They took him down to Caesarea and put him on a boat by himself, to go to Tarsus. If you think being a Christian is easy, study the life of Paul. Why Tarsus? It was the town from which he had left some years before as the bright boy, the head boy of the local school, ran away with all the school prizes, going up to Jerusalem – to the university. With a promising career ahead, he was going to be one of the most famous Jewish boys from Tarsus.

Now he was coming back, hunted by the Jerusalem Jews – a complete failure in his chosen career. He was coming back as an enemy of all the things of which he had been a friend. He was coming back as a fanatical Christian – back home to his own relatives and his old friends, by himself. We don't know that there were any Christians in Tarsus then, but he was coming back home to tell them about Jesus.

So I come to v. 31 and a summary of this chapter – only two letters long: *so*. "So the church throughout all Judea and Galilee and Samaria..." [notice how it was spreading already], "had peace." Of course they had peace! Their greatest enemy was now their greatest friend. The man who had started the persecution was now a Christian. Why didn't others persecute the church now? For the very simple reason they were so flummoxed, bewildered, caught off guard by the fact that their leader was now a Christian they didn't know what to do. So, for a period, the church had peace in which the church grew. "So the church was built up." Why? For the simple reason there is nothing builds up a church so well as an outstanding conversion.

My cousin Tom Rees, in his early days as an evangelist, was invited to go to a town in the Midlands and conduct a ten-day mission. He went and he preached the first two or three nights, and it was like preaching to wood. Nothing happened and he thought, "What's going to get this church and this mission going?" He finally did something he only did once in his life. He asked a local man, "Who's the worst character in this town?" He asked a few people this and he got the same name from all of them. So he went to the address of this man and he knocked on the door.

He said when the man came to the door, "I'm Tom Rees and I'm preaching at the church down the road," and the door began to close. He said, "Hold on a moment. I will give you ten shillings if you'll come and hear me preach." The door opened again quickly. He said, "What? Ten shillings to come and hear you preach?" Tom said, "Yes, that's all. Just come and hear me preach tonight." The man said, "Done." He went to the pub first and he said, "You know what, there's a preacher up at the church who's giving you ten shillings to go and hear him preach." So all his pals came to see this strange preacher. That night the man was converted. The mission took off like fire then!

So in Acts the church was built up, edified and walking in the fear of the Lord. Why? Because there is no argument so unanswerable as the argument of a changed life. This is the one thing that the unbeliever cannot stomach. He may be able to tie you in knots on other grounds, but he cannot deny a changed life. He can't argue it away. Not only was the church built up in the fear of the Lord and the comfort of the Holy Spirit – it was multiplied. A church that is *dividing* is the opposite of what God wants it to be. We are to be a *multiplying* church so the church was multiplied.

This wonderful testimony occurs twice more in the New Testament. Paul was never tired of giving his testimony. Thirty years later he was still giving it. On the last occasion when he gave it he was standing before a king. At Saul's conversion, God had said to Ananias, "...he is a chosen vessel of mine to take my name before Gentiles, *kings*, and the people of Israel." Thirty years later, Paul said, "... King Agrippa, I was not disobedient to the heavenly vision." That to me is the most moving sentence of the whole testimony. It is one thing to have a heavenly vision, quite another thing to be obedient to it. It is one thing to be moved in church and long to be a saint, and long to devote your life; it's another thing to get on and do it.

But it was fourteen more years before Paul began to be a missionary to the Gentiles. It may be that you have heard the call to be a minister or a missionary, and it may be years before that call is fulfilled. He calls you to be obedient to the heavenly vision.

Finally, we see this man forty years later. He is sitting in a Roman prison, chained and awaiting execution. He is still suffering for the name of Jesus, still bearing the name of Jesus to the Gentiles and to kings. He is going to give it to Caesar in a few weeks' time. He is writing a letter in which he says: "I have fought the fight. I have kept the faith. I have finished the course. I was not disobedient to the heavenly vision."

13

The First Resurrection
Read Acts 9:32–10:35

I hope that some day you will have the privilege of going to Israel and visiting the land about which Acts was written. I recall the first time I landed at what was then called Lod Airport. Lod is the modern name for Lydda. It looked like any other airport in the world of course – the usual refreshment lounge, interminable waiting room, and so on. Yet I was standing in Lydda and all sorts of associations of that place came to mind.

It was of course at Lydda that St George slew the dragon. Lydda was Philistine territory and they worshipped a god called Dagon. It is almost certain that the legend of George and the dragon is a corruption of Dagon, that Philistine god. What is certainly true is that it was very near Lydda that a young man of my name slew Goliath, the Philistine giant. It was also in Lydda and nearby Joppa that a man called Peter slew death and disease. I think that was a greater victory than anything of George and the dragon or even David and Goliath.

Why is it that – having got us all excited about Paul, and having told us that Paul is going to be the missionary to the Gentile world and take the gospel all over the place – we have got to go back to Peter? The reason is that Luke wanted us to be quite clear that it was Peter who first took the gospel to the Gentiles. He did not want us to think of Peter as a kind of Jewish missionary and Paul as a Gentile one. He didn't want any division in our minds between the great apostles of God. He showed us that in fact it was Peter who not only preached the first sermon to the Jews, he also preached the first sermon to the Gentiles. This fisherman who had been trained by Jesus for three years was the man who first took the truth about God and about men and about Jesus *outside* the Jewish circle. Had he not done so, and had no-one else done so, Christianity would not have been your faith unless you are Jewish. It might have been just a little Jewish sect kept within that race and locked away from the rest of the world. But Peter, and later Paul, saw to it that you could get the truth.

Peter travelled from Jerusalem, up in the hills, down to Lydda and Joppa on the coast. Then from Joppa, right up the coast, to Caesarea. Three amazing things happen en route which we will now look at.

First, Peter is on a tour among believing Jews. The reason is that he was the first pastor of the church. We must not play down the fact that Jesus gave him the leadership of the early church, and that he *did* build his church on Peter first, and Peter *was* the first pastor shepherding the flock, feeding the lambs of Christ. Peter had the terrible experience of seeing his flock scattered. The church in Jerusalem, of which he was pastor, had scattered, and it was all due to Paul. They had fled, with what belongings they could manage, to all kinds of places. They scattered everywhere. Peter was going the rounds, trying to pick up the threads. He came to Lydda because some of them had gone there, so he was visiting.

He arrived and found there in the church a man who had not been able to do a thing for himself for eight years. I don't know what that man felt like. I have spoken to some people who have been paralysed. It is one of the most frustrating experiences in the world not to be able to do a thing for yourself—he couldn't dress himself, couldn't feed himself, couldn't do a thing. He was a Christian believer. He couldn't do anything for other people either, and he couldn't do much for the Lord, and he lay there.

Now here is Peter, who has no qualifications except that he knows Jesus is alive. When he looked at this man, he knew in his heart what he had to do. He didn't have to say, "I'm terribly sorry that you're like this." He didn't have to say, "Well, God will have some compensations for you." He didn't say, "Well, you can at least pray for us." What did he do? He went and stood by that bed and said, "Aeneas, Jesus the Christ heals you. Arise and make your bed." It was only because Jesus had risen that Peter could say that – you cannot tell a paralysed man to rise unless you believe Jesus rose. Peter was very careful in his choice of words at that crucial moment. His using Jesus' name is important – it is Jesus who heals you. When he said "Arise", the man could have said "I can't", but Peter was giving him the opportunity to exercise faith, and was doing what Jesus had done before him. To say "Rise" to a paralysed man is to say: *believe* that you can get up, and you will.

What Peter also told him to do was: make your bed – which seems very practical. It meant to roll up the mattress and to carry it away, and to take away the wooden frame on which it lay. Why did Peter add that? For the very simple reason that he wanted this man to realise that *health was going to bring work* – that when Jesus made him well again he was going to have to do things for himself and for other people. He had not worked in eight years. Some people can get to the point where they actually enjoy bad health. Do you know what I mean by that? Would they rather lie there and not be healed rather than get up and have to do for themselves and not get all the attention? Jesus once met a man like that who said he had been lying there thirty-eight years and couldn't get well. Jesus asked him, "Do you really want to be well? Would that man really enjoy good health and working for his living again? As a result of that question the man was healed. Here is Peter saying that Jesus can heal – he is alive and he is here. Get up! The implication is: get up and then get down to business and make your bed, do some useful work and look after yourself. No wonder that this incident caused many people to believe in and turn to the Lord. Do you notice that Peter didn't become a star, a hero? The crowds didn't say, "Have you seen Simon Peter? Isn't he wonderful?" The crowds turned *to the Lord*. Of the little village (which is what it was then) of Lydda, and a nearby village of Sharon, it says they all turned to the Lord. They would have thought: if the Lord can do that, he can help me too.

Some people claim that such healings were of physical symptoms produced by mental, emotional or spiritual disorder – psychosomatic. But we will move on to another incident which could hardly be psychosomatic because the "psyche" part was dead, and the "soma" part was just left ("psyche" here meaning "life" and "soma" meaning "body"). Because while he was there Peter got an urgent message from a nearby group of Christians who had also fled from Jerusalem (they were meeting in a house near the sea).

This time it was a lady of good works and charity. She was full of that kindness and practical help which is one of the loveliest things you'll ever meet. Furthermore, we know she devoted her life to helping widows. When you bear in mind that a widow in the ancient world had no pension, might have nowhere to live, was unemployable, and literally was completely bereft, you realise why in the scriptures we are told that true religion is to look after widows and orphans, the two groups of people in the ancient world who had nowhere to go and often no-one to look after them. This dear lady devoted her life to widows in a very practical way – making clothes for them, helping them to work, helping them to make some money. It is a lovely picture.

There are two things I want to point out: first, her good works did not make her a Christian. She did them *because* she was a Christian. This is the difference between doing good things in order to get to heaven and doing good things because you are going there. Secondly, good works and charity are no guarantee that you will not fall sick and die. Christianity was never meant to be an insurance policy, but many times I have been asked, "Why should this happen to me?" Let us not regard religion as an insurance. Christ never promised that.

This good woman, who was so busy helping others, fell sick and died. They laid her out and they sent for Peter. Now I wonder what on earth they wanted Peter for. Why do you think they sent for him? To take the funeral because they felt he would give her a good oration? Did they think he would be able to comfort the relatives? Did they possibly imagine that when he came he would do what he did do? He came into this house, went upstairs, and there was the body laid out and washed. The widows around her, weeping, showed Peter the clothes she had made for them. It is a very moving scene and Peter must have wondered what to do in that situation. To this uneducated fisherman there came a thought so startling that he told everybody to leave the room. They left. Peter was alone with the corpse, he knelt down by the bed and prayed. God then gave him the words and told him what to do. Peter was to tell her to get up. Can you imagine the feelings in his heart? He had never done such a thing before in his life, but he had been present on some occasions when Jesus had done it – with a little girl of twelve, Jairus's daughter, with a widow's son, and with one or two others. Peter had always been there, indeed, Jesus had once shut everybody out except Peter, James and John.

Peter, now alone in that room with the Lord and with the

body, now knew what to do. He got up and he did a thing, which requires tremendous faith. He said to her dead body, "Tabitha, arise." Her eyes opened and she looked up at him. I don't know if she knew him, but I am quite sure she smiled, and then she sat up. He took her hand and he lifted her up, and he took her downstairs to the others. You can't explain that away in psychosomatic terms! You can't explain it away at all. You've either got to say that happened or it didn't. You have either got to say, "Jesus Christ who rose from the dead can raise from the dead," or you've got to say, "It's all a complete fairy tale, and no-one in their senses would believe such a thing." I believe it happened, I believe that Peter was only doing what Jesus had told him to do.

That does not mean that every Christian is called to rush around and stop every funeral and put the undertakers out of business. Peter only did it to this one woman. Furthermore, he only did it once to her and she is now dead. So we must not get this out of proportion.

There were those there who didn't believe. When the miracle was of *healing* they all believed it. When it was a miracle like this it says that many did, but quite clearly there were others who didn't. You are still free not to believe in the resurrection from the dead, but if Jesus has been raised from the dead then any other is a lesser miracle.

You are going to be raised from the dead. Most of us will have to wait for that day when, with a mighty shout and the trumpet sounding and the archangel calling, the dead will hear the Lord's voice and come forth. Everybody will believe in resurrection from the dead in that day, but it is difficult now.

Have you noticed that in these two simple accounts Peter is echoing what Jesus did in the Gospels? Again and again we read the very words that Jesus uses – particularly, the word "rise". That is the word of command. Peter is just doing what Jesus did before him – helping a paralysed man to walk, calling a corpse back to life. On the night before Jesus died he said to Peter and the others: "The works that I do, you will do also." I think that is the most amazing thing Jesus ever said.

Peter is now going to face something even tougher. What could be tougher for a Christian than to overcome death itself? Well, the very fact that Luke only spends a brief paragraph on the paralytic man, and a slightly longer paragraph on Dorcas, and two or three pages on the next thing that happened to him, shows that the biggest problem that Peter was yet to face was something even harder to cope with than death. In a word, it was prejudice – his own.

There is only one thing harder than learning, and it is unlearning. It is far harder for you to learn that something you believe in is wrong than to learn to believe in something that is right. Peter had been brought up a Jew, and he had been taught that there are certain very deep divisions in food, in animals, and in people. Some are clean, some are common and not to be touched. Now every parent that I know teaches a child this division in some way – "Don't touch that, it's dirty." Every child grows up with this knowledge that some things are not to be touched. In a Jewish household some animals were unclean, not to be touched and not to be eaten. To keep pigs was the rock bottom level of the social scale. There were certain foods Peter just couldn't eat, having been brought up never to touch them.

He had been brought up to think of some people in the same way. The tragedy is that in our Lord's day the Jews thought of everybody who was not a Jew as common and unclean, someone you shouldn't have in your house; someone into whose house you should never go. Peter was brought up with this deep, ingrained instinct: "Don't eat that kind of food; don't mix with that kind of people." Peter would have to unlearn that if he was ever going to take the gospel to them. It was harder for Peter to face that and to deal with it than to face death or disease. In a wonderful way God had to prepare him before he could have overcome this prejudice.

The other person involved with this now was Cornelius, a centurion. In the Roman army a legion had 6,000 men, a cohort had 600, and a century had 100 men with a centurion over it – in other words, the Company Sergeant Major. We are told far more about him than his rank. He prayed constantly. Not only that, but he was a very generous man, giving his military wages to other people in need. That is rather rare among company sergeant majors, but the greatest thing that stands out about this man, and the reason why he prayed, and the reason why he was generous, is this: *he feared God*. The sergeant majors I have met seem to fear no-one, not even the commissioned officers. They were a law to themselves and had no fear. Yet here was a Gentile who feared God. He was neither a Christian nor a Jew, but he was a man who feared and believed in a God to whom he would answer for his life. So he was going to live right and pray to this God – wherever he is, and whoever he is. His thought would be: I'm quite sure God would have me share the good things of life with other people, so I am going to do this because I revere God.

There are many who are genuinely trying to pray, who give, and who, deep down, do fear God and pray – but when an answer comes, it really shocks. Cornelius feared God before he got the answer, but when he got an answer one day he was in terror. He prayed, but one night he was praying and it was the ninth hour, which makes it three o'clock in the afternoon – not a time when you normally have hallucinations. Suddenly he got a reply to one of his prayers. There in front of him was a figure standing and saying, "Cornelius take down this name and address" – an extraordinary reply.

Do you know that God knows you by name, that he knows your address, and that he could give your address to someone else? I've had that experience in my ministry, and been told by God to go to a particular address not knowing why I should go there, but just knowing I should go to number so-and-so on such-and-such a street, then finding that God had a need there that needed meeting, and that needed somebody to go. God knows your name and address and every single thing about you.

He said, "Cornelius, I've heard your prayer. Here's the answer. Send for a man who is lodging by the seaside in Joppa in the tanner's house." Cornelius, terrified though he was, as soon as the vision ended called two of his slaves and a devout soldier who shared his views about God, and said, "The three of you go straight away to Joppa." I am sure he sent the two slaves to carry the man back. If you get a clear reply from God in prayer, act on it straight away. Do something about it while it's still fresh and clear. So they set off.

Peter is up on a rooftop at midday, high noon, with the sun straight overhead. In the Middle East if you are on a rooftop at midday you cannot be there in direct sunlight, so they stretch an awning which may be a piece of sailcloth from four posts, and you lie down under it. The last thing Peter saw before he closed his eyes would have been what is referred to, literally, as a "sail".

It is remarkable that he was in the house of a tanner, a man who makes leather, who is therefore dealing with carcasses. To the strict Jew it was already an unclean house, and Peter would have been a bit worried about some of the food he had already eaten. He was hungry and wondering what the tanner would give him for lunch, and whether he would have to say, "Well, I'm sorry I can't eat that kind of food."

You can guess all the thoughts revolving in Peter's mind as he falls into a trance. He sees a great sheet, let down by the four corners, and in it are animals he has been taught never to touch. Now, for the first time, somebody tells Peter to rise. He has been saying to a paralytic and to a corpse "rise", now the voice from heaven says, "Rise Peter, kill and eat." Like the old Peter who said to the Lord once, "You'll never wash my feet," he said, "Not so, Lord. For I've never eaten anything common or unclean."

Peter takes so long to learn, doesn't he? The Lord wants to do something with me, and I might say, "I've never done such a thing. I wasn't brought up to do such things. It's against all my training, all my background, and all my feelings. I can't do that."

Notice that God tells Peter something three times. Peter, who had denied the Lord three times, and three times told the Lord he loved him, was three times rebuked again. If God has said things are clean you mustn't say they're unclean. If God has told you to take something, you mustn't shrink from it.

You know the sequel. There were the three men down at the gate and Peter invited them into the house. Two hours earlier he would have kept them outside the gate and shouted over the wall. Now he says come in and sit down. Then, when he went with them to Caesarea, he went straight into the house of Cornelius. He had never before crossed the threshold of a Gentile house. Cornelius has the wrong attitude to Peter, as Peter, prior to this, would have had the wrong attitude to Cornelius. Cornelius realised that before him was a man who is known to angels, and whose name and address God knew – and he fell down and worshipped him. Peter said, "I'm just a man, get up."

I will never forget seeing the statue of Peter in Rome. It

was a bronze statue eight feet high, and the toe is worn away with people kissing it. There is just a stump of a metal foot – so many people have got down and licked that toe. Peter would have loathed that, he was just a man, the servant of God. Cornelius was like a lot of others. You can never think too much about God, but when you are first seeking after him you can make too much of someone else, one of God's servants. Cornelius introduced some of his relatives, friends, slaves and soldiers. They had gathered because they wanted to know the truth, and God had told him that Peter could tell them the truth.

Peter's words were magnificent. He begins to explain that he now thought differently about others: that God had shown him he should not call anyone common or unclean.

We see again the great truth that God has no partiality. This Jewish fisherman, brought up to despise and scorn a Gentile soldier, had been shown a great truth by God. Those he had thought were unclean were not.

Prejudice is one of the greatest problems in the world today. It lies behind so much violence, causing men to fight one another when it is so obviously the silliest thing to do. The cure is this: "God has no favourites." He is neither more fond of black or white, Jew or Gentile, civilian, barbarian, bond or free. Peter says, "I perceive that God has no favourites and that in every nation the man that fears God and does what is right is acceptable to him." That is a revolutionary statement.

Prejudice is so powerful a thing in our world for destructive purposes because men do not fear God and therefore only do what is expedient. The great need in politics in our nation, I believe, is for men who will fear God and do what is right instead of fearing men and doing what is expedient.

If God has no favourites there is nobody who is outside

God's love. There is nobody to whom we do not have a duty
to say: "Jesus Christ died for you."

14

The First Gentiles and Peter's Defence
Read Acts 10:34–11:18

A man once walked round a cemetery reading all the tombstones, and finally he went to the grave digger and asked in which cemetery they buried the sinners, in that part of the world! It seems at most funerals that everybody is going to heaven. You will get to heaven and to glory provided you fulfil the conditions, and there are two conditions Peter starts with in this sermon. He says, "I can see that in every nation a man who fears God and does what is right is acceptable to him." That is one of the trickiest texts in the whole of the New Testament. If it were the *whole* truth then, frankly, Jesus need never have died. If that is the whole truth there would be no point in talking about Jesus Christ, because if a man fears God and does what is right then he's in.

But it doesn't quite mean that. We have to look at this text very carefully indeed and not make it narrower than God has made it, nor make it broader. It does not say, "God accepts everyone." There is not a word in the Bible ever to suggest that he accepts everyone. It does say that, "God accepts anyone who..." – and then come the conditions. The first condition is *not* "...who believes in God." Most people I meet do believe in God. I very rarely meet a convinced atheist. I meet a few agnostics, but nearly everybody is at pains to tell me they believe in God – but that is not even the first condition here. The first condition is not to believe in God, but to *fear* him. That is the first step towards reality.

Somebody asked me, "But isn't fear wrong?" There is nothing wrong with fear if it is a healthy fear of the right danger. Your children need to have a healthy fear of traffic and of fire, and the beginning of a man's dealings with God is to have a healthy fear of him. There is danger to a person in God. Should we fear God because he is powerful – because, being God, he can push me around? No! *The healthy fear of God that is not a phobia is the fear of displeasing him by doing wrong.* I was never afraid of my earthly father because he never in my presence lost control of himself, but I had a *healthy* fear of him. And that was a very different thing because I knew that my father was the sort of father who dealt with wrong. That is a healthy fear and one of the things that psychologists are telling us today is that there are many young people who only wish their parents had punished them, who only wish they had had an earthly father who took wrongdoing seriously. Even if they rebelled and deserved punishment, they would rather have had the punishment than the sort of earthly father who never takes wrongdoing seriously. This causes psychological damage in later life.

The person who starts by fearing God – and the punishment of wrongdoing – has taken the first step into a real relationship to God. *One of the things that is desperately missing today is a fear of God.* The idea that you can sow wild oats and get away with it later—"There's nothing to be afraid of; there's no judgement; there's no punishment in the next world; there is no next life anyway, so you don't need to be afraid"– this is no way to find God. But Peter is telling us that anyone can start finding God if they fear him. That is step number one.

Step number two is to realise that it *does* matter how you live, and that you start trying to put it right. He who *does what is right*, and a man who does this is at least seeing that God is a moral God, that he is a *good* God in the deeper sense of the word, and that therefore he demands good lives in us. Now let me affirm straight away that these two things don't save a man, they don't get him to heaven, but they get the attention of God. For the word "acceptable" which Peter now gives, does not mean "saved" or Peter would have said that. If anybody who fears God and does what is right is *saved*, then there is no need of the cross, no need of the gospel, no need of Jesus, no need of the church, no need of the Bible – if you fear God and do what is right, you would have enough.

But the word "acceptable" means "to get a favourable hearing; to begin to get an answer to your prayer; to begin to get through in conversation." God will begin to talk to a man or woman who fears him and does what is right, and this is precisely what Peter saw. That is where the gospel begins. It does not end there, but that is where it starts. Paul began that way, Augustine began that way, Martin Luther began that way, John Wesley began that way, Billy Graham began that way. You read their lives. If you could have asked them how they first began to get serious with God, you would have found that the fear of God and an attempt to straighten out their lives was the first step.

Would to God that we saw more of both! No wonder God isn't real to people—they don't fear him, and they don't realise they should be straightening out their lives.

But those two things do not take anyone far enough. They are a grand beginning. God will talk to them, help them and reward them with further truth that will save them, just as the angel came to Cornelius and told him to send for Simon Peter, who would tell him how to be saved, making it quite clear that although Cornelius feared God and did what was right, he was not saved yet.

Cornelius had seen moral reality – that *he was bad and God is good* – and he was going to do something about it; he realised that you can't play around with God. Now God was going to help him. But there are two things that a person

ACTS

does *not* have who fears God and does what is right. The first
is this: *someone who fears the punishment of God and does
what is right has no peace*. This is a fact of life. Why don't
they have peace? For very good reasons. First, you are never
sure if you are right *enough*. How can you be sure that you
have done *enough* good? They are never quite sure, and deep
down they know they haven't – so they have no peace, they
struggle and strive to straighten out their lives and cannot
get any nearer to that peace. So we can see why Peter spoke
of "...preaching peace through Jesus Christ." This was to be
the good news that Peter brought – that peace which comes
through the Lord Jesus Christ.

Mere belief in God never brought anyone peace of a deep
and lasting kind. *You need to be led from fearing God to the
forgiveness that is to be found in Jesus, then you find peace.*

Of course the other reason why a person who tries to do
what is right never has peace is that even if he manages to
live a perfect life from now on, that would not deal with
what is on his conscience from the past, the things he did
in his earlier years, even if he could live a straight life now.
So a man who fears God and tries to do what is right still
needs Jesus.

Another thing he doesn't have is *power*. He struggles and
strives, and finds that although he tries to do what is right,
he can't. He hasn't the power to achieve it, and that is why
he needs the Holy Spirit.

In summary: if you begin by fearing God and doing what
is right, that's grand, and a first step in the right direction.
But you will not find peace that way and you will not find
power, because you have only found a "third" of God and
you need all of God if you are going to be saved, and all of
God is Father, Son, and Holy Spirit. If you fear the Father
and try and do what is right – no peace, no power; but if you
find the second person of the godhead, Jesus Christ, there

is peace because your past is forgiven and it is as if it had never been; and if you find the third person of the godhead, the Holy Spirit, then there is power to achieve what is right. So if you are going to know full salvation, wherever you begin, you need ultimately to know Jesus and the power of the Holy Spirit.

Peter would not have entered the home of Cornelius a few months earlier. As a Jew he would never have sat down to share a meal with him. But now he knew that anyone in any nation can *begin* by fearing God and doing what is right.

Some conversions are shallow and superficial because people, before they were converted, never faced up to moral issues and the reality of the God who punishes wrongdoing, so they have never found the joy and peace of forgiveness. They professed faith in Jesus. They said, "I'm going to follow him; I'm going to belong to him," but they didn't know the joy and the peace that comes from knowing that all those wrong things on your conscience are literally forgotten and finished with and will never be brought up again. That is peace, because it is *the peace of a conscience that's clear*. Then, facing the future, those who know the Holy Spirit know power.

Consider Peter's sermon. Here we have a perfect summary of what the gospel is all about. He doesn't mention the church once, because the good news is not the church. He refers to the prophets, but the good news is not good news about the Bible. Nor is it good *advice*. It is still as true now that a preacher's task is not the provision of good advice but to preach good news about Jesus – about a *person*. This is the strength of the Christian faith: we don't have to preach ourselves, we preach Christ Jesus. If we preached ourselves, our hearers would very quickly be disillusioned. They would find out we are just sinners—poor people who do the wrong thing. But if I preach Jesus I am quite safe because no-one will ever be disappointed in him. There are three levels of understanding Jesus, and they get deeper. The first level is Jesus *of Nazareth*, and Peter uses that phrase – a man who lived in a particular place in a particular time. But if that is where your understanding of this person ends – on a biographical level – you will not find peace in that alone.

The next level deeper is *the Christ of Israel* and Peter uses that phrase too. That means Jesus was not only a man living in a particular place, he was the final fulfilment of a thousand years of expectation: a whole nation looked forward to someone coming to get them out of their troubles, to be their king and lead them, and he was the Christ (Messiah) of Israel. Even as he died, it was written on a notice above his head: "The King of the Jews." But that is not a deep enough level for you to find peace. The third level of understanding – Jesus, *Lord of all* – means Lord of you; it means Lord of every nation. It means Lord of every person. So now at last we have got to an understanding of this person that affects my life. He is the one who is going to judge the whole world, and we are all going to see him one day as Judge. That is how Peter preaches him here – starting with Jesus of Nazareth, saying he was the Christ of Israel and then that he is Lord of all.

Therefore everyone is one day going to have dealings with Jesus Christ, whether they know it now or not, because Jesus is Lord of all. Who reigns over the earth? Who has the real power? Jesus Christ does, for he is Lord of all. Things only happen on earth by his permission. *Now this is Christianity – preaching a person who is Lord of all.*

Yet there are certain facts about that person which are basic to understanding him. I notice that Peter didn't preach the *personality* of Jesus; he didn't even preach the *character* of Jesus. He preached certain *objective facts*: Jesus began his ministry at his baptism at the age of thirty, and from then on he fought the devil for three years. God was with him, the devil was against him, and Jesus won every time. That is a simple statement, but I don't think you will ever understand Jesus unless you believe in a personal devil. You will never understand what Jesus was doing for three years until you believe that there is a personal, intelligent being in the universe who is directly responsible for many of the troubles of mankind.

When Jesus met a sick woman, he said, "Look at this woman. Satan has had her in his grip for eighteen years" – and Jesus set her free. He was conscious of fighting a battle with the devil, and he won the battle every time because God the Father was with him. Moving rapidly through that, Peter comes to the heart of what we need to know about Jesus: that men tried him and judged him and believed that he deserved to die. They heard that he was saying he was God, and therefore, believing that was blasphemous, they thought that according to the law he deserved to die.

But Jesus died appealing to a higher court, a higher Judge, believing he would reverse the verdict and release him from custody within three days – even the custody of death. So Jesus died with his case in the hands of God the Father, and three days later God did reverse the verdict and released Jesus from the punishment. Which means, quite simply, that if that is true then we must accept that Jesus is God. We must accept that what he said about *himself* was true, and what he said about *us* is true. We must accept that one day every one of us will stand before Jesus. We must accept that he can do anything he says he can do, including forgiving you, which brings me to the end of Peter's sermon. I am sure it is a very condensed summary of what he said, but you see the gospel. The gospel really begins with the baptism of Jesus, which is why so many can believe the Christmas story and not become Christians. It is not his birth that saved anyone, but from his baptism and the beginning of his battle with the devil, through to the cross and the resurrection, it is here that you see the meaning of the whole thing. And now Peter is teaching that this is the choice: either you face Jesus some day in the future to be punished or you come to him right now to be pardoned. If you come now you will find peace; if you don't come now you will never find it. This is the good news: Jesus, who will judge you, is prepared to take your case now and forgive you. That is the gospel, and millions of people all over the world have come to Jesus Christ and said, "Take my case now, and I beg for pardon" – and found peace. That is the good news Peter offered to Cornelius, a man who feared God and did what was right. Many people in the world would say, "What more is required that a man will get to heaven? He fears God and does what is right." But Peter was pointing to something more: *you need forgiveness and you need power.*

Jesus had the power – he was anointed by the Holy Spirit. He went about doing good and he wasn't trying to do good because he feared God – he was anointed with power so he went about doing good. Cornelius needed to be forgiven his past and anointed with the Holy Spirit, and then he could go about doing good as Jesus did. Could it be simpler? It is straightforward; it is based on facts, not on theories, opinions or philosophy. Here are simple, straightforward facts. Jesus was baptised—that is a certain fact. He was anointed with the Holy Spirit—that's a fact. He went about doing good, healing those that were oppressed of the devil—that's a fact. They hanged him on a tree—that's a fact. An angel rolled the stone away and he came out again, God reversing the verdict—that's a fact. And you are going to meet him one day as Judge—that's a fact. And you can come to him now for forgiveness—that's a fact.

Isn't it wonderful to be able to talk about facts – real things that are true? No sermon has ever had such an immediate effect on its congregation! There was Peter busy preaching and suddenly out of the blue something happened. It stopped Peter's sermon dead – just like that. I don't know if he was going to go on preaching. I have the feeling he was, from what he said later, but suddenly something happened. The listeners, Gentiles who didn't belong to the chosen race of Israel, as they heard *believed* – and suddenly the power came, just descending on them. The Holy Spirit was poured out and fell, and they spoke in tongues and extolled God. That is exactly what had happened to all the other Christians up till now – and it was happening to these Gentiles.

Those who have no knowledge or experience of the gift of tongues get all tied up in that part of it, but I want to tell you that the biggest miracle is extolling God. The tongues were the means; the end was worshipping God. There can be demonic tongues, which curse God. There can be psychological tongues, which do nothing to God or for people. But the real gift of the Holy Spirit praises God. That is why it is given. But the important thing is: here are people praising God who once feared him but are now loving him. That is the difference that the Holy Spirit makes.

Fear is transformed into love because perfect love casts out fear. Until you have found peace with God, worship is drudgery. I do not blame an unbeliever who comes to a service of worship and says, "How dull and how dead," because we come to extol God. But here are Cornelius and others filled with the Holy Spirit and no longer just *fearing* God – for now they are *loving* him. They have found peace with God and so now welling up within them is *praise*, and out it comes in glorious God-given language.

Peter stands back and then turns them all into Baptists! Who can stop them being baptised now? I meet some people who say that if a person is filled with the Holy Spirit and believing in Jesus, they don't need baptism—but don't you listen to them. This is the very best way of expressing such a faith. It is declaring: I believe in the death and resurrection of Jesus; I know it to be true because I have died, and I have found new life in the Holy Spirit, and now I want to express this and identify myself with his death and resurrection – I want to be buried and I want to be raised.

There are several things that are needed to make a person fully a Christian – four things that belong, in a sense, to Christian initiation: *repentance*, which only comes if you fear God; *faith*, which only comes when you hear about Jesus; *baptism in water*, which he commanded for every believer; and confirmation by being *sealed and anointed with the Holy Spirit*. These people had obviously got three. They had repented – this man fears God and he has straightened out his life. He believes, obviously, in Jesus. Look at their faces. They have already been confirmed with an anointing of the Holy Spirit. Now they have to have a baptism service, and Peter stayed a few days.

When Peter got back to Jerusalem he was in trouble with the members of the church of which he was a pastor. They did not like their pastor doing such things, mixing with all sorts of people. The believers challenged him concerning those he had been mixing with. They were shattered. So Peter gave them an account of the events. It had not been his decision – God had given him a vision. Peter had got a message; three men had come to him and told him that an angel had spoken to Cornelius, and he had gone and preached to them and, as he had preached, exactly the same thing had happened as earlier did to Jewish believers. God confirmed them, and if God confirmed them, who was Peter to withstand God? That was a powerful defence, and he stuck to the facts. This is the final test: the fellowship of the Spirit is the test of real human relationship, and if other people have the Spirit, you must meet together. If the same Holy Spirit is in them as is in you, you cannot keep away from them, and so Peter said it was God, and I thank God that the Jerusalem church members got over their prejudice. At first they were silenced, because you can criticise somebody else, but you can never argue against an act of God. Then they rose to the occasion. God gave *them* the Holy Spirit just as he gave to us? Then they glorified God that Gentiles were going to belong to the people of God, and in that moment they caught a vision of a church that would include every race, every colour, every background, and that is the church as it is today. When you get to heaven you will be amazed at the great multitude that no man can number, perfectly united in the fellowship of the Holy Spirit.

God could come to anyone and bring peace through Jesus Christ and give them the power of the Holy Spirit. Most of us are Gentiles to whom God has granted repentance to life, *real life*. And that is why it is not enough just to believe in a God, and not enough simply to try to live a good life, and try to help your neighbour and not do anybody any harm. That brings no peace and it brings no power, but God the Father, God the Son, and God the Holy Spirit together can bring you all the power and peace that you need.

15

Barnabas's Mission and Peter's Escape
Read Acts 11:19– 12:25

As we are seeing, the church spread amazingly rapidly to every little town in the Middle East. Yet there was a complete lack of organisation. There was no headquarters with a group of Christian salesmen meeting together to say, "Now how do we open up this market or that." There was no concerted policy. There was no planning, as far as I can see. Jesus had told them, "Begin at Jerusalem, then Samaria, then the uttermost parts of the earth," but as far as I know, they never held a single committee meeting about how to put that into practice.

They were very well off in Jerusalem, and they might never have got on with the job if Saul had not started persecuting them after the death of Stephen. That is what started the first big wave of outreach. They didn't plan to open up a new depot in Antioch, but that is what happened, and Antioch became the next centre from which the ripples spread out, and we are going to see how that was done. It looks like an accident, just as a miracle looks like a coincidence but isn't. When we look closely we find that it was not an accident.

God is the strategist. He is the one who planned it and who managed to spread the gospel so rapidly, and it was he who brought about the circumstances. Within a few months then, they were scattered, not only throughout Judea. They were spreading up the coast. They had reached Phoenicia, that maritime nation, which was already trading with Cornwall.

The believers spread into Cyprus, which was a cosmopolitan island. Every ship called there, so there was the possibility of the gospel spreading from there. But above all they reached Antioch.

I want to describe Antioch for you. It was the third largest city in the Roman empire. Every nation had a little corner of Antioch. There was a Jewish quarter and a Greek quarter, and it was the most immoral town in the world. It was packed with nightclubs, gambling casinos and drinking dens.

The main religion in Antioch was at a pagan temple which had barracks full of ritual prostitutes who served the men of Antioch. Now this was the town of which many people would have said, "You'll never make headway in a town like that. You'll never establish Christianity there." Yet the church was in Antioch, like a cluster of chaste snowdrops growing on a foul rubbish heap. In that city, for the first time in history, the word "Christian" was used. We will have to ask why, and ask how they got started.

I cannot tell you who started the church in Antioch. We have no names. Much of the work of God has been done by people who have not been remembered. We have some names of great saints, but here is a group of people we do not know anything about. We know that they were on the run for their lives. We know that they were concerned to save their families, but we know that while they fled they talked to people about the Lord Jesus. And they talked to Greeks, to people who had no Bible. They talked to people who had never heard about God. They talked to people who were utterly pagan, and I am sure they must have wondered how they would get on. Starting from zero they had nothing to build on. It was the first time anybody had heard about Jesus who did not know something of the Old Testament, and to the astonishment of the believers it worked just as well with Greeks as it had with Jews. A great number turned to the Lord and believed, and there was a church in Antioch. Jerusalem was terribly worried about this, and wondered what would happen.

Let me give you a modern parallel. A man in a town in the north of England bought an old barn, and he opened a youth club, and the youngsters poured in, and they came to the Lord in considerable numbers. So he said, "You must go along to the nearest church," which they did. They came back very quickly and said, "They don't want us, and we don't fit in there." So this man said, "All right, we'll have to have the church here." So in the barn they had a church and it was a church entirely made up of teenagers – including the leaders. A lot of suspicions were aroused: "How could they run a church? They were so new to it. Who would teach them what was what?" Yet they did.

It is astonishing how many of us are suspicious of new groups starting up. It may be the work of God. We might ask, "How can it possibly survive?" Yet we go and look at it and the grace of God is there. When I was a chaplain in the RAF I got an urgent signal from the chief chaplain in Cyprus saying, "Go to Bahrain in the Persian Gulf. The most extraordinary things are happening up there and you must stop it." When I got there the station commanding officer said, "There is no chaplain here, and there is a corporal who started a church, and he is baptising airmen in the swimming pool" – and so there was a great scandal.

So I went to see the corporal, and I found there a group of thirty or so young men, all of whom had come to the Lord. This corporal had just told them about the Lord Jesus, and there was a church, and he was indeed baptising them in the swimming pool. What could one say? I preached to them the longest sermon I had ever preached. I preached to them for three and a half hours at their request, because they said, "We want as much as you can give us, because we won't see you again for another two to three months." I came back thrilled! I'm afraid I didn't reply to the signal from Cyprus because I didn't know what to say!

The church at Jerusalem was a bit suspicious—"Greeks running a church? Why, they don't know the scriptures well enough! Greeks turning to the Lord? We can't make this out; we had better send someone down to see what's happening."

Praise God they chose the best man they could have chosen, a man with such a big heart – a good man. That means he had a generous mind as well as a generous hand. That is what the word "good" means in the Bible. Barnabas was a man full of the Holy Spirit, and therefore he was a man who was not full of his own ideas. Here was a man full of faith. He could believe that anything was possible to God, and therefore they chose the best person in their church to go and see. He came down and he had only one thing to say to this little group of Greek Christians: keep right on the way you are; hold on to the Lord; you have started the right way – *keep* on the right way. He was going to tell them at Jerusalem how thrilling it was to see a Greek church.

Of course, the problem arose at this point as to what to call this church – indeed what to call these people. You see, they were not Jews and hitherto all the Christians had been Jews, and therefore you just called them,"Jews who believed that Christ had come" to distinguish from the Jews who didn't believe it. Now they were given a nickname, and there have been nicknames given to Christians ever since. "Baptist" is a nickname that stuck somehow; "Methodist" was a nickname for those who were so methodical in their Christian life. "Quaker" was a nickname for those who trembled before God.

"Christian" – that was the name that they called the believers in Antioch and it meant people who follow Christ. Christ is their God, their leader – he is everything to them.

They preached the Lord Jesus, and to pagan people that meant "The God Jesus", not just a human leader, not just a great teacher or healer.

In those days they had two sorts of preacher. There were teachers whose job it was to teach the truth, and Barnabas spent twelve months doing that. But they also had prophets, and they didn't prepare a sermon, they could stand up and give a direct word from God to the congregation – a revelation of something they needed to know in their situation. One of the men who came from Jerusalem to Antioch was the prophet Agabus, who said that God had told him that there was going to be a famine in the whole world, something nobody else knew. The historians tell us how it came about. For years the Roman farmers had been taking out of the land without putting anything back. A well-fed empire had been taking too much from the soil, and what happened in the Midwest in America creating the gigantic dustbowls, happened in the Roman empire in the days of Claudius. Nobody knew that this was going to happen except a little bunch of Christians in Antioch. When Agabus told them about it, their immediate reaction was a lovely one. It was: we must help those who are going to be most badly hit. And they thought of their fellow Christians in Jerusalem who were already finding it difficult to go shopping, and even to live. They wanted to take a collection before the famine came. Barnabas didn't come down from Jerusalem and say, "Will you please join our denomination?" He didn't come down and try to get them to apply for membership in some federation. He came down and simply rejoiced in the grace of God, and it was they who wanted to be in fellowship with this other church of which they had now heard. Their hearts went out to fellow believers, and the job Barnabas and Saul had before they became missionaries together was to be joint treasurers of the Famine Relief Fund for Jerusalem. This is the fellowship they had in the New Testament. It was not an organisation or a machine. It was a fellowship between local churches and it is a lovely kind of relationship to have. Barnabas didn't try to create this, it happened spontaneously and naturally.

From Antioch the ripples were now going to spread out until they reached Rome. And the church was mobile all this time, spontaneously expanding – a group of people who, wherever they went, preached the Word to whoever would listen.

Now we come to Acts 12. What was happening in Jerusalem all this time? I have a little cold shudder that goes up and down my spine whenever I read the name "Herod". What a family! This man's grandfather was the Herod the Great who slaughtered hundreds of innocent babies to try to kill Jesus before he was old enough to be king. His uncle was the Herod who put John the Baptist to death to please a dancing girl. Another member of this family was the Herod whom Jesus called "a fox", before whom Jesus stood and had nothing to say – a Herod who dressed Jesus up in some of his cast-off clothes, laughed at him, and said, "Look at the king now!"

So here we have the last of the Herods, and this man had been the close pal of the mad emperor Caligula in Rome, and by greasing palms in the right quarters he had bought the throne of Judea, and his policy now was to please the Jews. This Herod was an extravagant money-spending, luxury-loving, lustful man. To keep the throne he tried to get on the right side of the Jews. Most such people with tremendous ambitions for personal power like to find a scapegoat, a minority group that they can ill-treat and blame for everything that goes wrong. This dictator looked around and noticed the Christians. He made inquiries about them and learned they were not very popular. So he decided to be popular by getting rid of them, and he took James the brother of John and killed him with the sword – of the twelve he was the first one to die for the faith, but not the last. Do you realise that three or possibly four years previously, when a young man in his twenties fishing in Galilee responded to the call of Christ, he was signing his own death warrant? Within four years he was dead.

I have heard many sermons on this chapter, as you may have done, on Peter being in prison. They have all been so full of the marvel of the Lord getting Peter out of prison that they have forgotten about James who didn't get out, and I want to underline this first: sometimes God does not get his people out of trouble. Sometimes his purpose is fulfilled in a different way. Sometimes his purpose is fulfilled in martyrdom rather than safety or protection. Sometimes he saves a person from death, and sometimes he leads a person to certain death. God knows what he is doing. John was to be the last of the apostles to die – and from all we know he died peacefully of old age, but James was the first apostle. Why did God call two brothers, letting one die and one live? Why, on this occasion, did he let James die and keep Peter alive? We don't know, but we believe that we shall see the whole pattern spread out, and one day we will understand why. If only we will realise that God has a different pattern for everybody's life, then we won't be troubled so much when things happen that we don't understand.

Let us turn back to Peter. Having put him in prison Herod could not have executed him immediately because it was the Passover and he was anxious to please the Jews, so he kept Peter there. And the church held a special prayer meeting for Peter. They had time to do this – and Peter was there for some days. What did they pray for? That he would be given grace to bear it? That he would be a brave martyr? I don't know, but I have the feeling they probably prayed that he wouldn't die. He was their pastor, they felt they needed him, and Peter was lying there in prison. Look at the situation. On the one side: chains, an iron gate, padlocks, four squads of four soldiers—sixteen soldiers, and you would have said, "That man is in the top security wing, and he's there to stay." On the other side, only one thing: prayer, that's all. The first profound lesson we learn from this is that prayer is the mightiest thing in the world. Prayer changes things. A praying believer is a more powerful person than the greatest military leader on earth. All the resources of heaven are ready to help. Then Peter woke up. He must have been in a complete daze, putting on his clothes, going out to pass the gates.

Of course, if you don't believe in angels you really must wonder what this is about. Why shouldn't we believe in angels? There are intelligent beings in the universe other than man. We don't need modern scientists to start arguing about that. We know there are. They are called angels. Don't get the idea of creatures with wings and nightdresses, and long fair golden hair that has just been shampooed. God's angels are superior to us in strength, beauty and intelligence, and they are there to help, whether you are aware of that or not. It is not just a childish thing to remember that angels guard you while you sleep. "The hosts of God encamp around them that fear him." Angels make good locksmiths – they can get a man out of a security block, and they got Peter out. No wonder Charles Wesley, when he became a Christian, felt that his chains fell off and his heart was free, and picked up this theme to express his wonderful joy.

But now comes the funny thing. Peter knocks at the door of the prayer meeting, and the girl called Rhoda, who answers the door, is so excited that she doesn't even let him in! She comes flying back to the others and tells them he is there. And they said, "You're mad!" They couldn't believe her. One point to be made here is that God is able to do exceedingly, abundantly above all that we ask or think. The blockage is on our side. We sometimes can't imagine a thing happening. We pray for someone's conversion, then they are converted, and we say: "Well, how on earth did that happen? I just can't believe it! They're changed? I'll believe that when I see it." Have you ever noticed with what a surprised tone we always tell each other about answers to prayer?

When Rhoda insisted it was Peter they thought that it was his angel! They could believe in angels more easily than they could believe that Peter was at the gate, but Peter came in and they saw the answer to their prayers. Peter had found it difficult to believe, so we mustn't blame them. But let's remember, when we go to prayer, we should expect to have an answer. Let us believe that when we pray we are not just talking to ourselves. We are not trying to exercise telepathy. We are praying to an Almighty God, and nothing is too hard for the Lord. Let us hold on to Peter coming out of prison as an example of that. Of course, the result of his getting out was that all the sentries were put to death. It is amazing how an evil man like Herod can cause so much suffering.

There came a great day when Herod overreached himself. He went too far in the sight of God, and Herod did something he should not have done. What happened? A great festival was held and from my research I think I know what the festival was. It was now about the year AD 44, and a festival was proclaimed in every part of the Roman empire. It celebrated the successful invasion of England. So that puts you right into Acts 12. King Herod had his own festival, and two nations who wanted to make peace with him (Tyre and Sidon) were represented at the festival.

Herod appeared in a silver robe which shone in the sun. He spoke to them and it went to his head and he spoke as if he were a god. The people said, "It's not a man speaking, it's a god." We needn't go into the gruesome details as to what happened then. Dr Rendle Short in his book *Modern Medicine and the Bible* describes the medical situation. This man at his peak – who thought he was God and who accepted worship from this crowd of people during this festival to celebrate the invasion of Britain – was eaten with worms and died. It was not even *after* he died that he was eaten with worms, it was before. What an end! That was the last of those Herods who at every stage had opposed Christ. They had given themselves titles like "the Greatest" – "Herod the Great", these men who had been guilty of murder, incest and almost every other sin in the book. Filled with ambition for power, the last in the line finishes up eaten by worms, but the next sentence is: "But the Word of God grew and multiplied."

It does not matter what happens: the Word of God grows and multiplies. Do you know that there are more Christians in the world today than there have ever been before? The church is growing more quickly today than it has ever grown in two thousand years. Kings and dictators may strut on to the stage and they finish up eaten by worms, or, like Adolf Hitler, by having petrol poured over their bodies in the ruins of Berlin, or, like Benito Mussolini, hanging upside-down from a petrol pump in Milan Square. That is what happens to those who try to be little gods, but the Word of God goes on. Empires rise and fall, dictators come and go, people want to have a kingdom for a thousand years, but their kingdoms go in less than twenty-five, and the kingdom of God goes on. The Word of God grew and multiplied. You may kill the apostles, you may persecute the disciples, they may have to run for safety – but all you do is spread the gospel.

16

Barnabas and Saul in Cyprus
Read Acts 13:1–12

Imagine a missionary society considering a candidate to go out and preach the gospel overseas, and it is reported that there are some serious hesitations about him. For a start, he is not of a very prepossessing appearance and he suffers from some physical handicaps, perhaps even deformities. He has not got a very good record in the sense that he has never stayed in one place more than eighteen months. In fact, most of his stays have been a few weeks. He has usually got into trouble with the authorities within a few days of arriving in a place, has been in and out of court, and indeed had a prison sentence or two. The appointments committee listens and sadly shake their heads and turn down someone like Paul, one of the greatest missionaries the world has seen!

The first half of this book is about the acts of Peter; the second half is about the acts of Paul. There is no mention of anything John said. James is beheaded fairly early on and most of the other apostles are not mentioned.

Acts concerns the acts of the Holy Spirit, and we are going to see how he took Saul of Tarsus and what he did with him over perhaps thirty years, and how Saul took the gospel all the way to the capital of the then-known world and finally finished up in chains in that city. If you took Paul to Rome, even in chains, you have taken the gospel – and the gospel is not bound. It is going to spread from that prison, which it did – even into Caesar's own household, but I am jumping ahead!

You could give Acts a subtitle: how they brought the good

news from Jerusalem to Rome. In the first half, the centre is at Jerusalem and concerns the good news spreading out from there, but in the second half there was a new centre. Once the ripples spread out as far as Antioch, that in turn became a new centre of ripples which then spread out from there, and that is how the gospel goes. The circumference of the mission becomes a new centre of a new circle of influence, and the ripples go on and on, spreading in every direction until now the gospel is heard around this whole Earth. There are hundreds of millions of people alive today who profess to believe in Jesus Christ. It is not a day of small things. This is one of the biggest movements the world has ever seen. It started with a few people like Peter and Paul.

Paul was converted in Acts 9. He would not have put it that way. We have the account of that amazing conversion. Paul was a missionary before he was a Christian, but an anti-Christian missionary. Such a fanatical Jew was he that he was prepared to leave his home and leave his land and go to another country to speak against Jesus Christ and get Christians arrested and put in prison. But little did he dream that when he set off as an anti-Christian missionary he would finish up as the best-known Christian missionary.

Some of the finest Christians I know are those who were the most antagonistic to Jesus before they were converted. It seems as if the very energy of someone who will fight God can be used by him. It is as though God tells such a person: you're going to fight for me. You can speak, and you are not afraid to voice your convictions even if they are the wrong ones. Well, you go and voice *my* truths. God has a way of arresting you in your tracks, stopping you short and saying, "Right, about turn! Go my way." He met Saul and told him as soon as possible what he was in for – he was sending him out to Gentiles to tell them about him. Saul knew that from the day of his conversion. He didn't go out as a missionary for many years, but he knew from the day he became a Christian that one day God would say "Go."

So why did he not go when he was told? He was not only called of God to be a missionary when he was converted, three days later, when he was baptised, he was filled with the Holy Spirit—that is as important as his conversion, though many forget to mention it. There are many today who would say that if someone was converted, called and filled, he should go. But Paul knew better – he knew that God had a lot to do with him yet. It doesn't mean because we are called and filled with the Holy Spirit that we have got to go straight off into mission. God may have a lot to do to prepare us first.

God sent that Saul off into the desert for three whole years to do a bit of hard thinking, to get his mind straight, so that when he spoke he could speak clearly – so that he could make the gospel plain. It took that long. Even then, when he came back he was not ready for his missionary work. He had to learn to integrate into normal church life and submit to the discipline of his own fellowship. It is vital before anyone sets out on mission that they have achieved integration with the fellowship. It is not until chapter 13 that Paul actually went to fulfil the call he had received some years earlier as recorded in Chapter 9. The reason why he set off in chapter 13 is that at last his church said "Go". We are told by the Holy Spirit that the time was ripe, so I take it that God has put this in the Bible as a pattern for our example.

I believe there are two mistakes being made today. One is for individual Christians who have been called of God and filled with his Spirit to go off without the church's commission. The other is for the church to send people off who have not been called of God. I thank God that when he called me to be a preacher of the gospel I had to wait. This was because my minister said, when I told him I felt I was called to be a minister, "Go away and come back in eighteen months and tell me if you feel the same way." I felt a bit hurt at that. Weren't ministers needed? Aren't you glad to have me? I was ready to go at the drop of a hat, but the time came when my fellow Christians said, "You must go." The inward and the outward call confirm each other. We can mistake our own impulses for the call of God. So Saul, who knew on the day of his conversion that he was going to go as a missionary to the Gentiles, had to wait many years until one day, in the church of Antioch, the Holy Spirit said: now you can send these two for the work that I have already called them to.

The first three verses of chapter 13 take us to Antioch, which, as we have already seen was a city with a bad reputation. Almost certainly, the prodigal son went to Antioch when he said to his dad, "I'm leaving you, give me some money." He went and he wasted his money in riotous living. It was almost certain that he left Galilee and went straight north for about a hundred miles to Antioch. The amazing thing is that in the middle of that city there was a little group of Christians, and what a lovely mixture they were. There was Barnabas, a Cypriot, with a great heart and a generous hand – everybody loved Barnabas; there was Simeon, an African. That man had become a Christian on the day that a Roman soldier made him carry the cross of Jesus. We are told in Mark's Gospel that he had two Christian sons, Alexander and Rufus. Amazing that he was just in Jerusalem that day, and a Roman soldier looking around for someone to press into compulsory service, saw this African and gave him the cross to carry. Out of that situation came faith. He must have found himself wondering who this poor suffering man was, staggering in front of him, up the road. He became a Christian, and here he is at the church of Antioch.

Then there was Lucius a Roman, quite different from the others; and Manaen, a man who as a child had actually lived in a palace and been brought up with a prince. He had been adopted by Herod's father and he had been brought up with Prince Herod. What a background! Finally Saul, a Jew from Tarsus, trained as a rabbi. Could you get a greater mixture on earth of race, religion, class, background, culture, yet they are all so happily together they can use nicknames of each other. It is great, a marvellous demonstration. If you have a church like that, it will be missionary-minded for a start because you have people in it from other countries. There is a living demonstration that people from many backgrounds can live happily together in one fellowship. We misunderstand if we think God wants uniformity among believers. If God wanted uniformity he wouldn't have made us all so different. He wants us all together in one family, accepting each other.

We have already mentioned two kinds of ministry – that of prophets and that of teachers. A church needs both: the teaching of God's eternal truths that apply everywhere and those whose mouths will bring a message from God to that group of people in that place at that time to tell them what to do. These members we have mentioned had these ministries between them. Now they were praying and they were fasting – the denial of their physical appetites that they might stimulate their spiritual appetite. It is strange that much of the modern church seems to have forgotten prophecy, and many also seem to have forgotten fasting – by which I mean a church being willing to say, "Let's do without food and give ourselves to earnest prayer for this matter." So they fasted and worshipped, serving and ministering to God.

People who see that fasting and prayer were meant to be partners are likely to hear God speak to them – did you realise that God wants ministering to? He wants serving and that is why we attend church services – not primarily to render service to each other (though I hope that will happen as well), but to serve God by giving him our attention.

It was as they fasted and prayed that God told them to send out their best two members. Maybe we would hear God speak more often if we were willing to give him our undivided attention, scrap other things, and say, "Lord, have you anything you want to say to us?" We must concentrate our whole attention on God. So they forgot about their meals and they went on: Lord, tell us what you're saying; tell us how to do this, when to do it.

Finally, they took those two men and they laid hands on them and said, "Go." The laying on of hands is the most precious practice. We should do more of that too. It is an act of identification. It's saying, "You are part of our body. We're all one body and I'm identifying with you." So our missionaries from our fellowship are part of our body somewhere else. It is also saying: Lord, we are people in bodies as well as spirit, and so, as we put part of our bodies on this person, will you send something of your Spirit through our bodies to him or her? The Lord can do this. He can use ordinary "common or garden" hands as channels of his grace. What do you do when your child needs to feel comfort? Do you not take your hands and let comfort go to them through your hands? What do you do when somebody is bereaved and in dreadful distress? Don't you hold them and let the hand express your sympathy? God wants us to do this when he calls someone to service – to let our hands express his love and our unity in the body. So they sent them off and the great mission began.

It was such a small beginning – just a little meeting and a few prophets and teachers – but God spoke, and when God speaks you never know what is going to result. It was a cobbler in Northamptonshire who gathered just a handful of friends about him and he spoke to them about a whole world that was without Christ. He had a little globe of the world, which he had made out of bits of scrap leather and which he used to pray over, and that cobbler said to his few companions, "What are we going to do?"

God spoke to them and said, "Take a collection and start a missionary society." They took a collection. It was about four pounds (then a significant sum of money). The Baptist Missionary Society began that day in that room. It was the first missionary society in this country. Within ten years there was a Methodist Missionary Society, a London Missionary Society and a British and Foreign Bible Society. Missionaries were going out from this land but it started with a cobbler calling a few friends together and listening to God. Nobody knows what is going to happen if a few people get together and mean business with God and say, "Lord, if you want to tell us something, then tell us." One of the results of that little meeting at the cobbler's was that William Carey had to go to India. It is dangerous to be serious with God – he might send you!

So there began in Antioch the greatest missionary outreach there has ever been, which is still the pattern for every other outreach, and still tells us more about mission than any other book. Let's turn to the last few verses.

They set sail for Cyprus. It was known as "Macaria", which is the Greek word for happiness, blessedness. Happy Island, they say, because of the climate, though it has not been very happy in its history for other reasons. (I have only been there for a few days, but it is lovely.) It was a bustling island with copper mines and shipbuilding in those days, densely populated, and a Roman-occupied territory with a proconsul or governor in charge. Why did they go there? I believe it was because that was where Barnabas came from. Here is a profound principle in mission. Have you ever thought that you would be willing to go to Africa or China, but not where you live? Have you ever felt that if only you can get away from all those who know you and start preaching under a palm tree somewhere else, you would really manage much better? A missionary once said to me: "One of my greatest disappointments was that when I arrived at the country to which I had gone, I disembarked the same person who had set off!"

When Saul of Tarsus was converted, where did he go for his first mission? Tarsus! When Barnabas joined Saul, Barnabas coming from Cyprus, where did they first travel to together? Cyprus! Do you get the message? It is hypocrisy to go and preach elsewhere if you have not let it be known where you are that you have found Christ. That is where mission begins – right where you are. God wants you to be in mission *here* before you start going off *elsewhere*. He wants you to start with a people among whom you were brought up. He wants you to let your neighbours and friends know. That is what Matthew did, and what others have done.

So they went to Cyprus. Now look at the method of their mission. They went in a group. God doesn't usually lead people to be loners. There are a few exceptions but when Jesus was on earth he sent them out two by two. Have you ever been house-to-house visiting by twos? What a comfort it is to have someone else with you, isn't it? You feel that much bolder. You can imagine two of the disciples sent out by Jesus to deal with demons and sickness, walking down a road together, hoping they wouldn't meet a possessed or a diseased person, then seeing one and then Peter saying, "You do this one Andrew and I'll do the next." Andrew saying, "Well Peter, I'm sure you'd be better this time, you try then I'll do the next." Two of them go up to a person, maybe hesitating, then saying, "In the name of Jesus...." Then eyes opening as something happens – the encouragement, the joy! I believe that God's pattern for mission is that we should do it together, not just as individuals.

They took along Barnabas's nephew, John Mark. He

wasn't much help to them and he later cried off, but at least they took that young man to learn, and the three of them set off.

Notice that they didn't start Sunday Schools – they went for adults rather than children, and I believe that to be a divine strategy. They didn't start welfare services, getting tied up in a lot of social and political reform. They went straight for the main target: to tell people the good news. Though our mission to the world includes many other things – it includes helping children, welfare, serving people in their practical needs – the main thing that mission is concerned about is getting people saved from their sins by preaching the good news of Jesus. So they went straight for the main thing and do you notice how they did it? They looked around for people who are nearest to God and started there. That's a strategy for mission. They made for the synagogues, which were groups of people who already believed in God but did not yet know forgiveness of sins through Jesus Christ. The most fruitful field for evangelism in this country to begin with are nominal churchgoers who are not yet Christians – people who already profess to believe in God but who don't know Christ. Start there. They are among those who already fear God, and they are the most fruitful field to begin with. Start with those who acknowledge who God is in some way. Say: "I want to tell you about God's Son Jesus, and how you can know him." There is a strategy here. So, working through the island, they finally came to the greatest opportunity in that place for the gospel. They found themselves invited to the governor's palace.

Billy Graham came here to these shores in his twenties, full of fire, shouting and wearing loud ties, and a few people listened to him. I can remember his first visit to Newcastle and nobody knew his name. He was just a Youth For Christ evangelist travelling around. Some of the young people thought he had a bit of spark! The day came when he had an invitation from Her Majesty the Queen: "Come to Windsor and tell us your message." You never quite know how far your message is going to go! You never know what opportunities you may have.

Saul and Barnabas found themselves unknown missionaries, Christian Jews, preaching from synagogue to synagogue and it came to the ears of the governor, a sensible and intelligent man, and he invited them. Any sensible and intelligent person will want to hear about the gospel and listen. Because this was the greatest opportunity yet, they ran smack into opposition. This is not unknown. As soon as a real door seems to open, you find yourself in trouble. It came about through a magician. One of the characteristics of the Romans was that they were so practical that they were superstitious. They were influenced by dreams, astrology and occult powers. Any Roman worth his salt had a soothsayer. Shakespeare has captured the superstition of the Romans perfectly in some of his plays – Julius Caesar is a good example. Romans didn't like to go to battle unless the stars were right. That sort of thing is happening again now in our age. There are world politicians who have their own private soothsayers to tell them whether to make this or that political move. Indeed I am told that political representatives at the UN who go to discuss world peace and security consult such people before they go. What a world!

The apostles ran right into this extraordinary figure. He was a renegade Jew so he had known the truth. He even had the most unusual name: Jesus-son. His dad was called "Jesus"! What a terrible coincidence! Or was it a name he had given himself because he heard something about Jesus' power? I don't know but what went wrong was that this man dabbled in the occult. My brother, my sister, don't you dare dabble in that for anything at all. Young people don't even play with it. Never try playing with a Ouija board. Don't read your horoscope. Don't play about with levitation or with knocking on tables or glasses or anything else. Never touch it. This man, brought up a Jew with the knowledge of the one and only God, should have known better. When the truth of Christ comes into that house, this man is found opposing Jesus, for there can be no reconciliation whatever between the occult and our Lord Jesus Christ.

On a number of occasions, situations were brought to my church office for help. There was need, and when we had begun to get into the matter we came up against occult influence. You feel there is a barrier there, and the people are in need but it has all become so twisted and perverted. This man who called himself Elymas the magician opposed Paul. Believe me, if we go out in mission and talk about Jesus Christ, you do get opposition from occult powers. There is so much of it around and those powers are bitterly opposed to Christ.

Here we have Paul the missionary of light confronting the powers of darkness. Which gives way? There is no question about the answer to that one. Paul, mincing no words, spoke bluntly. He said, "You're called son of Jesus are you? I call you son of the devil. You are an enemy of all that's good. How long are you going to go on blocking what's right? I'm going to stop your evil influence straight away." Then Paul's first miracle was a miracle of turning a man blind. We tend to think a lot about the miracles that make a blind man see and do good, but the Bible also contains miracles that do harm. As he spoke to that man, Paul felt the power of the Holy Spirit coming upon him and knew he could do with that man anything he wished. He knew that with a word he could strike him dead; that if he said, "Drop dead," the man would. He felt the power surge into him. I can almost imagine him saying, "Lord, what do you want me to do to this man?" He did the same thing to Elymas that Jesus had done to him, Paul. He said, "God is going to turn you blind for a time." Now that was obviously an act of justice. The man deserved it, but it was an act of mercy too. On the one hand it stopped the man from telling fortunes any more because he needed his sight to tell fortunes for the governor, to study the tea leaves, to look at the stars. He needed his sight for his job. Paul robbed him of that ability and he took his sight away by the power of the Holy Spirit. The second thing is that Paul knew that if you shut a man up in darkness like that, he has got to do some hard thinking – and he shut him up with God.

The Venerable Bede, who was a Christian in Jarrow about nine hundred years ago, said when he read this story: "The apostle remembering his own case knew that by the darkening of the eyes, the mind's darkness might be restored to light." But the result of that miracle of harm was that a Roman governor was on his knees. The governor now believed. What a fish to catch! No wonder the devil didn't want that man caught, because if the governor is caught, the devil knows that a lot more people are going to sit up and take notice. I believe that occasionally God wants a man of influence and greatness to become his. Normally God works with the nobodies, calling those of us who are nothing, and he makes us somebody in his sight. What a glorious thing he does! Paul says, "Look at you in the church – not many noble, not many wise." Notice he doesn't say, "none noble, none wise." Occasionally God, in his amazing purpose, looks at a man of great influence and says, "I want that man too." It is usually in that case that Satan fights with everything he's got, because the convert may be a person who is going to be a great influence for good. When the governor was converted it meant a lot to Paul.

Paul did two surprising things after the governor's

conversion. First, he sailed away from Cyprus. He felt there were enough people to get on with the job so he went somewhere else, and that is a divine strategy. When you are missioning, don't go on hammering the same people, don't go on fishing in a pond that has no fish. Move on. When you have caught enough for them to go on doing the work, conquer fresh fields.

After his conversion, Saul changed his name. He was given the name Saul when he was born in Tarsus and he was brought up a Jew. I don't know if he was particularly prominent in public service in Tarsus but they made him a Roman citizen. When Saul becomes Roman, the name is Paul. When Saul leaves Cyprus he is never again called Saul, always Paul. It was changed after the Roman governor was converted. Why? Well, here is a lovely thought: the Roman governor's name was "Paul"—Sergius Paulus. He was Paul's first big Gentile convert. I can see the way Paul's mind worked, I think. He had been called Saul after the first great ruler of his people, the Jews, King Saul, who had come from the same tribe of Benjamin. Saul did not turn out to be a good king and I think Saul of Tarsus may have been a bit embarrassed that he was named after such a ruler. But when the governor became a Christian, Paul knew to whom he belonged now. He changed his name to that of a Gentile ruler. Luke slips in brackets, "Saul who was also Paul". Paul was even prepared to change his name that he might be more identified with the people to whom he came.

There is one little word to mention: "seen" or "saw". When the governor saw, he *believed* what he had heard. When people can see the results of what they have heard, they will believe. That, too, is a divine strategy. Paul gave Sergius Paulus an "audio-visual" presentation of the gospel. We must preach the word, but that is not enough to convince. It is when people see the effect of instruction from the

Lord in other people's lives that they will believe. It may be a negative effect when they see the result of someone rejecting the gospel – that can be evidence. But there is also the positive when they can see a life that has changed. Others want to see the gospel as well as hear it. They want to hear the good news but they want to see the power of it. You can't engage in mission without the Holy Spirit. You may preach until you are blue in the face, you may give out tracts, you may say the right thing, but they want to *see* and God wants them to see.

17

Paul Preaching in Antioch
Read Acts 13:13–52

The mission to Cyprus having covered that island within a few weeks, Paul and Barnabas, having led the governor to Christ, then felt that they had established the work of God there and they moved on to the mainland.

If you are a Christian you have a mission and God has sent you to do something, and does not expect you to report back until you have done it and are able to say, "Mission accomplished." Christ was able to say, as he died, "It is finished." Mission completed. He could then report back to his Father in heaven that he had done all that he had been sent to do. Did you ever think of Jesus as a missionary? He was the best one ever. He said, "The Father sent me" and the term he used was the root word for "mission". Then he said, "As the Father sent me, so send I you." *You* are a missionary. I wish we had not fallen into the habit of reserving the term "missionary" for those who go overseas. From the mid-twentieth century onwards, gradually the word "mission" changed so that we realised that we are meant to be missionaries right where we are.

We cannot just rush into mission. We have to know what our objective is, and what the strategy is that God has planned to reach that objective.

The life of Paul has so much to teach us. The best way to learn anything is to stand at the side of a master in that job. See how he does it and learn from him as we study his approach to mission. Having left Cyprus, they crossed that little bit of the Mediterranean to the north of the island, landing in the area we now call Turkey, which the Romans called Asia Minor.

The astonishing thing is that they began their mission in a synagogue in a place called Antioch. Here a map can be helpful. If you have a Bible with a map at the back, then look at it. Why is it surprising that they began in a synagogue in Antioch? I am going to draw out from that broad report of what happened, two profound truths for every missionary concerning you and your situation. Why Antioch? If you look at the map, it is not on the coast, so it was not the first place they came to, but right in the interior, four thousand feet up, on the north side of a range of high and difficult mountains (called the Taurus Mountains) which stretch like a crescent between the coast and the interior. Why did they begin their mission there? There were people living along the coast in the area called Pamphylia, with towns like Attalia where they had landed in Pergas – large towns, so why did they move on? The answer is that Paul fell ill. Pamphylia is a low-lying, flat, swampy area full of mosquitos, and it was terribly unhealthy. When the three of them landed – Paul, Barnabas, and the young John Mark who was helping them – Paul fell ill. He does not say what it was but it was almost certainly malaria, which was the scourge of Pamphylia. I want to point out that in the Word of God there is no guarantee whatsoever for the Christian that if you are engaged on the Lord's business you will be free from sickness. It depends what is going to serve God's purpose and glorify him best. Falling sick faced Paul with a dilemma. He could either get straight back on board a boat and sail for Cyprus, and I am sure the governor of Cyprus would have had a spare bedroom in which he could recover, or he could sail back to Tarsus, his home town, or his home church. So one option was to go back. The other alternative was to go on and get up into the healthier climate of the hills, even though it meant crossing a high mountain range – a sick man climbing over mountains to get to that high plateau beyond, and to get well there. That is what Paul did. If he was tough, John Mark was weak. The young man had had enough. When the mission gets tough you will find that weak Christians leave it.

When it is hard going, start a programme of reaching out into the street, or house-to-house. Everyone will come at first for the novelty, and the weak will go back. Poor little John Mark had had enough and he went off home to Jerusalem. I am afraid that led later to an argument between Paul and Barnabas, which made them split, for John Mark was Barnabas's nephew. I am glad that at the end of his life when Paul was in prison, he said, "Send John Mark to me." So they were reconciled.

I once heard an amazing testimony from a woman whom the Lord had healed of blindness, polio, epilepsy and a withered leg. But the part of her testimony that made me worship God most was not that – wonderful though it was to hear and to see – but her telling of the years when she had been ill, when these things came upon her one by one. She had been to one institution and hospital after another. She believed that the sickness had taken her as a missionary into a place where the gospel had not been taken. So she went into one institution at Godalming and there was no Christian there and she thanked God – the illness had meant she had taken the gospel there. They had listened to her because she was one of them. I am not surprised the Lord healed her because she had used the sickness as a way to further the gospel. What is a person's first reaction when they are told by the doctor, "You've got to go into hospital"? The understandable, natural human reaction would be: I wish I didn't have to go in. I just wish it would get better. But the second thought might be: does God want a missionary in that hospital? That might decide whether one asks for a private room or goes into the public ward. But do you see that sickness can in some instances further the gospel? That is the lesson I want to draw for you: within his overall plan to take the gospel somewhere it wouldn't otherwise reach, God can do this through adverse circumstances. That transforms your attitude to these things. God can and does heal, but he sometimes uses sickness too.

We need to be praying: Lord what is *your* plan? What are *you* saying? What do *you* want to do? He got Paul up to Antioch because Antioch was on the main Roman road from Europe to Asia. The world and his wife went through Antioch, and if the gospel were established there, then it could go to the ends of the earth quickly. It was a strategic place. Paul might have been down in the swamps of Pamphylia, but God got him up into Antioch and used the circumstances to further the gospel.

Writing to the church in Antioch later, Paul says: "You know it is through sickness that I came to preach to you first and I was a wreck when I arrived and you felt so sorry for me. You wanted to give me your health but that's how I came."

Sometimes God can use a weak, sick person to get across the gospel. When Joseph de Veuster, that brave Dutch Christian, went out to the little island of Molokai in the south seas of the Pacific, he went out to an island with many lepers. He preached to them about the love of God and they laughed and sneered. "Love of God, and here we are, outcasts on this island!" One day, making his breakfast, he tripped and fell, and the boiling water from the pot poured down his leg and he didn't feel it. He saw that he was now a leper, but they began to listen then. They received the message. The little leper colony of Molokai became a place of hope and joy. They called him Father Damien. Be encouraged if your circumstances are adverse – if you think: I wish I wasn't working in this place; why doesn't God clear a way out of this difficulty? Pause, and say, "God, are you trying to put the gospel somewhere? In this difficult office, where people are at each other's throats – do you want a Christian here?"

They began to preach in Antioch, and it says, "They began in the synagogue." Why the synagogue? Because there were two groups of people there that God could start with. First of all there were Jews – who were scattered all over the world in little groups or ghettos if you like, in Greek towns and Roman colonies. You could nearly always find a synagogue where there were Jews meeting and studying the law of Moses. They were trying to live right and failing miserably, but believed that God was God, and that he had spoken to men. Paul started his missionary work among them. Why? Because he was a Jew, and again, remember that you start with the people who are like you, people you know and understand. Are you a businessman in your fifties? Then start with businessmen in their fifties. Are you a young teenager and you have found Jesus Christ? Then go out and tell teenagers. So Paul, though he felt indebted to the whole world, went first to his own people. He could talk to them. He knew the way they thought, their deep feelings and the scriptures. He understood, and he wanted to share Jesus with them.

As we have noted, there was another group in the synagogues of those days who used to sit in a separate part of the congregation: the "God-fearers" – seekers, who believed that Jews were on to something, dissatisfied with their own religion, they were not yet totally convinced but came to listen. We can look around at our society and ask where the God-fearers are. Where are those dissatisfied with their own religion, seeking after God, wanting to know, not committing themselves, but interested? Many people are seeking a reality beyond themselves and beyond this life. Paul went to Antioch and looked for the people searching for a new dimension. We, too, need to look around for those who show some signs of sensing need, of inadequacy, of dissatisfaction – and start there. Do you see the principles emerging from this?

Here we are reading about events of two thousand years ago and God is saying: now you know what to do. The message they preached! We now have a sermon. It is the only full report we have of any of Paul's sermons. (We have extracts of others.) We can learn a great deal by analysing it, but first, before we split it into bits and look at its parts let us look at the thread that goes right through it. What is the theme that ties it all together? What's he preaching about? About God! Twenty-one times in this brief summary Paul says "God...." From the beginning to the end he is talking about God as a living, active God, working in space and time – in history. He is talking about what God is doing. What he has done, is doing, and is going to do. We are going to preach about God if we are going to enter into mission. One of the slight imbalances in modern witnessing is to talk a little too much about Jesus and not enough about God. In a sense, until you really understand the basics about God, what Jesus has done for you will not make much sense.

Jesus pointed to God all the time. He came to bring us back to God. He is the way – but the way to God; the truth, but the truth about God; the life, but eternal life in God. All the time he was pointing men to his heavenly Father. We have got to get people to realise there is a God and that Jesus is his Son. Otherwise you'll finish up with "Jesus people" who don't know God. It may sound a little extraordinary but that is why we used to have shows on in London ostensibly about Jesus, where none of the casts knew God. It was an extraordinary phenomenon. God is the subject of our testimony, and Jesus is the way to God because he is the Son of God and the Saviour.

Let us split Paul's sermon up. There are only three parts to it. I was always taught that three points are a good pattern for a sermon. It is about as many as people can remember. The three points are: Israel; Jesus; you.

First, *Israel*. Paul simply summarises the history of Israel over five hundred years. It was the greatest period of their history to which they still look back with longing every Passover, every main feast: from Moses to David; from slavery to liberty; from being a downtrodden people in Egypt to being people who could lift up their heads in their own land with their own king.

What is Paul trying to do? Three things I think, and you have got to learn to do them. He is beginning with things they are familiar with, starting where they are. If you are going to be in mission, you have to understand where people are, and begin by talking about where they are, and how they feel and what they think, and something they are already familiar with. Then you are likely to help them to where you are. Don't just start where you are and say, "You should be over here." But there is something deeper. Paul is wanting to talk to them about God before he talks to them about Jesus, and that may be something we need to learn to do. But the most important thing to remember carefully, and it may never have struck you before, is that *Paul always began every sermon or message he gave by telling people what God had already done for them.*

Before he spoke about what God wanted to do for them, he brought from them a feeling that they were already involved with God and that he had already been good to them. If Paul is talking to those who are not Jews, those who have no Bible, he could say: look at that sun, who do you think sent that sun today? – God did, and you should be grateful to him for that. Who gave you your food today? God did.

Could you learn from that in your witness? When you go

to someone, tell them what God has already done for them. Show them that they are already indebted to him; they are already related to him. It is not as if you have a God they have never heard of and have had no dealings with and you are trying to persuade them to adopt your religion! You start by saying, "Look what God has done for you already."

In other words: God is already touching your life, he is already being good to you, and I have come to tell you something more of what he wants to do for you.

Do you see the approach? Brilliant – and you find this when Paul went to Athens and Corinth. In Athens he said, "You know God has already spoken to you. You've got an altar to him – to the unknown God." It meant: you are already in some way in touch; I have come to tell you his name. Could you learn to do that? Go to people and say, "God is already dealing with you. God's already given you his goodness. He's already helped you. Now I've come to tell you that there's something more that he wants to do." What a lovely approach.

So Paul goes through the history of Israel and delivers his message: God gave you fertility. From one family you became two and a half million in Egypt. God gave you liberty. He brought you out of Egypt with a mighty hand. God gave you maturity. He endured your foolishness for forty years in the wilderness, but you grew up and you matured. God gave you security. He destroyed seven nations and gave you your own land. God gave you stability. He sent judges to rule your affairs. God gave you sovereignty and gave you a king, a man after his own heart who did God's will. God had given them so much, but there was more.... That was the approach.

Israel knew she had not got all she needed because after David the nation went to pieces, and the reason was sin – selfishness, greed, pride, lust, anger, idolatry, envy eating up the hearts of the people – and they lost their land. They struggled under one enemy-occupying power after another but God had not brought them all that way to drop them. The thing that they really needed was a Saviour, and he had promised to send that Saviour. When God promises anything, you can trust him to keep his word. It is still the first part of the sermon and he has not mentioned Jesus yet, but he has got these people involved with God, thinking about God. He has got them grateful to God. He has got them open. What next?

What is God going to do next? They are already excited to hear, and now he tells them that God sent the Saviour. Paul is right into his subject, and they are willing to listen and ready to hear because he has led up to it so beautifully. He has not gone up to them and slapped them on the shoulder and said, "Are you saved, brother?" He has gone up and said, in effect: Did you realise that God has been dealing with you and been good to you and helped you all these years, but he has got something more. I've come to tell you what he wants to do for you now.

So next he is going to speak about Jesus, but he refers to John first. John the Baptist was the last prophet of the Old Testament, the first prophet of the New. He was the man who offered the whole of his people an opportunity to make a clean start. That's great. It is where you begin with people. The good news begins with John's message of repentance and baptism. Do you want to make a clean start? Nothing could convey that more than baptism. But John himself admitted that the desire and intention to make a clean start is not enough, so he said, "There is somebody coming after me who is much greater...."

To seekers today who may be God-fearers and trying to live a good life, you can say: "Do you want to make a clean start? Jesus is the one you need."

Do you notice what Paul says about Jesus? He didn't talk

about his birth, marvellous though that was. He didn't talk about his teaching, wonderful though that is; he didn't talk about his miracles, great though they are. He talked about just two things: Jesus died and he rose. That's what you need to tell them about Jesus.

Tell them that people so misunderstood our Jesus that they didn't see that he was their Saviour. Tell them that people put him on a cross and killed him and said: away with him, he is a bad man, he doesn't deserve to live.

But tell them, too, of how God said that is not true – he raised Jesus back to life. Do you notice that the apostles never said: "Jesus rose from the dead"? They always say, "God raised him from the dead." It was God's doing. He was not going to let men stop his purpose of salvation. God was not going to let men end it all in a cemetery. That is when God's power begins to be seen: when men have done their worst.

So that's what we need to say next: the greatest thing that God wants to do for you he has done in Jesus by sending him to die and rise again.

That cross and that empty tomb can save you, and so we come to the third point in Paul's sermon: *you*. It is at this point that you need to notice carefully that Paul offers both the positive and the negative.

He tells people the consequences of believing what he says, and he warns them of the consequences of rejecting what he says. Both are needed.

We preachers today are under some pressure – sometimes from church people – to keep to the positive and never be negative. That has been said to me. You know: "I like you when you're preaching on positive things, on God's love, on heaven, and on salvation. I don't like you when you are preaching on hell and judgment. You shouldn't frighten people. You should love them into the kingdom and not frighten them with the fires of hell." But Paul gave both, and Jesus gave both! When Jesus finished the Sermon on the Mount with his teaching about loving others as we want them to love us and so on, he finished off by saying there are two roads: one to life and one to destruction; there are two trees – one bearing good fruit, the other one bad, and the latter will be cut down and burned. There are two houses: there is the one built on the rock and it will stand when the storm comes, and the other will crash. You will always find Jesus finishing with the alternative – and so, too, with Paul. The positive side is great, Paul offers them forgiveness and freedom. He said, "In this name of Jesus, forgiveness of sins is preached to you." Oh what a great gospel it is — forgiveness, that the wrong things done can be forgotten, wiped clean, taken away, buried in the deepest sea, so that God will never again mention them. That's great news.

But that's not enough because he forgives all my sins of this past week – what about next week? Paul says that the good news is that you can now be set free, while the Ten Commandments never set you free. Trying to keep the Ten Commandments, trying to live a good life, never sets you free from sin. Forgiveness and freedom come through Jesus – but the negative side is serious. People say, "Don't frighten people into the kingdom of heaven." Why not? We need to preach about hell and judgment, and Paul's message is: beware if you don't believe this. The same kind of situation you can read about in the prophet Habakkuk who warned Israel that the Chaldeans were going to invade their land and take them off and they said, "Rubbish, that couldn't happen here." They didn't listen and they died. That is what happens when you preach about Jesus. You have got to say to someone, "Now you've heard about Jesus. If you believe in him you can be forgiven and free from sin, but if you don't, you'll die."

You might say, "Well I could never end up in hell.

Judgment won't happen to me." There is this kind of euphoria – it will never happen to us, it's always the next chap! Judgement *will* come. So Paul finished with this dark fork in the road, and was offering the choice: now you've heard; you've got to go one way or the other.

I am not surprised that they followed him down the street when he went home. I am not surprised that on the next occasion the place was jammed, and there were people outside trying to hear. What is this – an answer to our problem? The message addressed the longings of our hearts. No wonder they came back.

Consider the division they caused. All went well for a time. People were interested, and this is what I have found happens when you preach the gospel. When you talk about Jesus, people are interested at first. The crowds who came to hear Jesus built up to five thousand people fairly quickly – in a matter of months. But after a time the interest divides and opposition begins. Jealousy gets into somebody – about the numbers – and things begin to get said about the message and about the messenger. It is part of the price you pay for having crowds hear the gospel that people will say things to try and discredit. It made Paul all the bolder and he went on preaching, but finally the Jews, alas, must bear responsibility and I say this advisedly: through the last two thousand years Christians have been guilty of doing dreadful things to the Jews in the name of Christ. The memory of the Crusades still lives in modern Israel, and we ought to repent of what has been done by "Christian" countries to Jews. (Germany is still thought of as a "Christian" country in Israel.) But I want you to remember the other side of the coin: that the greatest opposition to Christians has been from Jews. There is opposition to Christ in Israel today that is trying to stamp out Christianity in God's own country.

It was true to say some decades ago that, tragically, the

opposition to the gospel came most fiercely from religious people. If you go out and tell your town about the gospel of Jesus, opposition may well come from religious people, and you must be ready for that. In the twenty-first century, opposition is also seen to come from state authorities.

It finally came to the point where they so rejected Paul and Barnabas that those missionaries did the right thing that Jesus told us to do. When there is a clear and positive rejection of the gospel and people have made up their minds they are not going to listen and not going to accept, then move on. Shake the dust off your feet. Don't take anything from them – not even dust! Move on, because there are others waiting to hear.

But that is only one side of this account, and the other side is that the Gentiles were glad. Why? Because they heard the good news that they didn't need to become like Jews to be saved, but they did need to become like Jesus.

Paul and Barnabas left the city. They were kicked out by the authorities and the influential women in the place. Did they feel it had been a failure because they had been kicked out? No. *The disciples were full of joy and the Holy Spirit.*

18

Iconium, Lystra and Derbe
Read Acts 14

One of the first gifts that the Holy Spirit gave was the gift of boldness. Have you noticed that? It was the most frequently given gift in the early chapters of the book of Acts – sheer courage. As we have seen, Paul, having been taken ill in the malarial swamps of Perga had climbed up and over the mountains to the high plateau rather than go back home. Having been thrown out of Antioch, surely now he is ripe for a vacation. Will he take a little time off? No! What's making this man tick? What's driving Paul? What is his motive? His motive is that he wants to save as many people as he can. He feels in debt to the world. The common outlook today is that people feel the world is in debt to them, that the world owes them a living. But Paul says, "I'm debtor to everybody, Jew and Greek, doesn't matter who. I owe them the gospel." Did you ever realise that if you go out and seek to win your neighbour for Christ, you are not doing them a favour you are discharging a debt? If you were paying back a financial debt to your neighbour, you wouldn't think you were doing them a favour, would you? You would think they were doing you a favour in waiting for you. Paul says: "I've got a debt to pay and I'm going." More than that he says, "There will be a curse on me if I don't." Did you know that? He said, "Woe is me if I preach not the gospel." That word "woe" has lost a lot of its horror but it means *cursed*. It is the opposite of *blessed*; it is the opposite of beatitude. It is a malevolent curse, and Paul says, "If I don't preach the gospel, I'll be under a curse." There was a custom in India that when a new Christian is baptised, when they come out of the water they say, "Woe is me if I preach not the gospel." Paul had another motive too. He said, "There's something inside me that *constrains* me. The love of Christ constrains me. I have just got to go.

When you've got to go, you've got to go, and he did. So far from taking a vacation, far from saying "I've done my bit; I leave it to the younger ones now," he went on from Iconium to Lystra, to Derbe, and he didn't know it but he was going into worse trouble than he had known thus far on the missionary trip. We are going to study what happened next.

The first characteristic of Paul's mission can be summed up in one word: *forward*. As long as there was new territory to conquer, new people to reach, Paul wasn't going to turn back, he was going on forward. He soon ran into opposition. Tragically, a person cannot reject the gospel without becoming anti-Christian. You can't remain neutral once you have had a chance to follow Jesus. You can't go on as if you've never heard. You become defensive, you build up a resistance, and you begin to attack the Christians. That is why those who didn't believe what Paul preached became "anti". They said evil things about him. What do you do when you are slandered? It doesn't matter what they say about you – you stay.

The Lord honoured their staying by giving a new dimension to their ministry. From now on there was a double testimony there, and I want to underline this. The double testimony was this: *as they witnessed to the Lord, the Lord witnessed to them.* As they witnessed to the Lord with words that reached people's ears, the Lord witnessed to them with signs and wonders that reached people's eyes. The testimony was strengthened by God himself, and as has been pointed out already, the world needs to see as well as hear the gospel. When they can see the results of the gospel, when they can see lives changed and know this is real, and that there is something in this, it is what the world is looking for. I meet some young adults who are clapped out at twenty-five, worn out, they tried everything, they are miserable, they are cynical. But, "They that wait on the Lord shall renew their strength; they will rise up with wings as eagles." That is the promise.

When people see as well as hear, something happens. When the double testimony comes, when God does wonderful things that have no explanation except supernatural power, then people sit up and take notice. So they stayed longer, and God helped them even more and testified to them. Mind you I have to add – that still did not convince those who did not want to believe. There are those who say, "Well, look, if God is a miraculous God, you perform a miracle and I'll believe." Jesus saw through that kind of request again and again. The people who demand a miracle for proof wouldn't even believe if they saw one. They would try and explain it away. Jesus said, "Even if they have someone rise from the dead, they won't believe." He did rise from the dead and people still didn't believe.

But when God is testifying to those who testify to God, some will believe and the mission will succeed and it will be completed. God will have people from that place. So, though slandered, they remained.

Now we come to a sudden and surprising twist. The next sentence says that they *fled*. Hold on a moment, where has that courage gone? Have they lost touch with the Lord? The next sentence says that when they learned they were going to be stoned, they fled. I want to tell you now something that you may find difficult to understand. When it is right to go, it sometimes takes more courage to run than to stay.

Missionaries in Congo, when the Belgians left, were faced with this appalling dilemma: should they go or stay? The missionaries were greatly exercised, even divided in their opinion, because they knew that if they stayed, they would almost certainly be martyred. If they went, they would be safe. They wrote home to the missionary societies and said to the headquarters, "What do we do? Will you give us some guidance? Will you tell us: should we come home with our families, or should we stay?" But the societies, for the most part, rightly said to the missionaries: "You must sort it out at that end and seek God's will." Some stayed and were martyred and some came home. When should one flee? When should one stay and be a martyr? It is the most difficult question for any Christian to have to face. I want to point out that the Lord Jesus on at least four and possibly five occasions ran away from death, escaped from it – hid himself in the temple when they wanted to stone him. Why did he do that? It was not because of any lack of courage! The answer is this: if death is coming to you and your work is not finished, you must move on. But if your work is done, you must stay – that is the deciding factor. Paul and Barnabas, realising that their death was now an accomplished fact in the minds of the rulers of Iconium, knew they must go, for their mission was not completed.

Jesus, on those occasions, slipped out of the crowd and hid himself and went on – his time was not yet. That does not mean he lacked courage. He had the courage to be thought a coward. He had the courage to flee when it was right. Because when the moment came for his mission to be completed, he set his face steadfastly to go. When Paul's time came for his head to be severed with a Roman sword, he went with head held high I'm quite sure, but God's time was not yet. We need the wisdom to know when to go and when to stay if they are just slandering us, but if we can go on talking and we can go on preaching the gospel, then let us stay whatever they say, and ask God to testify to the truth of our message with his wonderful acts. But when death stares us in the face and we believe that God has yet more mission for us to complete, then we must go. We must come back when we can, as Paul did.

What wisdom and what courage – both to stay and to go. I hope that might just help. If you are in a difficult situation, unsure whether to stay in that impossible circumstance, whether to stay in that office, in that shop or wherever you are, the question is quite simple: is your mission completed in that place? If it is, then go. If it isn't then say, "God, I'm going to stay, and you testify to me, and do wonderful things in this place." Paul left Iconium but he left such a very deep impression that about seventy years later somebody wrote up an account of what he had done there. The manuscript has been discovered in Iconium, which is the modern railway junction of Konya in the middle of Turkey, and it is called *The Acts of Paul*. This is what the writer said, referring to a relative: "*And he saw Paul approaching, a man small in size with meeting eyebrows, a rather large nose, bald-headed, bow-legged, strongly built, full of grace, for at times he looked like a man and at times he had the face of an angel.*"

So he left Iconium – mission completed – and moved on to Lystra. From Antioch to Iconium was a ninety-mile walk. From Iconium to Lystra was another eighteen miles down the military road, and here is Paul, trudging on in the heat along dusty roads – which may well have aggravated an eye disease if he suffered from that. He could have got the dust under his eyelids and aggravated trachoma which seems to be what he describes in his epistles.

Paul is a man with a single purpose, and he has got to fulfil it so he comes to Lystra, a very different place. There are no Jews there, no synagogue to start in. It is a pagan town through and through. The inhabitants had all kinds of myths and legends and worshipped many gods and goddesses, but particularly two: Zeus and Hermes.

We now meet a poor crippled man who had never been able to walk all his life. His feet were twisted and weak. There he sat in the road, and Paul and Barnabas were preaching in the open air because there was no synagogue and they could not go into the pagan temple. Christians will preach in any circumstances – if they are turned out of one place they will preach in another. The cripple heard them and Paul looked into his face and saw something. Now we know from the story that the cripple was going to be healed, but I want to underline something else which was important. Looking into the man's face, Paul saw that he had the faith that was needed to be healed, so he said: "Get up on your feet." There is a very important principle here. You see, what we often call faith may not be faith. It can be that you have so desired or even despaired of health that you persuaded yourself to believe that you will be healed; or it can be from being in a big crowd where there is a strong emphasis on this. One thing is vital. No-one who has talked themselves into believing nor anyone who has been talked by others into believing had this: something about a person who has been *given the faith to be healed*. Paul saw it and knew that God would do something in this situation. You find this again and again in Jesus' ministry. You find that after he had healed a person he said, "Your faith...." The healed person had the one thing needed – the faith. Not the urgent desire, not the human convinced mind, but the faith, and that was why when Jesus went to Nazareth he could do no more than heal just a few sick folk – because the faith that was so needed was not there.

We can't try and work it up. It is the gift of God and when it is given, a miracle is going to happen, and it did and the cripple leapt up on his feet. Paul and Barnabas, not understanding the local dialect, didn't know quite what was happening – flowers around their necks, bulls brought up. What's going on? The most dangerous thing for an evangelist is to be popular. This was a far greater danger to Paul and Barnabas than any other situation they had been in yet – to have the adulation of the crowds, to be worshipped, to be looked up to.

When Billy Graham went to Cliff College, a woman pressing through the crowd was heard to say, "I just want to touch the hem of his garment," and she was reaching out for Billy. It can happen. A servant of God can have adulation, and believe me his soul is in mortal peril if he does. Paul and Barnabas saw this, and then suddenly they realised what was happening – that these people were going to offer the bulls to them. Straightaway, Paul dealt with this situation – another moment of supreme courage – telling them that they were just men who had come to talk about the living God.

I have mentioned that Paul's fundamental principle of preaching was always to begin where people were, and to tell them what God had already done for them. In this way he was saying: you are already related to the God I am talking about; I have just come to tell you more. It is a very simple and lovely approach. Not: you have nothing to do with God, you're far away from God, you're on the other side of a great gulf and I've come to bring God to you.

When Paul was with the Jews he took them through their Jewish history, quoted their own scriptures and showed them that God had liberated them from slavery and given them their own king and land. But when he was with Gentiles, he didn't quote the Bible, he didn't talk about Jewish history. He started where they were and he started with two things that every Gentile knows about: *creation* and *conscience*. He lets his hearers know that he has come to tell them about the living God, to take them away from worthless superstition. The living God is the God who gave you your food this morning. Have you got any human happiness in your family and in your love for each other? God gave you that happiness. Now that is quite a start, isn't it? It is in your approach. It is saying to people: God has already got a care for you. But it is most revealing that Paul says: "God up till now has let people go their own way."

This is the picture of God I want you to convey to the people *outside* your fellowship; it is the picture of a God who has let people go their own way but has gone on being good to them. He has kept in the background in their lives, and yet he has kept in touch. He has let people go their own way knowing that they will choose the way that leads to destruction; he has let the nations go their own way, knowing they will invent their own religions and follow their own gods.

He let me go my way and choose my own life and make my own decisions and yet still gives me food and happiness – though not food for the soul, and not totally satisfying happiness, but we are foolish if we say that there is no happiness among unbelievers. There is. Watch a couple of unbelievers in love. What could you say to them? You could go and say, "Are you happy together? Do you know it was God that gave that happiness and made them male and female?"

A wise preacher, Paul begins with this theme. God has given you good things even though you have turned your back on him – and he is then going to tell his hearers more about the living God, inviting them to leave superstition behind. He has come to invite them to turn to the God who is *really* alive – because their gods are not alive. Paul wants them to know the living God and to know that he has come to save them.

I can guess what Paul was going to say next but he was interrupted. I'm quite sure he got them absolutely ready for just one word: the God who gave you food and happiness wants to give you forgiveness and a Saviour. But he never got there. The crowd went wild; they wouldn't let him say any more and it was a very tense situation. I have noticed this, that when people are in danger of receiving too much adulation for Christian service, God reverses the situation radically and quickly. He rescues them from it. The only way that God could get them out of that hole, that trap of human worship, was to bring Jews over from a hundred miles away who swayed the crowd. Nothing is more fickle than mob hysteria so that the very crowd who were going to sacrifice to Paul and Barnabas decided to make a sacrifice of them, and Paul was stoned.

I marvel at the Bible — it just describes it in a few words with no account of anybody's feelings or description of the wounds or the pain. But I don't feel I am wrong in just making you dwell on this. Imagine being stoned. A man cowering while they pick up rocks and throw them as hard as they can, cutting him, breaking him until finally one hits him at a vital point and he slumps unconscious to the ground. Then a crowd coming up with rocks and throwing them down on him until there is no sign of life or breath and he is lying in a pool of his own blood – that was what happened to Paul on that morning.

Then they took him by the feet and dragged him through the streets with his body banging on the stones. They dragged him outside the city and threw the corpse onto the rubbish heap. So that was what Paul went through. When he referred to it a few years later in one of his letters, all he says is, "Once I was stoned." Very few people have ever lived through that. The disciples gathered around and Barnabas looked down at that body. I suppose he was already thinking in his mind about what he would say at the funeral – "the bravest man I've known". Then suddenly they saw a spark of life, the flicker of an eyelid. He's alive! Paul sat up and he stood up. That was a bigger miracle than the cripple.

Bleeding, bruised, broken – but he walked back into Lystra. What courage! What a man of God! "Now Paul," we might say, "you're ready for a holiday now. We know a good convalescent home in Cyprus."

But Paul would say: "There are people in Derbe without the gospel. Let's go."

Imagine it—here's the man sick in Perga and Pamphylia, climbing the mountains to get his health back; Antioch – kicked out of the city; Iconium – kicked out of the city; now Lystra – stoned and left for dead. Forever afterwards, his body could not be the same again. Writing to those same churches in what we now call the letter to the Galatians, he says, "I bear in my body the scars of the Lord Jesus." But he went on preaching. Can you imagine it? He preached to Derbe and many people were won for the Lord.

I say it very hesitantly but I believe that the days may not be too far distant in this land when Christians will face physical violence. There will be people who will hate Christians and attack them physically.

If you trace this missionary journey on a map, you will find they have been almost in a complete circle. They started in Antioch of Syria (don't get the two Antiochs mixed up). They went down to Cyprus and through that island. They crossed the Mediterranean to Attalia, went up over the Taurus Mountains to the other Antioch (of Pisidia), then to Iconium, then to Lystra and Derbe. Can you see what is happening? They have almost completed the circle, and all they need do is go through a pass of the Taurus Mountains called the Cilician gate, and back to Tarsus and back to Antioch. So what does Paul do? He says, "Right – about turn! We're going back that way." Think of that! You see Paul knew something terribly important, and I want to emphasise this about mission. What is our mission? Well people say to get folk converted, to bring people to Christ—amen to that. That is fifty percent of our mission. What is the other fifty percent? It is to go back and strengthen them and grow them up. Christians of all people should not be guilty of bringing babies into the world and leaving them on a doorstep. Our mission is not just to bring people to the new birth by the grace of God – not just to bring them to Christ but to see that they grow up, to see them through their problems, their first struggles, seeing them through those first anxieties that every Christian has – to go back and help them, to nurse them, to build them up.

The missionaries had been right round the circle and had left Christians everywhere. Now it was time to go back home and tell them how many have been converted. There was now to be a second stage in the mission. Back into the places that had thrown him out: back into Derbe, back into Lystra, back into Iconium, back to Antioch and even back to Perga where he never even preached because he had been sick and he had missed out on that town, so he went back and preached there just to catch up. What a man, what a strategy, what a mission! But what was he doing? He was going back to see that they were growing up in churches. One of the commonest misunderstandings I hear today is that you can be a Christian without being in a church. The world is interested in Christ but doesn't have any place for the church.

Now I know the church's failings – probably better than others! The minister hears most of them sooner or later and gets blamed for a good few of them. I know what's wrong with the church and I know our history isn't great, but I know this: that it is God's will that we are born again into a family – that we should be in churches. The church is a family of God, the body of Christ, and you are not a New

Testament Christian until you are right in a church.

So Paul went back and you notice the word "churches" comes in. It was Jesus who first used the word "church". It was Jesus who thought of having churches. It was Jesus who gave himself for the church and bought her with his blood – and this is extremely important. So Paul went back to strengthen the churches because Christians are strong when they are in churches that are true to the pattern of the New Testament, and so he strengthened the believers.

How did he strengthen them? By telling them they were in for big trouble! Never believe the evangelist or the preacher who says, "Come to Christ and your troubles are over." Believe those who say, "Come to Christ and your troubles have just begun." Your past sins are behind you but your troubles are in front of you. Paul went back to those new Christians now when they would be at the end of the honeymoon stage. They would be down to earth again now, and he could tell them that it is through much tribulation that we should enter the kingdom – that it is tough down here. Now Paul could show them scars that they had not seen on his first visit to them. Through many troubles we are going to enter the kingdom. It was tough for Paul and it was tough for Jesus. Jesus promised that in this world you are going to have tribulation, that means big trouble, but be of good cheer! I'm not taking the troubles away but I'm going to give you grace to overcome the world because I've overcome it. Cheer up.

So that is the way to strengthen people – not to tell them it is going to be easy, not to tell them to relax, but to brace them for the fight. To do what Churchill did during the war when he said to this nation: "Blood, tears, toil, sweat, that's all I've got to offer you." But he was strengthening the nation when he did it, and that is what strengthens young Christians. "It's going to be tough. You're going to be a misfit in society.

You are a pilgrim passing through and people will not like you now. You'll be laughed at, you'll be ridiculed, you'll be frustrated, you will have trouble, but you're on your way to the kingdom of heaven. Be of good cheer."

"Blessed are you when men revile you and say all manner of evil against you falsely for my sake ... that's what they did to the prophets." That's what Jesus promised.

You are on your way to glory if you are having big trouble. So Paul strengthened the believers but he did something else for those churches—he appointed elders. This is a vital feature of New Testament Christianity. If a Christian is going to grow up, it is absolutely essential for them to be in the care of elders.

I still meet people who say to me, "I can't find church membership anywhere in the New Testament and that's why I'm not a church member." My one reply to them is to ask a question, "Then who are your elders while you flit around from one place to another, or just come as a perpetual visitor? Who are those to whom you are going to look for guidance, for help when you have decisions to make and problems to get over? To whom are you looking to help you to become mature in your outlook?" Paul knew that new Christians need elders who are recognised and appointed for the task. I ask you to consider the pattern of mission for the church. God's will is that the mature should guide the immature. That happens in an earthly family and should happen in a church family. Seek to be in churches with elders so that we can grow up together as families in Christ. That is part of mission and the way that God has ordained for us to grow.

Having established the new churches, Paul set sail for the old church. He went back to the church that sent him out, to tell them what had happened. He didn't come back to boast about himself; he didn't come back to tell them what he had done or Barnabas had done or what John Mark hadn't done.

He came back to tell them what God had done. That is the kind of report we want to hear in churches, because if people report on what God has done then God gets the thanks. But if you report on what Christians have done, then the Christians get the thanks. Have you noticed that? Think of the church annual general meeting in which it is reported that Mr So and So did this and Mrs So and so did that, and we're grateful to all the ladies who did that, and all the men who did the other. What happens? Then somebody says "Now a vote of thanks ought to be given" and up you get and you have a vote of thanks! But let us report what God has done. It is thrilling what he is doing. The Lord adds to the church daily those who are being saved. It is God's doing and it is marvellous in our eyes. Paul came back to report the cripple walked, and Barnabas told how they gathered around Paul's corpse, never expecting to see him again and he got up and walked back into the city. They reported what God had done for bodies. They reported what God had done for souls. Every place they went to, they said, "God chose people for eternal life." These dear people back at Antioch in Syria (the earlier one) had been praying for Paul and Barnabas, and they had been expecting to hear the report of what God had done.

When they came back, Paul not only said what God had done, he reported this: "He's opened a door to the Gentiles." Do you realise the significance of that statement? Do you realise that Antioch had been the first church that had been primarily Gentile Christians with just a few Jews? Hitherto, every Christian church had been more Jewish than Gentile. But now Paul is able to report totally Gentile churches. What's the significance of that? Just this: *Christianity had become a world religion*. Isn't that exciting? The Gentiles are believers, and now they saw the words fulfilled that Jesus commanded them before he left for heaven. When he gave them their mission he said, "To the uttermost parts of the earth". People who had been brought up as Jews steeped in the Jewish scriptures with a Jewish Christ must have wondered whether anybody else would be interested. Now the missionaries came back and said they are interested and they are Christians!

They remained at the church for about a year and enjoyed fellowship before the Holy Spirit said: off you go again; I've got another mission for you.

19

First Council in Jerusalem
Read Acts 15:1–35

Acts 15 administers a real shock to the system. It comes as an anticlimax after chapters 13–14 where the most exciting things have been happening, where Paul has been pioneering missionary work and leaving behind him converts and memories of great miracles, of a cripple who is now walking, of a Roman governor who is now a Christian, of a magician who has been blinded and is having a good think about what he has been doing, of Paul being stoned and left for dead outside a city and rising up from that condition and walking straight back into the city. It has been exciting, and Paul has now come back to the church which sent him out and told them what tremendous things have been happening, and they are all thrilled.

Then comes this chapter in which we find Paul and Barnabas engaged in a fierce, hot argument with their fellow Christians. We find that Paul is going to make a special journey all the way to Jerusalem to pursue that argument and to get it settled. We are going to see Christians in much debate with one another, spending a lot of time discussing the issues that have been raised.

There are two groups of people today who feel that this chapter is a tragedy and is something that should never have happened, something that is not edifying and should not occur among Christians. The two groups are those I am going to call the "activists" and the "pietists".

The activist is the person in those days (and today) who would say: "Let's keep off doctrine, it only divides. Let's not discuss theology, it only wastes time in debate and causes Christians to get hot with each other. Don't let's have meetings to discuss what we believe, let's get on with the job – let's get out on mission. Let's go out and preach and pray together, but let's not spend time discussing what we believe."

Then the other group that doesn't see any point for Acts 15 is the pietist group— those who have no room and no place for Christians to get together for meetings to discuss different points of view. They believe that you can settle all controversy by holding a prayer meeting and seeking a direct word from the Lord to settle the issue. They don't realise that there is a very important place for Christians to gather in a church meeting and to discuss openly and frankly their different understanding of the ways of God. Such people would not go to others for advice or consultation. Paul and Barnabas, why didn't you just seek the Lord and pray and get an answer? Why did you go and waste time in Jerusalem in a big debate?

So these two groups of people would say that Paul got himself involved in something that Satan wanted to happen. There are those who say that Satan loves to see Christians disagreeing about theology, about doctrine, about beliefs, distracting them from the main task of getting on with mission. There are those who say, "Please, don't let's discuss the gospel. Please don't let's get bogged down in debate because we shall be divided."

We are going to look at this chapter very carefully and see what the truth of the matter really is. Let me tell you how I believe the devil was behind this. The devil knows that the church can put up with most things from outside, and the more we are persecuted from outside, the stronger we get, and the more we go to the attack. Stone us, and we'll rise and come back into the city to preach. That is what happens

– but the devil knows that if he is going to stop the gospel being preached, he can't stop it from outside the church and he will have to stop it from inside. That is where he comes and attacks, and the way he will do it will be to change the gospel that is preached from inside the church and add things to it until the point is reach where it ceases to be the gospel at all. It is like putting luggage in a canoe. Have you ever tried this? Get in the canoe, and have people hand you all your luggage bit by bit until it piles higher and higher. There will come a point where you have added so much that you'll turn upside-down! This is what the devil seeks to do. He wants to add this, that and the other to the simple gospel of the Lord Jesus until the thing turns upside-down and tips you out. Paul recognised this. He had proved something tremendous. When he got back from his mission, he was able to report that he had transplanted Christianity into a Gentile culture and it was flourishing. That was great news because Christianity at that point ceased to be a Jewish sect.

Most of us are Gentiles, and Christianity came to us as a faith for us in our culture in our situation. It was Paul who showed that Christianity could be for anybody in the world.

The devil didn't like that one bit. He wanted it to be kept an exclusive Jewish faith. Paul had taken it out, so how could the devil pull it back in? The answer was he got hold of some Christians in Jerusalem with a strong Jewish cultural background, who had made the same mistake that nearly all of us make: they had confused their own culture with Christianity, and began to preach their cultural version, their background, their scruples, their principles, and teach them as Christianity. Now before we condemn those poor Jewish Christians who did this, just bear in mind that you and I are doing it all the time. We had missionaries who went overseas and went to live among peoples who, as one missionary put it, "Wore nothing but a piece of string." One of the first things the missionaries did was send home for shirts and trousers as if that was Christianity, as if that was somehow part of the faith. Those dear folk had had no embarrassment about the way they dressed until the missionaries brought some clothes to them. We have taken our Gothic archways, and you can see mud churches in the heart of Africa built of mud, where everything about the church is indigenous except the shape of the windows! Our predecessors have thought that was part of Christianity, whereas it is simply part of European culture and goes back to the Middle Ages.

We do the same thing in our own culture. We say, "Look at that young person coming to church dressed like that." They may be saying, "Look at those old people coming to church dressed like that!" Dress doesn't matter a brass button; it is part of our culture, as long as it is modest. That is the only thing the Bible says. So we confuse our culture, our background, our way of life in England with Christianity – and we bring our culture into our preaching, and we preach that. I have spelt that out because that was all these Jews were doing, but the devil was going to use it.

They came from Jerusalem to Antioch, which was a church in a Gentile culture that had grown up without a Jewish background, without Jewish customs, and they said, that unless you are circumcised, you cannot be saved. That is the point at which we go wrong and add something to the gospel. There's a simple gospel: repent of your sins and believe in the Lord Jesus, and you will be saved.

So they came from Jerusalem to Antioch, and their message was: unless you adopt the Jewish culture, unless you adopt our practices, our customs – this minor operation of circumcision [for which there were very good hygienic reasons in a desert land in the Middle East] as part of your religion – then you can't be saved. You'll never get to heaven.

The big, important question is this: what must I do to be

saved? That is a question you have to sort out before you go on mission. It is a question you have to be agreed on before you go out preaching. You must settle that absolutely before you can unite to evangelise the world. Your answer to it will tell you whether you are free in the gospel and in the Holy Spirit.

So Paul fought this thing. He had a fierce argument. Paul didn't mind arguing with a fellow-Christian if something important was at stake. For Paul, this was the tip of the iceberg. Or, to change the metaphor, it was the thin end of a wedge. Adopt circumcision, and who is to stop you saying that all the rest has to follow? Or again, using a metaphor from the Middle East, it is the camel's nose. It is the camel in the cold, desert air at night saying, "Can I put my nose inside your tent to keep warm?" and you say, "Yes, all right then, I'm sorry for you." "Can I put my head in?" "Yes." "Can I put my front legs in?" "All right then." "Can I put my hump in?" and very soon the camel's in the tent, and you are outside in the cold! Paul recognised that this was the camel's nose. When he got up to Jerusalem, his worst fears were confirmed because the very people who had sent these false teachers said not just that you must be circumcised, but you must be circumcised and keep all the Law of Moses. That is not just ten commandments, it is 613. I am sure you don't even know half of them, or couldn't recite them. Paul could see that this would have destroyed the gospel.

The gospel includes the great truth you are saved by believing, not achieving; by trusting him, not by trying to do something for him. You are not saved by what you do for God but by what God does for you. What is required of you is total trust in God, believing in his Son the Lord Jesus. That is freedom. It means I can begin to be saved *now*. I don't need to wait until I am perfect. I don't need to wait until I have built up a treasury of merit. I don't need to wait until I have cancelled out my past sins by future good deeds. I can begin to be saved right now, then I can try to be good – not in order to get to heaven, but because I am going there, and what a different motive that is.

Paul realised that once you start making rules to be saved, you kill a person's spiritual life. You damn him because he will never make it. Tell him, "You can get to heaven and be saved if you keep the Ten Commandments," and you have sent him to hell because he never will. He will break them – that is our nature and our weakness. We need a Saviour, not a standard.

So now we can see why Paul was prepared to argue with his fellow-Christians. If they were to go on teaching that, then people would not get saved. In these circumstances it is our *duty* to argue with our Christian brethren and to go as far as we can to stop this thing, however far that may be, because the gospel is at stake, and because the freedom of the individual soul could be lost.

In Jerusalem, Paul and Barnabas went to the top, to the very people who had started all this. They wanted to settle it and to stop it at source. They knew that a little poison can affect an awful lot of good food. When I worked on a farm I looked after some prized pedigree calves, some of which were very valuable. Imagine my feelings when I came down one morning, about four o'clock I had to get up then, and I saw half of the calves lying dead in the pen. One or two more were struggling, having fits. The farmer came in and he was shattered as years of breeding had gone. We wondered what on earth had happened. We presumed that they had been poisoned because the symptoms were of lead poisoning. We thought, "Where have they got this from?" and we began a detective search to get back to its source. We looked to the water pipes and to the trough, which were lead, but these had not been chewed. We wondered if enough lead had been dissolved from those into the water, but it didn't seem so. We searched and searched, and then we looked at the corn they had been eating. Finally we conducted a *post mortem* on a calf. We opened it up, and in its second stomach we found some little lumps of lead. They were cut up and shaved, little shavings of lead, and among them was an air gun slug.

Tracing it back, we found that the farmer had given his son an air gun for his birthday, and the son had gone into the barn, and had been shooting sparrows with it. He had filled the corn in the barn with lead air gun slugs. We had taken that, put it through the thresher, through the mill. We had ground it up for the calves, and we had been grinding poison in. We did not rest until we got back to where it was coming from, and then we destroyed all that corn. It was the only thing to do, the only safe way.

This is what Paul was doing. He was saying, in effect: Where did this poison come from? Where did it start, this cultural accretion to Christianity which is spoiling it? And he went right back to Jerusalem. What a challenge to them as a church: We believe that you as a church have sent out people who are giving false teaching. How did they deal with it? I want you to notice that they did not hold a prayer meeting. I underline this: *they held a debate*. There are times when this is the appropriate thing to do. There are times when a church should call a church meeting with its elders and leaders and thrash out a difference and be utterly frank about it and argue if necessary, but get through to God's will.

I hope you never get impatient or tired of long discussions in a church meeting. It is God's way of strengthening a church's convictions. It is his way of helping people to see the truth as they hear different points of view as it is discussed, maybe at length. I don't know how long this church meeting went on, but it sounds a long time. It says: "After a long debate". They let everybody have their say, and they heard everyone's point of view. Then they settled the discussion with just two basic appeals. This is how every church meeting should be settled and brought to a final conclusion.

Peter and James came in at the right moment with the right arguments. Here is what they are: number one, the argument from *experience*: what the Spirit does. Number two: the argument from *exposition*, what the scripture says. Either without the other is inadequate, but when these line up together you can be absolutely sure you have the answer, and the guidance you need.

So Peter stood up and his argument went like this: "I, Peter, was thrown by God into a Gentile situation. I didn't want to go; I had to have a dream first to tell me to go. I, a Jew, went into a Gentile home. You know what happened? God wouldn't even let me finish the sermon before he baptised them in the Holy Spirit. He wouldn't even let me tell them that I was a Jew. I just told them about Jesus, and before I could even get them in the water for baptism they were filled with the Holy Spirit just as we were on the day of Pentecost. Surely if God is prepared to accept them like that, why shouldn't we?"

That was a great argument. He was arguing from his experience of what God has done. He is not arguing from his feelings. By experience I don't mean feelings, I mean the facts. He was not arguing from *what he did* but from *what God did*, and that was the best argument of all. When we come to an impasse with a difficult issue, we should say, "What has God done about this? What has his Spirit said about this?"

Peter said, "When some Gentiles were baptised in the Holy Spirit, just as we were on the day of Pentecost...." Now that is an important principle: if God will accept a person, then we must. Some of the people God is touching today are people so different from us that we are sometimes a bit shattered when they come to our church. But if God has accepted them, so must we. If the Holy Spirit says, "They're mine," then so must we. You can't argue against the Holy Spirit's activity. But that is not sufficient to settle the argument by itself, for this reason: what we think is the work of the Spirit must always be checked by the word of scripture. Otherwise, claims can be made that the Spirit is moving which may not be true. So the next stage is the second argument from the Bible. James, the brother of our Lord, got up, and he was steeped in Jewish tradition. For James, the scripture backed up Peter's experience. Amos predicted that when God rebuilt the tabernacle of David, the rest of the nations of the world – the Gentiles – would come, and God would accept them as Gentiles. When James said that, it all fell into place. The whole church realised that God had settled the argument in two ways: *what he had done and what he had said.*

Frankly, when you get to that point, you don't even need to take a vote in a church meeting – and they didn't. If you take a vote it looks as if you are trying to find out the mind of the church, whereas what you are meant to do is to find out the mind of the Lord. When you have had a long debate, and when people have spoken of what God has done and said, then a wise presiding elder or chairman like James can say, "I sense what's right now; this is my judgement," and I am sure that as he said it there would have been nods of agreement all around the assembly. As he summed up the debate, they would realise that God had led them through the tangle of human argument to a clear understanding of his will.

So, thirdly, we come to the decision, and it is a surprise. Some superficial scholars have said that neither side won but a suitable compromise was arranged. I don't think that is the answer. What was their decision? It has two parts to it, as every church decision ought to have, because two principles are involved in this kind of issue: *liberty* and *love*. Liberty may point in one direction and love may point in another, and you must reach a decision that does justice to both. The first part of the decision was to repudiate the false teaching and say: we do not approve it; we do not acknowledge it; it is false teaching – nobody need be circumcised to be saved. So Paul won. We learn that there was great joy because the principle of liberty was upheld by the headquarters of the Jewish church. It was a historic decision: liberty, and they repudiated the false teaching, and declared that it is wrong that people should be told you have got to accept Jewish culture to be saved.

It is also wrong to say you've got to accept Western culture to be saved. It's also wrong to say you've got to accept any particular class culture to be saved. Christianity stands by itself, free of all cultures.

So far, so good The decision of the whole assembly was announced – I believe that the church ought to be nonconformist in the deeper sense. The trouble is that the "nonconformist" churches in this country are now desperately conformist. But a nonconformist church is a church that says: "We do not ask you to conform to anything other than Christ."

Then the surprising second part of the decision is this: we won't impose circumcision on you, but we do ask you to observe some rules of Jewish culture – things like not eating an animal that has been strangled. It is a surprise, this little added bit, isn't it? We thought they had just settled on freedom, and that cultural questions were not part of the gospel. Here they are, taking things straight out of the book of Leviticus and saying, "But would you please observe these?" Not circumcision, but some others. Why? You see, there is something more important than liberty, and it is love. Love says, "If a thing that I'm going to do is going to offend, and cause me to separate from another Christian, then I will impose a limit on my liberty. I will limit my own freedom so as to keep in fellowship with others." If this had not been added from that day onwards, there would have been two denominations that would have grown further and further apart. James realised that must not happen, and he saved the situation. He realised that in cities around the Roman empire there were synagogues where the word of God had been preached. Many Jews had become Christians, and because of their cultural background they would still have certain hesitations about some Gentile cultural patterns, particularly at the meal table. One of the things the early church loved to do was to eat together. I think we could do much more of it, having meals together. It would mean that they would have to have the Jewish Christians at one table with *kosher* food and the Gentile Christians at another table with other food. So James wisely avoids such a division. So as not to have to eat at separate tables, the Gentiles should limit their own freedom out of love for the others. Adapt your behaviour to others. Meet them halfway. This was not compromise. The gospel that was preached did not include any of these laws. They must not preach this to the unconverted: "You must abstain from things strangled." This was a matter of fellowship, and this is where Christians who love each other will adapt.

That is why Paul would circumcise Timothy. After going all this way to fight circumcision, he did that. But now he was doing it freely, out of love. Real freedom is not to say, "I'm free to do this," it is to be able to say, "I'm free not to do it." The way some people talk about freedom, it seems it is just to be free to do things that they want. But isn't it great when you are free *not* to do something? Real love says,

"I'm not going to do this if it is going to separate me from my brethren." So if you find that something in your culture is causing you to be separated from another Christian, you should examine your own culture. If you find that the way two Christians dress is keeping them apart from each other so they don't talk to one another after a service and just look at each other from a distance, and say, "Fancy coming to church like that," then maybe both of you should change your dress a bit. You are free to do that. You don't have to conform to your background.

It was such a wise decision that everybody was happy about it. It seemed good to the Holy Spirit and to us – and they reached unanimity. The principle was right and was established clearly, but in practice they were going to adapt it to the situation. Now that is the true Christian position – liberty and love, perfect partners together.

Having reached the decision, how best to convey it to the others who were concerned? Here there is a matter of public relations at stake. When a decision of this kind has been reached, people should be informed by written and spoken word. Both are needed, and you can see why.

First of all: the decision should be written down and then it is *fixed*. It cannot later be changed or misunderstood. It is a great thing to express something on paper and get it clearly stated. Thank God for minute secretaries. They are a vital part of church meetings – and somebody must have written this down. There must have been a secretary who took the minutes and wrote the decision down and wrote the letter.

Although the advantage of a letter is that it gets things stated in a way that is fixed, the disadvantage is that it is not very personal. It cannot convey the tone. It cannot easily convey the love behind it, and it can be misinterpreted and misunderstood. So, very wisely, having written the letter, they looked around the church meeting for two good people who would go with the letter and explain it, and help the others to feel the liberty and the love that they were trying to express. So they chose Judas and Silas, and off they went. Supposing they had just chosen two spokesmen and sent them, knowing what human memory is and knowing that our own thoughts and feelings can easily adjust things, by the time the message came out at the other end it could have been quite different!

What was the result of Acts 15? Was it a setback in the work? In the next chapter: "They delivered to the believers what had been decided upon by the apostles and elders in Jerusalem. So the churches were made stronger in the faith and grew in numbers every day."

Praise the Lord for doctrinal disputes, for men who are bold enough to say, "Let's settle the truth first and then get on with our mission. Let us decide what the gospel is and then go out." The vital need in all mission is to preach the same gospel. *I believe the greatest handicap to Christian witness in this country is not that the churches are disunited in working together, but that different gospels are coming from the churches.* One longs for the day when, whatever church you go to, whatever Christian you speak to, you hear one gospel: repent of your sin and believe in the Lord Jesus. Trust him and don't try to work your passage. Don't try to be good. Just bring him your life as a sinner and say, "God, be merciful to me, a sinner." We can make the social and cultural adjustments later. We can make that a matter of love. We are free to limit ourselves, free to adapt. But for the gospel, for Luke, this chapter was a great triumph, not a tragedy. It was a triumph for the truth, a watershed, from which Paul would go back to his mission with renewed confidence that the Christians were agreed on the truth and were going to go out and set people free with it.

20

From Asia to Europe
Read Acts 15:36–16:15

When I read about the missionary journeys of Paul, I take my hat off to a supreme juggler! He got a church going here, and then another one going there, and then he realised that one was wobbling and he dashed back or sent a letter, or he sent Timothy or someone else and got it going again. Dashed and got a few more churches going, then had to run back to these. In one place, listing all the difficult experiences that he went through, shipwreck, stoning, beating, all the rest, he finishes up with something that capped the lot – on top of all that, *the care of all the churches*. He kept them all moving. He would say: "Let's go back, let's see how they're getting along." So they decided to go back and that is the setting for this passage.

There are four principles of mission which we have to adapt and apply in our own situation. First of all, the principle of *mutual compatibility*; secondly, the principle of *cultural adaptation*; thirdly, the principle of *guided strategy*; fourthly, the principle of *sensible tactics*. Those four things I find in this passage.

Mutual compatibility
This is all-important if we are going to reach out in the name of Jesus Christ. Acts 15 is full of arguments. Some of them, as we have seen, were praiseworthy: defending the gospel; establishing the truth. We saw that the dispute, the contention, the dissension of Paul and Barnabas and those false teachers from Jerusalem, was a right and proper thing.

The argument that ends chapter 15 is not something we are so happy about, except to thank God that when he gave us the Bible he gave us an honest book. The saints are portrayed as human beings who can have arguments and differences of opinion, and can fall out with each other. Paul and Barnabas had worked together as missionaries, they had been around together such a lot. They had started life together as joint treasurers of a refugee relief fund and they had worked together as missionaries, they now had an argument and they split up. Thank God it is in the Word of God. It is an encouragement to missionaries who find this same problem.

What was the argument about? Well, it was over the young man called John Mark. You will recall that he had set out with them both on the first missionary track. When they had run into difficulty, when Paul had been taken ill, John Mark had got cold feet and ran off home. Whereas the sick Paul decided to go straight ahead up and over the Taurus Mountains to find health and to find new fields for God. Paul was not having him a second time.

The other side of the problem was that he was a relative of Barnabas, and blood runs thicker than water even in Christian circles sometimes. Barnabas wanted him to be given a second chance. Paul knew that reliable helpers were needed and so the argument took place over a weak Christian brother. Differences of opinion can happen over just that among elders of a fellowship. What to do with a weak Christian? Whether to encourage them and give them a second chance or to say, "I'm sorry, you've let us down in that position, we can't go on." So there was a division of opinion between them.

Now they very sensibly decided to divide. Paul and Barnabas, who had been together as missionaries, decided to go their separate ways. I think that is put in the Word of God to show us that we ought to be sensible. If we are to work in partnership we should be utterly realistic, and if it is not going to work out then let us go different ways. This may sound an extraordinary piece of advice to give, but there are many partnerships that should never have taken place and there are others that should be brought to an end, in Christian service. We get such a guilty feeling about ending a partnership that we feel we must push and push to make it work, and that somehow it is a failure and a defeat and an embarrassment to us in service if we cannot get along.

The church agreed with the decision of Paul and Barnabas and commended them to the grace of God. Praise God, do you know what happened? He got two mission teams out of it instead of one. Maybe if we push ourselves into impossible situations God could do much more if we recognised it and were sensible about it and said, "Alright, let's recognise the problem, and let's make other arrangements and spread ourselves more and commend each other to the grace of God."

This question of compatibility is very important. Partners are different personalities, God has made you differently and given you different backgrounds, so there will be adjustments to make. We should be sensible and not put ourselves in a partnership in Christian work that is going to strain our capacity of grace at this stage beyond what we can bear – that is not edifying.

Florence Allshorn, a young girl who went out as a missionary to Africa, was sent as the last of a long list of young girls to be the assistant to an elderly, unmarried lady missionary who was a bit of a tartar. She had upset all the previous girls. When Florence arrived she was shown into the missionary house, which was a single room and it was divided into halves. Clearly there was no barrier, but one half was beautifully furnished and the other was fairly bare. The elderly missionary said, "That's your half, and this is mine.

We don't get much privacy here, so I'll be grateful if you'll stay in your half." That was the greeting, and within a few days Florence was crying herself to sleep. So she sought the Lord about it and she said, "Lord, can I stay or should I go like the others?" The Lord did tell Florence in that case, "You can stay and you can cope." He led her to read 1 Corinthians 13 every day until she could love the older woman. She stayed and they became compatible and they became a team and they worked for the Lord there.

So the question is "Are we compatible?", not, "Are we identical?" For no two Christians ever are, in outlook or feeling or thought. Should we go on together? Because the one thing that is not edifying to the church or glorifying to God is Christians struggling to keep going an impossible relationship or situation. It drains nervous energy and ruins spiritual life. Much better to say, "Alright, we can't agree on this. We're brothers in Christ. Will you go on your mission? I'll go on mine, and may God bless us both."

As we have noted, God honoured such a separation very deeply, to the extent that in later years Paul sent for John Mark to come to Rome. So that was not an irreparable breach, it was a sensible facing of the facts at that stage.

So the principle of mutual compatibility is very important in working together for the Lord. If you are finding it impossible then be sensible about it. Don't just feel guilty and build up a complex and ruin your spiritual life – go and talk it over with someone and say, "Look, we're not working well together. What's the best thing to do in these circumstances?" Let the Lord multiply the work, maybe, by separating you for a time.

Cultural adaptation

This is the second principle, which is all-important to missionary work. Paul liked to work in threes; he liked there to be two mature men and one apprentice. That is a good pattern in mission and I don't know if any missionary society has ever taken it up: two seniors, one junior. Going off as threes, the junior one can learn so that someone can take over when the seniors leave the scene. John Mark was meant to be the apprentice but wasn't. So Paul set off with Silas. Silas was a more suitable person to accompany Paul on this second mission than Barnabas would have been. Silas held Roman citizenship, which Barnabas didn't. They soon found themselves in a position in prison where Paul could appeal for both himself and Silas, "We are Roman citizens and you have no right to put us in here." So God knew what he was doing through it all.

Paul was on the lookout for a young man to come alongside and learn the job and understudy the two missionaries. One day he met him – a young, delicate, rather shy lad, totally different from Paul, from a mixed background – a Jewish mother and grandmother, Lois and Eunice. They had taught this little boy, mother and grandmother, all they knew about the Bible. The father and grandfather were very different – Greek and pagans. But he had got the scriptures, his mother and grandmother had given him that. Timothy had been converted at Lystra on Paul's first missionary journey, and now a year later they could see that he had matured as a Christian.

There are few things more exciting to see in a fellowship than that. In a church where I ministered we had our staff meeting every Tuesday afternoon. We prayed for the people and talked over the work of the church, and time and again one of us would say, "Isn't it lovely to see so and so growing, becoming a stronger Christian, helping others?" What a joy it was, and in such meetings one thinks of the people God is bringing to your attention for positions of responsibility and leadership. Isn't Timothy doing well? I believe that Paul, with Christian love, said, "Timothy, my son, I'd like you to come with me. You are just the sort of lad I could use on this mission."

Timothy was subject to an extraordinary thing: Paul circumcised him. After all the fuss Paul had made at Jerusalem about circumcision, he went and did it. Not to save Timothy, but so that Timothy could save other people. It was a painful thing for Timothy for a few days at any rate, but it enabled him to enter a culture that otherwise would be closed to him. He was circumcised in order that, wherever they went together, Paul and Silas and young Timothy could enter a Jewish home without embarrassment. Timothy was willing to undergo that so that he might be a better missionary. Here is the principle of cultural adaptation – Paul did it for social, not for spiritual reasons. To save others, not to save Timothy.

Putting that in other terms: every Christian has to learn this, but particularly and supremely a missionary. I have been overseas and visited missionaries. There were some missionaries I went to, and I do not say this as a criticism but as an observation, where when you entered what was called the missionary compound you stepped out of the country in which you were and stepped back into England or America. The pictures on the walls were European, everything was European. The dress was European or American. There they were – living with the people – and I noticed that some of the nationals who came to those missionaries very quickly adopted Western culture. Western culture, as we have seen, is not Christianity. Some people laugh now at C. T. Studd and his friends growing pigtails in China, but they were trying to do something real.

On holiday in Cornwall on one occasion we were in a

little fishing village where there lived a retired Anglican clergyman who had been in Africa all his life as a missionary. In his hallway there was hanging an old portrait of himself presented to him by the church in Africa there when he left. It was a beautiful portrait, a real likeness and every feature was just right. There was one unusual thing about the portrait – his skin was painted black. When they gave him the painting, they said, "You are one of us." Wherever we go to win people for Christ we are going to have to learn the principle of cultural adaptation so that people sense the love and say: "You are one of us."

Where did we get this principle? Why do we emphasise it? Because that is precisely the principle on which the Son of God, the Lord of glory, became a man and cried as a little baby, and knew temptation and suffering and death as we know them. He became one of us, and that is why we feel we can go to him, because he is a high priest who has touched our infirmities, and understands and sympathises with our problems. It is because God the Son became like one of us that if we go out in his name we must apply the principle of cultural adaptation. As Paul and Silas and Timothy did this, so the churches were strengthened in their faith and grew in numbers daily. We are not throwing Christianity over a cultural gulf, we are saying, "We want to become like you, because we would like you to become as we are in Christ."

Guided strategy

This is the third principle. There is a great difference between where Paul wanted to go and where God wanted Paul to go. Maybe you have had my experience which is that if you tell God of a place you are *not* prepared to go, that is where he will send you! Many years ago I was pottering around a place called Guildford, and I saw the old Baptist church and said, "Lord, I'll never go there to be pastor. I just couldn't take that." That was how I felt – I am just being honest. So the Lord said, "Go to Guildford" – and I did!

Where did you say to God you wouldn't go? People have said, "I'm not prepared to go to Africa." And, "Lord, send me anywhere but the Arctic." The Lord may send you just there! Or have you said to the Lord, "I want to go to such and such a place," and he says, "No, somewhere else." Wilfred Grenfell dearly wanted to go to China but the Lord sent him to Newfoundland and Labrador. You study life after life and you will find that they felt this was where they ought to be. They said, "Lord, I want to go there and help those people," and God said, "There." My own sister-in-law offered to be a nurse in India but she spent her time in Angola and Zaire.

You see, the principle of guided strategy is this: "Lord, where do *you* want me to be?" There is no other principle involved. Paul said, "Let's go and have a mission in Bithynia," and God slammed the door. Paul said, "Let's go and preach in Asia, let's try going further north," and God slammed the door. God knew what he was about. I want you to notice the principles of guidance that came to Paul. Number one: the guidance of the shut door. If I ask a group of Christians how many have had the disappointment of a door slammed in their face, a door they thought was going to be the door of Christian service, most would identify with that. Somebody once said to me at such a moment: "Don't be so busy looking at the shut door that you miss the door that is going to open." Bithynia closed, Asia closed, and God was driving Paul further down the corridor to the door at the end.

Notice that guidance comes to those who are on the move. Physicists tell me that it is much easier to change the direction of a moving body than of a static one. If you have got a big, heavy, stone ball it will take you an awful lot of energy to start it going in one direction. But if it is on the move already then a little touch on the side and it will go in another direction. I do not believe that we should just sit and do nothing and say, "Lord, I'm going to stay right here till you tell me where to go." Paul would get going – let's be going forward, and let God shut the doors as we move. This is an active view of guidance as opposed to a passive one.

The result was that as God shut doors Paul finished up much further from the place where he started seeking guidance. He reached a place called Troas which is on the extreme western end of what is now Turkey, and he faced the waters of the Aegean Sea. That night he went to bed and as he lay in the night he saw a man. He realised the man was from over the water ahead of him, and was saying, "Come and help us."

Sometimes people have a vision of God calling and saying, "Go to that place." Sometimes they have a vision of people of a country saying, "We need help" – and that is a call. God speaks in a variety of ways. When we are quiet at night, when the busyness of the day is over, when we are relaxed, just lying down, that is a good place to be because the only place you can look is up. Sometimes then God says, "Go" and we know we have got to go.

How did Paul come to have that vision? Were there any previous incidents that led up to it? Were there any human factors in the vision, as there often were in visions in the Bible? They were so often related to things that had happened the day or the week before. Well, there is one little word that indicates it might be related to something human: "we". It is the first time it has been used in Acts. It had always been "they". From now on it is a personal diary kept by Luke, a medical doctor. Because it changes from "they" to "we", we know that Luke had joined Paul at Troas.

We know on other grounds that it is possible that Luke had been trained at the medical centre at Philippi in Macedonia. This doctor met Paul right there, and maybe they talked during the day of the doctor's home town, the needs of the people there, and the pagan immorality of the place, and Paul may have gone to bed with that conversation ringing in his memory. As he lay there, he saw a man from the same place. Am I speculating? It is interesting that the "we" begins here, and from now on Luke is part of the picture.

God can use all kinds of factors, human and divine, to bring us to the point where we know the Holy Spirit has called us. I am thrilled that in this passage the Holy Spirit is called the Spirit of Jesus. Those that get all worked up or worried about the Holy Spirit I think could very simply get over that if they just said the Spirit of Jesus. The Holy Spirit is the Spirit of Jesus.

Sensible tactics

This is the fourth principle. Sometimes our tactics are incredible. God calls us to use the *nous* he gave us. Do you know what that is? It is Greek for common sense. He tells us where to go but then he asks us to use our common sense as to how we go about the job. He wants us to think it through. He wants us to look where people are, when they are, how we can get through to them, where to gather them. What did Paul and Silas do? They took two very sensible steps, and we are not told that the Spirit had told them to take these steps. They landed on the other side, just two days' sailing later, which was a very small step for Paul but a gigantic leap for Christianity, because it brought Christianity to Europe, our continent. This was to be the radiating centre of Christianity for nearly two thousand years thereafter – what a gigantic step. When Paul landed on the shore at Samothrace he did not stay there, he moved on to Neapolis; he didn't stay there, he moved on to Philippi. Why? Because Philippi was the central town in that area and the most sensible thing to do if you are going to open up an area is to go for the main town in it. We should ask in our mission where the sensible place to begin is. Where is the place where, if something happened it would spread? When Paul had got a church established in a principal town he went away and left them to it, and it then spread to the surrounding region.

When he got to Philippi, what did he do? Again he found the most interested and likely people. Wherever he went in other cities he made for the synagogue, where there were people with the scriptures in their hands, worshipping the God of the Jews. He could begin with that, but there was no synagogue. Were there no Jews there? Evidently not enough to have a synagogue – you needed ten Jewish men for that. He was told there were a few Jewish women in the town. Where was their place of prayer? Paul and Silas went to meet them there: at the riverside, because that was the place where the women met to wash their clothes, and to buy and sell clothes, and that was the place they met on the Sabbath to pray. Have you ever thought of arranging with a few Christian lady friends to meet them somewhere on a particular time each week and just talk together about the things of God? See if anybody wants to join in. Why not? Think of where people might be, and go there and talk about the things of God.

Paul was so sensible, going to the place where there was most hope of finding people interested in God. They found not a man of Macedonia but a woman of Macedonia. Isn't that amazing? The vision was of a man and the first convert was a woman! Had something gone wrong? Well, we will see. The first man was going to be a jailer.

The lady was like a kind of Bond Street salon proprietress! She was – because purple cloth was terribly expensive. It was obtained from a special purple dye from shellfish. Kings dressed in purple. They dressed Jesus up in purple for his trial. There she was, praying with a few women doing the washing – what a situation!

She opened her heart – or rather the Lord opened her heart – to what Paul said, and this was the first convert in Europe. She opened her house and she brought her slaves, and she said they must hear too. Can you imagine it? This posh lady, if you'll forgive the expression, going down into the muddy river with her own slaves to be baptised, and God was there. The principle was of sensible strategy: go to the place where influence can spread. When you get there, look for the people who are most interested in God and begin with them and the church will be built.

Paul stayed with this lady for a time and I am sure it was a very comfortable and well-appointed home. God is so good to us – he was doing that to get them ready for the stocks in jail. God was giving them a nice few easy days in a feather bed first! No wonder Paul said "I have learned to be content in all circumstances."

21

Paul and Silas in Prison
Read Acts 16:16–40

One of the reasons we need to do a lot of Bible study is so that we can steep our minds in God's thoughts and learn to look at the world in which we live from his viewpoint rather than the world's. We don't always realise how much the world's ideas are pressing in on our minds all day long. It is essential that we drench our thoughts in the Bible and spend time looking at it until we can look out on the world and see what God is thinking about it and have his reaction and his thoughts.

There are two profound insights in this passage which are totally opposite to the world's way of thinking. I am going to put them in a rather complicated way first, and then explain them. Firstly: in God's thinking, the supernatural and the natural are to be kept together, whereas the world is forever separating them. Secondly, in God's thinking, good and evil are to be kept apart where the world is always putting them together.

Consider the first point: the world in which we live finds it very difficult to relate supernatural reality to natural reality – things beyond this world to the things of this world. So they do one of two things: they either deny the supernatural altogether or they keep it so far apart from the natural that the two never meet up. We have been through a scientific age in this land, in which people have tried blotting out the supernatural altogether. They said, "Unless you can prove that God exists with scientific proofs, we are not going to believe. Unless we can see or touch or taste or smell, we won't believe. The only reality is natural reality that science discovers. The only truths are materialistic truths."

So when they read the Bible and came to a miracle they said, "That must be explained away. That can't be true, it must be legend. How do we know that the Bible is an accurate record of what happened?" One way or another they reduced the Bible to a natural book of natural events that science could explain or explain away, and they lost the supernatural and only lived for the natural. But you cannot go on like that forever. Man longs for a supernatural world. He knows in his heart there are supernatural powers around him, and if you lock him up in a scientific materialistic world, sooner or later he will break out of that world and try again to find the supernatural. That was the case in the 1960s. For many years since then, people have been trying again to find the supernatural. They have done it in many ways. Thinking they have found it (in many strange, unhealthy ways), they are now separating it from the natural. Wanting to get out of the natural world, out of this world into that other world, they take a trip out into that world and call it "the infinite" and "the supernatural". So you get this sharp division between supernatural and natural, and you find people wondering which world to live in: the scientific, natural world down here or a supernatural world up there, which is another world altogether.

But the Bible puts the supernatural and the natural together. It teaches you to live in this natural world but to expect miracles. Live down here, but expect God to break through. Expect the supernatural to affect the natural. Expect a miracle when you pray.

What are we doing when we pray, but seeking to link the supernatural to the natural? What are we doing when we worship but seeking to bring these two worlds together? Here we are, natural people, flesh and blood people, subject to the law of gravity or you would be floating up to the ceiling! We are right in this material world, living down here, but we are here to seek the supernatural. The supernatural and the natural are held together so that you get an ordinary account in scripture about a couple of people thrown into jail by a tough jailor, and sitting there in the stocks. That is all a natural event. It is this world, we understand it all, and then suddenly there is an earthquake and things are happening. The supernatural has broken into the natural. The two have got related, and God is acting within time and space – within history.

Reading the Bible you can get the two worlds together so that you can relate the will of God to the washing-up. You can take heaven into your system, so that earth is transformed by the presence of things that are eternal. Now that is the first way of thinking that emerges from this passage. It is a natural event but shot through with the supernatural.

The second insight is that, in God's thinking, the good and the evil must be kept apart. Once again that is the opposite to the way the world thinks. So the world has got good and bad so confused that nobody knows now where the line is, and it becomes purely a matter of personal opinion. Indeed, there are those who have gone as far as to say, "There isn't a line. We are neither moral nor immoral, but amoral beings, and it is up to you to decide what is best for you and what you want to do" – and so on.

God wants evil and good kept separate. Bring together the natural and the supernatural, but keep apart the good and the evil – this is God's way of thinking about the world. And this comes out in this passage because here we have a person who has dabbled in the supernatural. We have a girl who has been exploring the supernatural world, and many people are doing just that today, and are not drawing any distinction between contacting good or evil supernatural powers. We need to warn people very seriously that both in the natural and the supernatural world there are good and evil forces which must be kept apart, and it is dangerous to dabble in them. Of course, people are doing it for many reasons. They do it largely for fun at first, but it quickly ceases to be a joke and it becomes very serious.

Let us take those two keys, unlock the scripture and see what this tells us. We left Paul and Silas in a comfortable bedroom in Lydia's house. Mind you, they took some persuading to take that room. It says, "Lydia prevailed upon us...." Paul and Silas didn't want "feather bed" Christianity with all "mod cons" and comforts laid on, but God was going to have them out of there soon.

It all happened the next day when they were going to the prayer meeting. A lot of things can happen on your way to a prayer meeting, and they met a girl. At first sight some might have regarded her condition as some sort of mental or emotional disturbance because she would shriek around the streets – but what she said showed that it was not mental trouble but spiritual. She had a power of extra-sensory perception. The growing interest in this is disturbing. I have heard of young people doing school projects on it, as well as on witchcraft and the occult. It is also a subject of research in some universities. Clairvoyance is a gift given by evil spirits to human beings so that they know things that are beyond the reach of the human mind – supernatural knowledge. This is the stage at which astrology, horoscopes, fortune telling, water divining and many similar activities reach the point where evil powers of the supernatural invade human beings. There comes a point where something true is said by an evil spirit, and that is where the laughter stops – when supernatural power is seeking to gain possession of a human life, to disintegrate that personality and destroy that person – and they will even use truth to do it.

For the remarkable thing here is that what this fortune teller said was true. The devil knows better than always to feed us with lies. He can put some truth in what he says, for that is how he hooks a person. This girl who was a fortune teller, and who was not a Christian believer, was shrieking after Paul and Silas: "They're servants of the most high God, and they've come to tell you how to be saved."

Now what's wrong with that? Isn't it a good bit of publicity? There is not a word there that is wrong, and shouldn't Paul and Silas have been glad that someone recognised who they were? They were not! It was a real embarrassment. It could have hindered the work of the gospel, and from this we learn a profound truth: that when evil spirits want to get hold of people, they feed the truth to them first, and then having opened their minds to their influence, they feed the lies afterwards. This is the devil's own method and he can dress up as an angel of light and he can give a first-class testimony!

Paul and Silas put up with it for a few days and then Paul got annoyed. That's the literal expression: he got "annoyed". Why should he be annoyed at someone with a message like that one, which was true? There are two things wrong with that girl's testimony. First: *the manner of her testimony was not edifying*. We need to remember that it is not only what we say, it is how we say it. Is our manner of testimony consistent with what we are saying? I have been thoroughly embarrassed by people giving a testimony in a way that was just not fitting for a servant of the gospel.

This girl was shrieking in the streets and we are not told to do that in Scripture. Yes, go on the streets by all means, but shrieking like this is not a fit manner of testimony. It embarrassed Paul and discouraged people from coming to hear the gospel. It kept them away, because people said, "It's madness." Paul lays down the principle in 1 Corinthians 14, for example: if everybody is speaking in tongues at once and not one at a time, somebody will come into your meeting and say "You're mad" – and you will wrongly put them off the gospel. You will not draw them. It is vital that we do things decently and in order, and that we treat people as people and don't shriek at them. It was embarrassing evangelism, and it was spoiling a good testimony from Paul and Silas. We ought to ask often that the Lord will save us from testimony delivered in a manner that will put people off and prevent the truth from getting through.

There is a second thing wrong with this girl's testimony: *the source of her knowledge*. It is not enough that we say the right thing or know the right thing. Where did we get that knowledge? Did we get it from the Holy Spirit or an evil spirit? As we have pointed out, evil spirits can feed you with bits of the truth, and the Holy Spirit was not telling this girl to say this. You can go out and testify for many reasons. It may be just an impulse of your flesh, it may be an impulse of the devil. It is vital that the source of your knowledge be the Holy Spirit, and that he be the teacher, and that he put the words on your lips. So Paul turned round on this girl and he said, "In the name of Jesus, come out of her." Jesus has all authority in the natural and supernatural realm, and because he is perfectly good he has all authority over evil in both places.

This girl was a slave. She had been bought and sold in the market place, but she was a slave in more ways than one. She was a slave to this occult power which she had dabbled in, and Paul liberated her. Now the testimony was no longer spoiled by this girl's activity, and she was free.

One of the saddest features of our world is that people want to make money and don't mind how they make it. There are those in our society who, as soon as they spot a human weakness, will exploit it. There are some who don't mind if they get their money from pushing drugs, knowing that they are killing people, and that is slow murder. They don't mind getting money as long as they can exploit. Believe me, when the Holy Spirit gets going, those people are going to lose money, and they are going to be hurt in the place where they are hurt most – their pockets and their wallets and their purses, and they are going to hate it.

Have you ever stopped to think and ask: supposing revival comes to your town, who is going to lose money there? Just think that through for a little while and you will get some very disturbing thoughts in your mind, but this is what happened here: this poor girl was being exploited. She had been bought as a piece of property, as a fortune telling machine, and there were men behind her exploiting her and getting money for it. They made a fortune out of her telling fortunes, and now she couldn't do a thing.

A young person told me of going to a spiritist séance, and when they tried to get messages through, their name was tapped out – a name that nobody else there knew. That young person told me how they said, "Tell me the name of my Lord" – and from that moment onwards they could get no more messages. That is what happens when Jesus is around. The powers of evil are helpless and they can't do anything more.

This is what happened here and the men saw their money vanish, and they fought hard and stirred up mob hysteria, and they grabbed Paul and Silas. They were furious, and they dragged them to the magistrates and told lies about them. They didn't say, "Magistrates, these men have robbed us of our living." They said, "They are Jews, and we are Romans and they are teaching us to adopt illegal religion, and they are disturbing the city."

If there is one thing the devil loves to put on people's lips when Christians are testifying, it is this: "They are disturbing our city."

One night a young, demented girl was shrieking outside a church building where I ministered, and I had letters from neighbours about the disturbance the church was causing – how peaceful the neighbourhood was before we came. We have to take note of complaints and see that the manner of our testimony is not a wrong kind of offence, but believe me, this is the most common complaint that will come when God is moving in a city: "It's disturbing!"

So Paul and Silas were whipped and beaten until their backs were red, raw, and bleeding, cut and bruised. They were taken into the jail, and if you have been in a Middle Eastern jail even today you know what sort of a place it was. They were taken into the inner security block. They were stripped of their clothes. They had their legs stretched and cramped in stocks, and they were left in pitch darkness in the smell, with the grunts and the groans of the prisoners lying round the walls. Rather a change from Lydia's home!

Again we remember that Jesus never promised an easy time for his followers. He never promised that you come to Jesus and you'll have a comfortable life. He said, "In the world you will have trouble, big trouble, but cheer up, I've overcome the world."

Notice the important lesson: it is not enough to seek the supernatural. The supernatural is real. Said a woman to me just after she had left her husband. "I've been to a spiritist medium to get comfort and I have had a message for my husband about some handkerchiefs in his drawer that nobody knows about except him." She continued, "You're not going to believe me, are you? You're a minister."

I said, "Yes, I believe you."

"Oh," she said, "Do you think there's something in it?"

I said, "I'm sure there's something in it."

"Oh," she said, "Then it's alright to go?"

"No, it is not alright to go. It's precisely because there is something in it that it's wrong for you to go."

She was seeking supernatural help at a time of tremendous need in her life, but it was the wrong kind of supernatural help. The trouble is that some of the messages that come through that channel have enough truth in them to convince that it is real, but it is the power of evil that brings that supernatural knowledge. Let us always be careful that we only seek the Holy Spirit, who is perfectly good.

Now we move to the second part of the account. I call the first part "tragedy" or "trouble". That is the word "tribulation" in the Bible, but one could also call it "triumph". They had been up against the truth from an evil source, and then lies from an evil source. You have really got to be on your guard when the devil can use both truth and lies against you, but they were going through part of what Jesus went through. He was wrongly arrested and was whipped unjustly. He was put through without a fair trial. They were sharing the sufferings of the Lord, and in the early church, whenever they suffered for his name, they rejoiced. It was an early Christian called Tertullian who said: "The legs feel nothing in the stocks when the heart is in heaven." It doesn't matter what they can do to your body, if your spirit is free you can sing. They were singing at midnight. They could have been having a good old grouse or getting depressed. They could have been sitting there and saying "Poor us" – especially in the early hours of the morning. That's when we think about ourselves such a lot, and get so depressed about ourselves. There they were, in the pitch dark, smelly, in pain, with the grunts and the mutterings of the other prisoners round them. "We'll sing hymn ..." – and sing they did, and pray. They weren't doing it as a testimony, they were doing it because they were worshipping God, but the other prisoners were listening. God had a new mission field for Paul and Silas.

He wanted them in the prison. There were people there whom God wanted to reach and to touch, so they prayed to God. Now here it comes: God joined in! You could hear in the singing – when God sings, it shakes everything, and he was joining in.

Now the scientist says: "No, it's purely a natural event. Coincidentally, there happened to be an earth tremor at that time." The Bible is full of such "coincidences"and no statistician would accept this number of coincidences! But that is how the natural man thinks. He says, "I don't believe that earthquake had anything to do with their hymn singing." We know better! You tell me an earthquake that opens every door in a building and loosens every chain that was fastened to the stone walls, drops every bar from every gate without hurting a single person! That earthquake was under complete control in God's hands, and God shook that building just enough to get the bars out of the door and to get the shackles out of the wall.

Suddenly they were all free, even the stocks are broken – not one life lost, not one person bruised, and yet doors cracking open. Don't tell me this is a natural event. I just find it too difficult to believe that explanation. Now see what happened: the jailor, big, tough, burly, probably a retired regimental sergeant major (they used to pension off centurions to look after the jails in those days), and he comes in. One of the rules was that if the jailor let one prisoner escape, he must pay the penalty of the prisoner. If a man was sent to jail for six months and he escaped, the jailor was put in prison for six months. And here he had some top security prisoners in the condemned cell almost certainly waiting to die, the door was open and he just wasn't going to wait for all the rigmarole of facing the court. He pulled out his sword and was going to do away with himself. Then came Paul's voice. Maybe Paul just saw him silhouetted against the doorway, and the sword poised, and Paul was just in time. He shouted quickly, "It's alright, we're all here." Fancy that, I don't know of any other prison where if the door suddenly shook open and the walls fell down, and the chains fell off, there wouldn't be one mad rush—a mass breakout. This is the second miracle here: those prisoners were sitting quietly in their places. Paul and Silas were simply sitting there – "It's alright, don't harm yourself, we're here."

The jailor, who had been filled with the fear of man, was now filled with the fear of God, and he asked the most important question a person can ever ask. The world asks questions like this: "What must I do to be rich? What must I do to be healthy? What must I do to be famous or popular? What must I do to be successful?" But the question that God is waiting for from everyone is: "What must I do to be saved?" Why did he ask it? He asked it because when you are at the point of death, they tell me, your whole life flashes before you, but you tend to remember the bad things you have done. And as this man thought he had come to the end of his life, he remembered his brutality, he remembered his selfishness, he remembered all the many things he had done. Now God was terribly real because he realised that God was in this place. It had something to do with those men singing and praying. He knew they were religious, and now he knew that their God was a real God, and he realised he was a sinner. I am quite sure all this came in a moment. The Holy Spirit can open a man's eyes in a split second to his whole life.

It takes a disaster like this to bring a man of that age to his senses. Lydia didn't have a crisis like this. She didn't need an earthquake to become a Christian. She was already quietly seeking the Lord as she went about her business. She had got a few women together to pray, and Lydia seems to have slid into the Christian faith as smoothly as a little child. As soon as she heard the truth her heart opened. But it can take an earthquake, a disaster, sometimes – it may mean a man has got to go right to the brink of his life before he will just say humbly, "What must I do to be saved?"

Paul knew what to say. He introduced them to a person. Believe, trust, and commit your life to the Lord Jesus. You will be saved, and if the people in your house will do the same, they can be saved too.

The jailor said, "Tell me more. I want to know, and will you tell my household too?" And he took them in. The word "household" would include slaves, servants, staff, all sorts of people, and they all listened. To take top security prisoners out of the condemned cell and into his own home, what a change! He was running the risk of losing his job and everything, but now he didn't care, now he wanted to hear more. Did they sit down in a circle, and did Paul preach to them? No, I think there's a lovely touch now. This great, tough jailor who may be the man who had beaten them, ill-treated prisoners, thrown them into the stocks and clamped the wood on their ankles, said, "Bring a sponge and some warm water," and while Paul talked about the Lord Jesus, this great big jailor washed his back gently like a little baby.

Can you see it? What a change! When God gets real to people, they do the most extraordinary things, but they are always beautiful things and lovely things. As he washed off Paul and Silas the caked blood and sweat, as he sponged them down, he listened. When he had finished, Paul said, "Now let's wash you" and he took them out and baptised them. The jailor was washing blood off, but Paul was washing sins away, and in the name of the Lord Jesus all in that household received the Word, believed and rejoiced.

Don't ever use the word "household" here to justify baptising babies. This was a whole household of people who all heard the Word, rejoiced, all believed and were baptised that night.

So through the early hours of the morning a whole situation was changed, and now this tough jailor and Lydia the seller of purple would be brother and sister in Jesus Christ. A new life had been given to a whole household, and Paul, Silas and all of them were singing again at dawn. The supernatural and the natural had got together and lives had been changed.

One thing I am quite sure about is that as we worship God today and as his Word is preached, unless the supernatural comes to the natural there aren't going to be changed lives. It is the result of God stepping in, the supernatural and the natural interacting, and in that meeting between heaven and earth new people are made by the Holy Spirit.

Day came and Paul sent for the magistrates. Now I used to think that this was a little bit of pride in Paul – you know, he wanted them to come and eat humble pie. But actually Paul wanted to make sure that no other Christian got the treatment he had from those magistrates. He wanted to teach them that as magistrates they must be just and fair and true. So he said, "Send for them. Tell them we are Roman citizens; that they are criminals now. They have committed an illegal act and they are liable to Roman law" – as they were. Those magistrates came in a hurry. They had already had a sleepless night and had regrets. They had already sent a message, "Set the men free," but Paul waited, and those magistrates came and said, "We're sorry." That would mean they wouldn't punish the jailor for what he had done. It would mean they would not throw Lydia in jail. It would mean the Christians in that place could be free. It would mean that they could live in peace in that city, at any rate for a time while those magistrates were in charge. They wouldn't make the same mistake again.

So Paul and Silas walked out into the light of day, sore

but rejoicing; tired but happy, praising God. They left the city because there was now a church there. There was now a man who would lead that church. There were other cities without Christ, so they moved on.

Don't ever believe that you won't get into trouble for witnessing, but do believe that when you get into trouble you will triumph in Christ, and you will often do it by singing everywhere you go!

Praise God that right where you are there is somebody he wants to reach through you, and praise God until he joins in and acts. You are not called to a picnic but to a battle. You are not called to a bed of roses, but a crown of thorns, and beyond that you are called to the joy that is set before us, if we endure, despising the shame.

22

Thessalonica, Berea and Athens
Read Acts 17

Everybody who knows Jesus Christ is honour-bound to tell others about him, to share the good news and tell anybody who will listen, but we need a little adaptability. What we want is a nice, easy, slick scheme whereby you can learn a few spiritual laws or a handful of texts and you are ready to go out and fish for men. Quite frankly, you might as well set off fishing with a bit of string, a bent pin, and a worm. You might just catch one, and the last lap might convince you that the bent pin and the worm are the right method, but it would be sheer luck if you did. You ask any fisherman and he will tell you that it's a skilled business, that you'll have to choose your bait, your spot and you may need to change your rod. Adaptability! While it is true that when we know Jesus Christ we can begin witnessing straightaway, we learn from Acts that when the apostles went out they had more than a little adaptability. They approached different people in different ways.

For example, it becomes patently obvious that Paul used the scriptures a great deal in personal witnessing when the person he was speaking to believed it was the Word of God, but when they did not believe, he did not use his Bible. That is what I mean by "adaptability". He still gave them the contents of scripture, but not in the same way. We see in Acts 17 that in the first half of the chapter he is dealing primarily with Jews, and the way he talks to them is totally different from the second half of the chapter when he is speaking to

Greeks or Gentiles. For the deepest division in the ancient world was between Jews and Gentiles.

When Paul went into a Jewish home, he could act like a Jew; when in a Gentile home, like a Gentile. He not only adapted his manner of life, he adapted his message. He didn't change his basic beliefs but he adapted the way he put them across. Sometimes we as Christians, when we witness, behave like a man I met in Lancashire who told me, "You've just got to accept me as you find me." In other words, I must do the adapting, not him. He said this to me in his own home, virtually: "You can like it or lump it; I'm not going to change for you, you can change for me." In the same way, if we go out determined, just with a nice little neat scheme to give them the works, whether it's adapted to them or not, whether it suits them or not, whether they're interested in it or not, then frankly we are going to be in trouble. If you are called, as you are if you are a Christian, to be a fisher of men, then the first thing you need to study is the fish, and to understand them, and to be able to meet people where they are, and to interest them. I believe that we do not have the right to witness to people solely because Jesus told us to witness. That is *part* of our right to speak to others. The other half of it must be to establish in *their* minds our right to speak. There are many ways we can do that: you can do it by meeting a need that they have, you can do it by making friends with them, you can do it by interesting them, and if they are interested in what you say, you have a right to go on speaking. But we need to earn the right in their minds to witness, and Paul is a marvellous example of this. He always began with their thoughts, their ideals, their hopes, dreams, fears, and their experience. Beginning there, he sought to lead them gently in an interesting way to the Lord Jesus Christ.

He didn't go and say, "A-B-C-D, that's what I've learned

in the school of evangelism. Now you pin back your ears
and let me give it to you."

On the day of Pentecost when Simon Peter and the others
were filled with the Spirit, some people thought they were
drunk, so Peter began his sermon by saying, "We're not
drunk, the pubs aren't open yet. It's only 9 o'clock in the
morning," and he had their interest at once. I want you to
notice that the most effective witnesses you hear are those
who bother to start where people are, and adapt themselves
to the people they are seeking to win.

Let us see how Paul did it. In the first part of the chapter
he went to Jews. Wherever he could find his own fellow
countrymen, he made for them first. There is a lesson we
have already drawn from Acts. Go to your own age, and
your own sex, and your own group first. They are the ones
you are most likely to get through to. So he always started
with Jews, and when he did he started with the scriptures,
our Old Testament. They already knew that is the Word of
God, so Paul quoted scripture to them, as Peter did on the
day of Pentecost speaking to Jews and to those who knew
the Old Testament.

To those who accept the Bible, quote it. To those who
will be impressed with what is written in it, show them what
is written. The other thing that the Jews had, which Paul
would latch on to every time, was a dream that had lasted
a thousand years – that one day God would send a man to
save them from all their troubles. Do you know that still
they hope for this, three thousand years after that hope was
born? If you are talking to a Jew, in many cases you can
start with this: "Are you looking for the Messiah?" In the
scriptures, God had promised he would send one, so there is
scriptural promise from the past and hope for the future, in
the Messiah. That word means, "an anointed one; a king".
In the Greek language it is the word "Christ".

So when Paul went to Jews he took their hopes and dreams of a Messiah and he put them together in Jesus, and that was the approach that he adopted. What a good approach it was with those who knew and believed the promise and so were looking for the Christ, the Messiah, and all Paul had to do was to draw those threads together and say: "I've come to tell you he's here. He's been, he's come."

But gathered around every group of Jews in the ancient world in their little ghettos, in the big cities of Thessalonica and Berea, there were others who were attracted to the Jewish God, because it was such a simple religion. Those who were used to having gods all the way down the street, statues, temples and shrines, and were utterly confused with all the gods that were believed in, they heard that the Jews believed there was only one. That made life much simpler, and religion much more straightforward, so they would gather around the synagogues, and those people were called "God-fearers" – Gentiles who worshipped God. One of the features in Greece was, of course, that the women were liberated. They were allowed to go out; they were allowed to follow their own ideas. They were allowed to go to their own meetings, and so you find throughout Acts 17, three times it is mentioned, that women of high social standing were there in the synagogue seeking God, and often among those women there was the most fruitful field for Paul's words.

The result was that when Paul told Jews that Jesus was the Christ, some of them believed. The trouble was that the others didn't, and one of the first things he ran into in Thessalonica was jealousy. Religious jealousy is a terrible thing, but not unknown. Let me tell you a modern form of it. Today people of all ages who have not been in church before, who have not known Christ, are coming to know him. Praise the Lord for that and they come into the churches. Praise God for that too, but what is happening in some of those churches? Some of those who have struggled for years to keep the place going say, "What is happening to our church?" Notice the little adjective: *our* church. "All these people coming in are taking over our church." That is jealousy, which is more than envy. Envy would say, "You know I envy these young people and others so fresh in their experience. I have never felt like that about the Lord." But when we start saying, "Our church is being taken over by these people," that's jealousy because jealousy resents losing something you have had, whereas envy is resentful that somebody's got something you never had.

So there was religious jealousy and it happens today and it will go on happening. It happened in the days of Jesus. The religious leaders saw prostitutes and publicans coming into the kingdom of God, and loving God in a way they had never done; and they had been struggling at their religion for years, and they were jealous for the religious emphasis was being taken away to other people. It is very hard when you have struggled to be loyal and faithful, and doggedly kept your religion going for years, to see people come and just take it like that, and that is what happened here.

These Jews had kept the synagogue open for years and suddenly it was full of people wanting to hear Paul, suddenly it was full of converts, new Christians, people eager to hear the Word and they had never seen such eagerness in their synagogue days. They had had this dogged loyalty – people sitting through the services – but now others were coming to hear, and there was jealousy. "What's happening to our synagogue?"

Jealousy does horrible things and they decided to get rid of Paul and Silas. They went outside and stirred up the mob. They got all the loafers worked up and they went to the house where Paul and Silas were staying. A man called Jason owned the house, and they couldn't find Paul and

Silas, so they dragged Jason and some of the Christians off to the magistrates, and they had to pay a lot of money to get bail and go free. Religious jealousy is one of the things you will meet if you preach the gospel. So Paul and Silas picked themselves up and off they went, but what was the charge made against them? It is a charge that Christians have been thrilled to acknowledge ever since: "These that have turned the world upside-down." What a charge! Of course, it is a false charge. What they should have said: "These that have turned the world right way up," but then if everybody's upside-down they don't just appreciate that that is what's happening.

In fact, they were accusing them of revolution, and every Christian is a revolutionary, but let's be quite clear what sort of a revolution it is. They accuse them of a political revolution by bringing Jesus in as a new king in place of Caesar, and that is a false charge. Christians are not *political* revolutionaries. They do not seek to turn the social order upside-down, because frankly they know that this usually produces a worse situation and a greater tyranny. Christians bring a *religious* revolution, not a political one. They seek to change people's ideas about God, knowing that if that can happen, the social problems will be sorted out.

So it is religion that suffers most when Christians are around. It is the outward form of godliness without the power that will get jealous of real Christians who are around, and it is a religious revolution that happens when the apostles hit town. What we want is a revolution in the heart.

Paul and Silas moved on to Berea. Once again they found themselves among Jews. Once again they took the scriptures. Once again they said to the Jews, "You're looking for a Messiah." Once again they said, "Can't you see that scripture predicts the kind of Messiah Jesus is?"

This time they met more open-minded Jews. We are told

something about these Jews that's lovely: they went home to check up on the preacher. I just hope that you check up on your preacher. You see, there are two ways of getting your Bible study. One is to hear the preacher one Sunday and then come back next Sunday to hear a bit more, and then the third Sunday to hear a bit more. Some of the Jews at Thessalonica did this, but at Berea they said, "That's not enough. We'll look into the Bible on Monday, and Tuesday, and Wednesday, and Thursday, and Friday, and Saturday, and we'll just see if this preacher is right, and if he's not we'll tell him so next Sunday." I will gladly challenge you to do that. Please check up on me, I am not a pope and I am not infallible. My Bible is the same as yours, but I am not an infallible interpreter of it. Will you check whether whatever I teach is in the Bible? If it is not, you can safely disregard my comment, and you can tell me I shouldn't have written it. When people check up on the preacher, shall I tell you what happens? In Thessalonica, where they just listened to Paul preach from the Bible every Sabbath, *some* believed. But in Berea, where many went home and checked up daily in the scriptures to see whether it was really true, *many* believed. Alas, the Jews in Thessalonica were prepared to send anti-Christian missionaries sixty miles to tell the Bereans they shouldn't listen to this fellow Paul. So off went Paul, Silas and Timothy? No, he didn't! He left the two there and he went off! You can check up on that – Silas and Timothy stayed in Berea and Paul went off by himself to Athens. In Athens he met a very different situation – a pagan, intellectual, cultured city.

What a city—you can still catch something of ancient Greece as you climb up the Acropolis and look at the Parthenon. When Paul arrived it was the greatest university city in the then-known world, renowned for sculpture, architecture, art, literature and oratory. It was a city that had given the Greek language to the world, which perhaps is one of the most expressive languages there has ever been, and God chose the Greek language as the one in which to write the New Testament.

This was a city where the great brains came. It was the city where Socrates and Plato were born, where Aristotle had lived, and where great poems were written, which we still read. This was the city where English education was forged, for our English education system owes more to Athens than to any other centre of learning, and still to this day our education is based on Greek thought.

To Athens came Paul. Was he going to pull out his scripture here? No. Was he going to talk about the Messiah, the Christ? Not at first, because he was now among people who didn't have the Bible and didn't believe it, and didn't have any desire or hope for a Messiah. Where was he to start?

Athens has three hills: the Agora, the Areopagus, and the Acropolis. The Agora was the centre of commerce, a marketplace, where the people gathered, a kind of super-market with long arcades full of stores. The Areopagus was the kind of university where they licensed the public lecturers, where they listened to any new philosopher and gave him a licence to speak publicly in Athens. The Acropolis was the centre of religion crowned by the Parthenon but with many other temples and shrines around it. When Paul got to Athens, what was the first thing he did? He had a good walk around the city. If you are going to go somewhere and witness, why not have a good walk around the town and notice things, and just look at the place with the eyes of Christ. So Paul looked around and he saw all this and he saw the religious idolatry: temples everywhere, and shrines – and it hurt.

Do you look around a city? Do you study the people? Do you see what they are like? Do you sit on a bus or tube train and look at the miserable, hard or lonely faces that you can see? As Paul went round the city his heart was hurt because as a Jew he had a memory of the very first two commandments: only one God, no other God beside me; no graven images. He knew that if you get the first two commandments wrong you are going to have real problems with the other eight; that if you get your ideas of God wrong, you are going to get your ideas of goodness wrong; that if your beliefs are wrong, your behaviour will go wrong. His heart bled for this city that was so superstitious, so full of idols, and along at the end of the street he came across a most unusual one.

It had no name on it and no statue of a god on the top. It was just an altar and it said: "To the unknown god." It had been there for five hundred years. It had happened that one day a pestilence came to Athens. A disease struck, people were dying like flies, and they said, "The gods are angry. Which one is angry? I wonder which one we've upset. How can we find out? How can we please them again? How can we placate him?" A poet called Epimenides made a suggestion: "Why don't we let loose a flock of black and white sheep and let them go down the main street, and where they lie down, the nearest altar is the god we have upset, and we all sacrifice the sheep." Great idea wasn't it? Until the sheep went down the street, past every single altar and not surprisingly sat down in a field at the end! Epimenides said, "There's a god we don't know about. There must be another one somewhere and that one is upset because we have forgotten him. So let's put an altar up, and we don't know his name, and we don't know what he looks like, we can put: 'To the unknown god'."

Paul, as he walked around the city, had found his sermon. This was the link – he had something that they were feeling after. You see, people are in touch with God, even though they don't know it. The people in your town, even though they may never go near church, are feeling after God in some way, and we have got to study until we spot the point at which they are searching after God.

Everybody has got a God-shaped blank in their human soul. Everybody needs God, and everybody is looking for a god in some way. They are crying out to the unknown god and they are trying to give him a name, and give him a face and a shape. So look around and say, "You're looking for someone aren't you? And I've come to tell you who he is."

Do you see how Paul was adapting his message, looking for some way to begin, something in the people to whom he was going, so that he could start where they were with their own aspirations and feelings.

Religious idolatry was one feature of life in Athens, but the other feature, rather strangely, was philosophical argument. They didn't have television so they had the Areopagus, the place where people gathered to hear something new, and they were always discussing one basic question: how to live, how to make the most of life, how to make the most of these years we've got. Everybody is interested in that. There were two answers being given to that question, which are also being given in England today. There was the Epicurean answer, and the Stoic answer. The Epicureans said, "Enjoy yourself, life is for pleasure. If there is a god up there, he's not interested in you. He's lost interest in you. So enjoy yourself. When you die, that's it. There is nothing of you after you're dead. So live for pleasure, but don't have so much pleasure that you kill yourself early. Just have enough pleasure to keep going, and don't hurt anybody else." Isn't that a philosophy that has come down for two thousand years and more?

The Stoics, on the other hand, believed not in emotional pleasure, but in rational behaviour: the main aim of life is to be self-sufficient; to be so much in charge of your own life that you need nothing and nobody else. Can you see what was happening? For the ancient Greeks, religion and life had got completely separated. They believed in gods. They believed the gods lived forever, but the people were here having to make the best of life without the gods, either by enjoying themselves as much as they could without hurting themselves or others, or by trying to be so stoical – we still use the word – that they didn't need anything or anybody. Isn't that strangely modern? Don't you meet people who are doing just the same thing?

Paul went into this situation and he preached Jesus and the resurrection, and they said, "This is new, this is something good. Come up to the Areopagus and be interviewed. So Paul had the chance to speak to the thirty top brains in Greece, probably the thirty cleverest men in the whole of the then-known world. Paul had to speak to them. What does he say? He starts by saying, "I see that you are already a religious people. You believe in the supernatural, fine. I see that you are not quite sure that you know all about the supernatural because I see you've got an altar to an unknown god. So you don't know everything about the gods. I have come to tell you about the one you don't know.

Can you see how he is easing their minds open? He started with something they have always wanted to know: the name of that god at the end of the street, and he has come to say, "I know him." Then he goes straight into nature, the material creation, because that is something they know about. He doesn't quote scripture but he is giving them scriptural truth. You see, it isn't always the person who quotes the Bible who knows the Bible. There are people who call at your door who can quote texts but they may not know the whole Bible. It is essential to know the biblical truth – not just text, but truth.

He says that the unknown god is the God who made everything. Did they think a god who made everything that is can be trapped in a shrine, dwelling in a house made with hands? Did they think God needs us? This is one of the biggest dangers of our human pride, that we think God *needs* us. He doesn't *need* any of us.

He wants us, and that is a different thing, but he doesn't need anything from you or from me. One of my favourite texts is in Psalm 50 where God says, "If I were hungry I wouldn't tell you."

Notice how Paul is beginning to address Stoic philosophy. He is saying that God is self-sufficient. Paul is also challenging Epicurean philosophy, because Epicureans used to say, "This world just happened," but he is saying, "God made it, and God is self-sufficient. He is the unknown god," and gradually he tells them what God is like. He tells them this: you live and you breathe – who do you think gave you breath? Who gave you life? This unknown god who made the universe gave you life and breath.

He begins to quote now, but still not from the scriptures. Who does he quote? He says, "Your poets say the same thing," and he quoted their poets. Do you see that this means that a Christian witness who is going to testify must not only read the Bible? He's got to read the paper; he has got to read other books. He has to read what people are thinking, reading and seeing, so that he can say: "Your very own poets are saying the same thing," and be able to take the quotes from their world, and their literature, and use them to glorify God. How adaptable Paul is! So, quoting their poets, he brings them to the sense that there is a great God who made everything that is, who doesn't need a thing from us but gives us everything we have got, and this God made all nations from one man.

Something that comes at this point is very important. Do you know that Greeks used to look down on people of other races? They used to say, "They can't even talk properly, but Paul is saying that he believes that all people on earth came from one man and that is a revolutionary idea. I believe that the idea of evolution is more responsible for racism than almost anything else. It was the idea that we have come from animals that has given to the world the idea of the struggle for existence.

Paul is conveying here that there is one God and one human race, and God is who decides where and when a nation lives. God is the one who draws the school atlas. God is the one who allows an empire to grow and then takes it out of history. God is the one who allots the times, the seasons and the habitations for the nations. It is God who is in charge of history as well as nature. He is saying: your own poets recognised that we are the children of God, for we are also his offspring as your poet, Aratus, has put it.

Then he begins to draw them closer. There are two things that every person on earth can know of God: creation and conscience. As Immanuel Kant, the Western philosopher, put it, "Two things convince me there is a god: the starry heavens above and the moral law within"— creation; conscience. Having spoken of creation, which they know, he goes on to speak of conscience, and he says, "You didn't know God until now, but now that God has sent a man who will judge you, there is no excuse. You are called to repent and turn from your evil ways."

From the material creation he turns to moral conscience. There isn't a person you talk to who hasn't got a conscience on something. I was speaking to some humanists and we got on to this. I said, "Are you telling me that you have always lived up to what you know to be right?" They couldn't say a thing. They would argue that people have different standards – agreed. That people's conscience tells them different things – agreed. They had argued that those who hadn't heard of the Ten Commandments shouldn't be judged for breaking them – agreed.

"Well then," they said, "What about those who have never heard?"

I said, "They've had a conscience, and my Bible tells me that God will judge every man by his own conscience, which is fair. Romans 2 tells you that, and that therefore every one of us must meet our Maker – this God who made everything, who gave us life and breath. This God has appointed a Man, we know his name, Jesus, to judge every human being."

At this point Paul had to say something that was going to cut right across Greek ideas. How can I meet my Maker if death is the end? Whether it is Epicurean or Stoic thought, they believed that when I die that's the end of me as an individual. So Paul said that there is vivid proof of this in one fact: God raised Jesus from the dead – the resurrection.

Here was one idea that the Greeks could not take – the resurrection of the body. When Paul spoke of the resurrection, that was it. They would not even register him as a lecturer. They wouldn't listen any more. Some of them actually burst out laughing, and to this very day those who believe that life is to enjoy, or life is to be master of your fate and captain of your soul, don't like the thought that they will rise from the dead to face their Maker – it is an offence.

Paul had led them from the beginning, their own altar, through to the point where he said: you will stand before God.

In a debate at the College of Law, students seemed keen to follow this topic through, so we went back for a lunchtime meeting to discuss the evidence of the resurrection. They came, I suppose, for three-quarters of an hour, they thought, but an hour and a half later they were still talking very earnestly. They got to the point where I felt I could say to them quite simply, "You will one day meet Jesus. You will one day stand before him, and you will have to give an account of your life to the Jesus you're arguing about now.

You won't have any doubts then that he's risen." There was a stunned silence, and the meeting finished very shortly afterwards. There comes a point where this has to be said, and at that point a division will take place. Various reactions will occur. That is not the place you must start.

You mustn't go up to someone and just say, "You're going to be judged," but if you start where they are and lead them through, tell them what God is like, tell them that they owe their very life to this God, tell them that one day they will rise from the dead and face their Maker, tell them that God is Judge as well as Creator, and they are ready to hear about Jesus then, don't be surprised if you get different reactions at that point. Whenever you tell people about God and face them with this certainty that they are going to rise and meet their Maker, some will say, "It's ridiculous, a day of judgement? What a joke. When I'm dead they can bury me and that's it." There is another group that says, "Well, maybe I'll come back next Sunday, it sounds interesting. I'd like to hear you again. You know, you're an interesting speaker; it's quite novel." Next week they will be listening to another dialogue, another debate.

But *some* believed. Among them was one of the thirty brainiest men in the world: Dionysius the Areopagite, one of those sitting on the council. He hurried out of the meeting, came to Paul and wanted to learn more, and he believed. And one of those leading Greek women who had been sitting in on the discussion came out of the meeting and said, "Paul, will you tell me more?" And one or two others came out and they said, "Paul will you tell me?"

I have heard preachers say that Paul was a failure at Athens, that he went away completely broken because it was all a gigantic flop, and that in this intellectual centre he was no good. Believe me, if I had an open-air meeting and one of the top brains in the country, and a leading woman, and some others were converted, I wouldn't say it was a flop. It is worth it for those who come, every time. So Paul took them from where they were, through to the point where they needed Jesus – and those who wanted to know more, he told them more. That is all we can do; that is what we *must* do.

What we need is a little adaptability so that we can take them from where they are, from their gropings after a god, from their dreams for something beyond, their hopes for a life after death, and lead them to God, tell them what kind of a God he is: that he has given us life and breath, that he is not far from any of us. We don't have to go a long way to find him. Tell them that this God will judge our sins, and calls us now to repent and turn away from the evil, and tell them that he has raised Jesus from the dead, and that Jesus is alive. Don't worry if some laugh, don't worry if some won't come to the point when you talk to them. Some will come and say, "Tell me more" – then just tell them about Jesus.

Finally, we need to note carefully, especially now that syncretism is growing, that Paul did *not* use the name of one of the other "gods" of Athens (or, for that matter, of the other Gentile cities) to translate the name of Yahweh, the God of Abraham, Isaac and Jacob, the God and Father of our Lord Jesus Christ. Missionaries may sometimes have been uncertain about what local word to use for God in translations. It is inaccurate and misleading to employ a name used for any other current deity (like "allah", for example). The name Jesus used for his heavenly Father was "Abba", and that is appropriate for a Christian to use in any language. Paul did not use a name of another deity, precisely because the one true God Paul knew was indeed "unknown" to the Gentiles of Athens. Christians could never worship Zeus! Paul knew this, and we must be clear on the point in our days, too!

23

Priscilla, Aquila and Apollos
Read Acts 18:1–19:7

Acts 18 tells us that missionary work is not one exciting adventure after another. I know Paul was flogged and shipwrecked and stoned, and I know that he had miracles happen. But there were some periods in his missionary work when it was sheer hard work—just getting on with the job. The Christian life is like that. There will be peak moments and exciting adventures, but there are times when it is just a matter of getting on and doing it for the glory of God. I hope you find this an encouragement, and if Acts 18 doesn't seem as exciting as Acts 16 or 17, never mind. It is all part of the total mission of God. Sometimes he can use the person who can go on doing the right thing without any excitement, without hitting the headlines but just doing a good job for the Lord.

Paul has moved from Athens to Corinth – from a university town, a place of learning, a place of culture, to a seaport, a very different social setting. From culture to commerce, from a place where people have lots of leisure to study and use their brains, to a place where there are dockers and sailors and sailors' girls on the street corner. The amazing thing is that the gospel was always easier to preach in Corinth than in Athens.

A few people had believed in Athens, but we don't read of the epistle to the Athenians. It was a day of small things. I am afraid it usually is, because one of the biggest barriers between a person and God can be their own intellect. The more educated they are, the more difficult it is for them to become as little children and accept the truth.

In Corinth there was a tremendous response. Paul was going to have a church here that would really hit the headlines – I'm afraid not always in the best way. It was a church that was going to give him more problems than any other church he ever had. There was going to be incest among the members, drunkenness at Holy Communion, divisions within the church, each modelled after their favourite preacher. It was going to give him headaches but it was going to be a church.

All kinds of people were going to come into it. If he hadn't gone to Corinth, and if he hadn't preached there and hadn't started that church, and if it hadn't had problems, you and I would not have those magnificent letters to the Corinthians. So praise God that Paul went to Corinth even if it was a mixed bag, even if he had problems. I would rather have a church with problems than one which has the order of a cemetery. Wouldn't you?

It was in Corinth where you had all kinds of people, all kinds of situations, and so notorious a town was it for immorality that if you wanted to insult someone, you called them a "Corinthian". Into that town came Paul all by himself. Silas and Timothy were still in Macedonia. Now when Paul came into a town which he had never visited before, he always looked for three places: a place to live, a place to work, and a place to preach. That was his method – utterly practical. This is part of the down to earth business of being a missionary. If God sends you to a place you have never been to, those are the three things you need, in that same order.

As Paul walked through the marketplace, he saw a man with the same job as he had. Now Paul had a trade. I believe that every Christian in full-time service ought to have a trade, and before you consider being a missionary or a minister or a full-time evangelist, you ought to have a job that you can do. Jesus did this – he was eighteen years a carpenter. Paul did it – he was a tent maker, and in Tarsus the main trade was sewing together Sicilian goats hair cloth to make tents. So he was a tent maker, and he saw a chap making tents so he got into conversation and found that this man was a Jew.

More than that, he found probably, and here I'm reading between the lines, that he was a Christian as well because he had been thrown out of the city of Rome by the emperor Claudius. In the Roman records it says that Claudius turned out of Rome a number of Jews who were getting stirred up about a man called Chrestus, which is probably the name "Christ" in a Roman form. So Paul found a place to live and a place to work.

Be very careful how you use the phrase "living by faith". Paul earned his living by tent making but Paul said, "I live by faith." There is a certain use of this phrase "I live by faith" which precludes most Christians from living by faith because they earn their living through a job. Now Paul said, "I live by faith in the Son of God" – but when he was short of money, he didn't pray, he got out his needle and thread, and he worked and made tents.

Writing to those Corinthians later (you can read all about it in 1 Corinthians 9), he said: I had a right as a preacher to live by the gospel, to expect those who benefited from me in spiritual things to support me in material things, but deliberately to give you an example of Christian attitude to work, you know that when I came to you I earned my living with my own bare hands.

So let us realise that whether God calls you to live by the gospel or by tent making or being a butcher, a baker, or a candlestick maker, you can say "I live by faith" if you are doing what God wants you to do and if you are in the place where he wants you to be.

So Paul looked for a place to live, a place to work – to

get enough money to keep himself – and a place to preach. As usual, he found a synagogue where they accepted his qualifications as a rabbi to get up and speak on the Sabbath, and this he did—all very ordinary, all very normal. I am afraid that what had happened in almost every other synagogue happened here, and the opposition began. You can't preach the gospel without arousing opposition. When you preach the truth about God, you split your audience down the middle – you can't help that. People can't remain neutral; they take sides. They either accept the truth or they fight it, but can't go away in the same condition.

Antagonism grew up in the synagogue because for the Jews to become a Christian was a revolution. Even though Jesus fulfilled all their scriptures, even though he was a Jew, even though he fulfilled the dream for a promised Messiah, a dream that had lasted a thousand years – still it meant a right about turn. People are not always ready to turn right around and follow Jesus Christ, so the opposition arose and the first form it took was the usual form of slander and libel. The devil was a liar from the beginning, and if there is one thing he likes to do, it is to tell lies about someone who speaks the truth.

The opposition grew to the point where Paul realised that he was going to be thrown out of the synagogue, so like a very wise man he jumped out before he was thrown out. He kept the initiative in his hands, and he said, "All right, I shake the dust off my clothes, I don't want any part with you." He turned right around and moved next door. That must have riled them no end. I mean, just fancy moving next door! More than that, the leader of the synagogue moved next door with him, and so did half the congregation. The services continued. Quite frankly, that is an explosive situation. It just needs one match to it and the whole thing will go up in flames.

Paul wondered whether he should leave Corinth. His policy was always, when he had established a church of believers and when opposition was rising: get out, so that the church could continue in peace. He did not want to stay and aggravate the situation. So would he move on and start another church elsewhere? Although that would have been his normal pattern, it strikes me in Acts that God has no normal pattern. He is always doing something different, breaking out of the pattern.

Paul saw a vision. I don't know what he saw – it doesn't say – maybe an angel, maybe the Lord himself. The Lord spoke to him through the vision, which would be while he was awake. (God is speaking to his people through dreams and visions today, just as he used to, and they have always got to be tested, of course.) God said to Paul, "Don't go. Don't give up. There are many people in the city who belong to me, far more than you have got already."

Notice this: before you speak to people, God knows who belongs to him. This is the excitement of going out. Haven't you discovered this? You go out, and you talk to people. You come across someone, and you feel that already God is working in their hearts, and nobody else has been speaking to them. It seems as if already God has got his hand on them, and all he wanted of you was to go and just give them a helping hand for the next step.

The promise to Paul was that if he stayed no-one would hurt him in that city. That was not a promise that God gave to Paul in other situations. God varies his promises. In some situations he doesn't promise safety, in others he does. So Paul stayed eighteen months, the church grew, and many more people revealed that they belonged to the Lord and came to know the Lord in faith.

This promise of God was severely tested when a new Roman governor came to the town – a great man. We know that he was handsome, intelligent, a very fair and good man called Gallio. But some Jews thought: "This is our chance, a new governor. He doesn't know the situation. Let's get him to throw Paul out of the city." They got together and dragged Paul before the courts. When this had happened before, Paul had been stoned and beaten. But God had promised Paul that no-one would hurt him in that city. They dragged Paul to the court and Gallio saw at a glance that this was not a crime, that Paul was innocent, and unlike Pontius Pilate, Gallio was not a coward. (Pontius Pilate knew that the right thing to do would have been to let Jesus go.) Gallio was going to show right from the beginning that he would be fair and just.

Gallio said, "This is not a crime against the Roman law. This is an internal matter. It's a matter of your Jewish religion; it's an argument about words like "Messiah" and "salvation" and so on. You settle it yourselves, nothing to do with me. Let that man go." Paul walked out of that court without a bruise or a scratch. It all rebounded on the Jewish leaders because the public, who had a little anti-Jewish feeling in them anyway, saw that Gallio was not going to side with the Jews and they jumped on old Sosthenes, the new leader of the synagogue responsible for it, and they gave him a beating. It is the first time in Acts that somebody trying to persecute Christians finds that it backfires on them and that they suffer for it.

It is probably because he was so grateful for God keeping his word and keeping him safe that Paul shaved his hair and took a vow of dedication. That is the only explanation I can come to for this. It was his way of saying thank you. So in the traditional Jewish way he took a vow and he shaved his head. Now it was time to go away, and he sailed across the Aegean Sea to a city called Ephesus, and here was another major seaport.

There was a Roman amphitheatre at Ephesus. You can still

see the ruins of it. The port has gone. The great harbour where the ships used to dock became silted up, so it diminished in significance. But Ephesus in Paul's day was a thriving place. There was life there, and all kinds of disturbing things happening. Towering over the city was a great big temple, which people have said was one of the seven wonders of the world. It was the temple of Artemis. Inside was a huge black stone, a meteorite that had fallen into the city of Ephesus. They looked at it, and like an artist, they saw something in the stone to be carved out of it. It was carved into a female figure with many breasts: Diana of the Ephesians, a fertility goddess, and this was in the temple above the city.

That tells you something about the city, too. Paul visited them, spoke to them, and the Ephesians said, "We would love to have you come and speak to us more often. Would you come back and preach for a few weeks or even months?" Paul said, "Well, yes, if God wants me to." The Bible says that you should never make any plans for tomorrow without adding "God willing". (See the Epistle of James.)

Paul, given an invitation to preach, said, "I should not accept that invitation unless God wants me to."

That is how we should order our lives. We should say, "If that's God's plan for me." How much time and energy we might have saved ourselves if we had stopped before we did something and said: is this part of God's plan for me? Does he want me to do it or not?

Paul came back after travelling fifteen hundred miles to Jerusalem, to Antioch, back to the churches he had started in Phrygia, in Galatia. Those two feet of his carried him everywhere! Notice again that he was always going back to home base, always trotting back to the church from which he had come, to tell them all about what he was doing.

Then he was always going back to the people he had led to the Lord, to help them on. What a pattern of evangelism:

back to home base, back to converts, on to new fields; back to home base, back to converts, onto more new fields, and gradually extending the frontier of his mission. What a man! I think Paul is the finest missionary there has ever been. We all have a lot to learn from him.

So Paul came back to Ephesus – and a very deep challenge for us. While Paul had been away from Ephesus, someone else had been there. An unusual man called Apollos, a Jew who knew something about Jesus, knew about the baptism of John the Baptist, and knew his Old Testament very well indeed – a Jew who had lived in Egypt, had great enthusiasm and great eloquence. He arrived in Ephesus and he started speaking about the Old Testament, John the Baptist, and Jesus. He really could put it across, and the people in the synagogue listened, among them Aquila and Priscilla. After the first Sabbath service, they went home, had a chat over lunch, and they found that something was missing from that preacher's preaching. What was missing? We are not told what they saw was missing, but I can have a good guess from what comes later. I guess that Apollos had gone so far with the account of Jesus but not quite far enough. He had left his Jewish background, he had been baptised by John the Baptist, or by a follower of John the Baptist, he knew that Jesus was the Messiah. But that is where he had stopped. Aquila and Priscilla did absolutely the right thing about the situation.

Notice what they did. When you feel that a preacher is wrong or has missed something out, or is not preaching things quite right, what do you do? Go and tell everybody else and have a good old discussion of the preacher with them? No. Invite him to lunch and correct him. That is what Aquila and Priscilla did. How wise! Very quietly and lovingly they told him about the things that clearly he didn't know. They corrected his understanding, and filled out the whole picture. I deduce from the next incident that they told him about the Holy Spirit. Anyway, they corrected him. Apollos was a big man, and he accepted their correction and instruction. They would have encouraged him to take the full message to Greece. Apollos went off and it says he was a great help to the people. He was able to use the gift that he already had in a new way, in a new setting.

Now we have the background to what I want you to notice. We have learned quite a bit as we have gone through chapter 18, but now we are coming to the crunch. Paul, after all his travels, came back to Ephesus. Looking around for a place to preach there, he found a little house group, twelve men, and they were talking about Jesus. He thought, "I'll link up with this group," but then he felt there was something missing.

At this point, I have got to tell you quite frankly that this next passage of seven verses (19:1–7) is one of the most controversial, and more argument has arisen over it than over many passages of scripture. It is because people are re-thinking their own attitude to God the Holy Spirit that this has become an area of controversy. For that reason, I am going to go through it verse by verse. In v. 1, "Paul came to Ephesus" you notice it mentions Apollos in the context, (there were of course no chapter or verse references in the original) so it follows straight on. "When Paul came to Ephesus he found certain disciples." Now that word used in Luke and Acts by itself with no qualification always means *disciples or followers of Jesus*. Professor F. F. Bruce, a New Testament professor who belonged to the Brethren, and whose writings I have found enormously helpful, says that undoubtedly these disciples were Christians in the sense that they were followers of Jesus. How far they had got is a question we are going to have to ask. I believe they got as far as the twelve disciples got before Pentecost. They were disciples, they talked about Jesus, they sang about Jesus.

They tried to live the life that Jesus would have them live, and yet Paul found that there was something missing.

Paul asked these disciples a crucial question. They seemed to be followers of Jesus, yet there was a dimension not there in their life and so he asked (v. 2): *"Did you receive Holy Spirit when you believed?"* That is asking if two things happened at the same time. If I say, "Did you wipe your feet when you came into church?" that is asking if two events occurred simultaneously. They are not one and the same event if you ask a question like that. But if I say, "Did you wipe your feet when you entered the building?" that's saying, "Did this happen when that happened?" Or I could say, "Did someone shake your hand when you entered the building? Did the two things coincide?" The question that Paul is asking can mean nothing else but: "Did two things happen at the same time? Did you receive when you believed?"

That is a very big question. There are some who today would say: "Paul, that's a silly question. It makes no sense. It's like saying, 'Were you born when you were born?'" It's like saying, "When you came into the building, did you come into the building?" as if the two things are the same. But Paul's question shows that in his mind they are not the same. They *should* happen together, and in normal Christian experience they *would* happen together. But he is asking them, *"Did they* happen together?" He's not asking them a theological question that they must go and look up commentaries and books to answer or even look up their scriptures to answer. He is asking, "Did those two things happen together?" Because Paul knew, as we know today, that they *need* not happen together. It is God's will that they should. It is God's will that when we believe, we receive Holy Spirit.

Notice that I keep missing out the word "the" before "Holy Spirit". In the Greek original, the word "the" does not occur in the question. He does not say, "Did you receive *the* Holy Spirit when you believed?" The omission of that word changes it from what I would call a quantitative to a qualitative question. To put it more simply, he is not asking, "Did the person take up residence in your heart when you believed?" But "Did he pour out power into your life when you believed?" That is an extremely important distinction. Did you, when you believed in Jesus, have a manifestation of the power of the Spirit? Because if they had said yes, then Paul would have said, "Well then, what's happened to it? Where's it gone?" But, in fact, they didn't say yes. Their answer was a rather peculiar one. Their answer is literally, *"We have not heard that Holy Spirit is."* Many have assumed that this means they were totally ignorant of the Holy Spirit, that they had never even heard those two words before. I don't think that's true, and I go along with the majority of commentators who believe that Paul's question means something else.

John the Baptist talked of Jesus Christ, and he talked of the Holy Spirit. Anybody who had been baptised by John had been told, "Now this is only a baptism in water, and there is somebody coming after me who baptises in the Holy Spirit." So anybody baptised by John would be looking forward to something more. The meaning of the question, or the answer, "We have not yet heard that the Holy Spirit is," is this: "We didn't know that that had begun to happen. We hadn't heard that what John predicted was now available," and that indeed is how it is translated in many Bibles: "We have not heard that the Holy Spirit has been given."

Here we come across what Paul was missing. I'm going to put it this way—I believe these were genuine followers of Jesus who were living a two-dimensional Christian life. They believed in God and they believed in Jesus to an extent – not fully, as we will see in a moment. The dimension that was missing from their following of Christ was the power of Holy Spirit. That is why Paul put his finger right on the spot and realised straightaway what was wrong.

Now the next question, the next verse, is very significant. Paul says, "What kind of a baptism did you have?" It is patently obvious from that question that, for Paul, baptism in water and the Holy Spirit are linked. If you study the New Testament, you will find that in thirty passages that mention baptism in water, sixteen mention also the Holy Spirit. People ask me, "What is the connection between the Holy Spirit and water baptism?" There is clearly some link. These people said, "Well, we had the baptism of John." Now Paul understands. He can see where they got stuck. They had repented of their sin, and washed it away in John's baptism, for that was all it was about. They were trying to live the life that Jesus would have them live, trying to live his way. But it is not a matter of trying to live the way that Jesus taught, it is a matter of believing *in* that Jesus. John was just getting people ready to believe in Jesus. Apollos knew the way of the Lord; Apollos had been teaching in Ephesus. But it was the *Way* – it was not that *full identification with Jesus* that shares his death and his resurrection, and enjoys his gift of the Spirit. Christian baptism takes you right into an identification with Jesus in his death and burial, in his risen life, and therefore prepares a person to receive his gift of the Spirit. This is how far they had got. So Paul could say: "Do you believe in Jesus? Are you trusting him? Are you identifying with him in his death and burial and resurrection? Then let's get you properly baptised with Christian baptism." So they were baptised in the name of Jesus. Do you notice that there is a difference between a baptism that is simply washing away sin, repenting of the past, and a baptism in the name of Jesus that is *identifying* with him?

Now we come to the crucial verse. Those who believe

that you receive Holy Spirit power automatically, as soon as you believe, are confounded by v. 6. If all that these disciples needed was to become fully baptised believers in the name of Jesus, then Paul was finished with them in v. 5. If you can receive Holy Spirit power unconsciously, without being aware of it, then nothing more was needed than their water baptism in the name of Jesus. But it is precisely at that point that I believe many disciples today have got stuck and need to go one bit further, because they still could not have answered his original question. They were now full believers; they were now baptised believers. But if you had still asked them at this point, at the end of v. 5, "Did you receive Holy Spirit when you believed?" they would still have had to say no. So Paul now deals with that. One of the most expressive forms of prayer is to touch the person you are praying for. That is the meaning of it. So Paul prayed for them and he laid hands on them.

Three things were done in the next few moments: Paul did something, the Holy Spirit did something, and the twelve men did something and that is what is meant by the question that Paul asked. He laid hands on them, then notice that Holy Spirit came upon them (notice it doesn't say "into"), was poured out on them, fell on them. There are many different phrases used in the New Testament. Then they began to overflow. Is it not when you are so happy you are bursting with joy that you overflow from your *mouth*? When you are sad, isn't that where you overflow? Have you heard? Do you know? When your first baby was born, and you saw and cradled that little baby, didn't you wonder why everybody in the street didn't ask you about it as you walked down the road? Where did your pride overflow? Out of your mouth, in the way you talked!

When the Holy Spirit came on them, they overflowed – not the same sign maybe for all of them. I am not going to be among those who say it must be this or it must be that. The Bible has a lovely variety. In this case, sometimes they were speaking to God in languages they had never learned, and sometimes they were speaking in their own language to man. But they overflowed! The Holy Spirit did come upon them. They were no longer "flat" Christians; they were solid, three-dimensional Christians. They were not perfect; they were not mature, but they were complete.

Paul's missionary method was this: to make sure his spiritual babies have everything – to set them off with everything that God has for them to walk by. So Paul never rested content until every one of his spiritual babies could answer one simple question: "Did you receive Holy Spirit when you believed?"

Somebody else had brought them a long way, and he took them the rest of the way. I have indicated that it was probably Apollos, because judging by what they said, they had been students of Apollos. In this case, Apollos planted, and Paul watered, quite literally. Later, he says at Corinth, Paul planted and Apollos watered. That is so often what happens – one person, one minister of God, one servant of God takes you so far, then another servant of God is sent along to take you a little further. My Christian experience owes a great deal to different people of God. But I have to say that I was a Christian many years before someone talked to me about the Holy Spirit. Isn't that a shame? Maybe when someone did talk to me about him, they sensed a dimension missing.

I thank God that he uses different people to take us further, and that one man gets you repentant, and another tells you about Jesus, and another takes you a bit further than that. Another baptises you, and another says, "Now, how about the Holy Spirit?" It doesn't matter who is used of God to do it. What God wants is *complete* spiritual babies, not perfect, not mature, but complete, setting off with life in every dimension that he wants.[1]

If Paul came to England today and went to the places of worship to preach, do you think he would say in our English churches: "Did you receive Holy Spirit when you believed?" Do you think he would still need to ask that question? Or do you think he would say, "Now, you are the sort of Christians I am used to. You are the sort of Christians we had back in the New Testament days. You have got all the dimensions of life. Yes, you still have problems, yes, you've still got ignorance, you have still got to grow and become mature because receiving Holy Spirit power doesn't mean that you have ceased to be a baby. You still have a lot to learn." But with all of that, would Paul say, "Yes, you are living in the full dimensions of New Testament Christianity"? Or would he say, "I'm a bit puzzled; here are groups of people in Britain talking about Jesus, following Jesus, and yet where is the power? Where is the supernatural dimension?" I have the feeling that of many of us, he would say, "Did you...? Did the two things coincide?"

My next question is: what would you reply if he asked *you*? It is essential that you be absolutely honest. It is just a simple question: did the two things happen to you? I would have to say, "No, they didn't, but I caught up on it later." Would you say: "Paul, that's an invalid question, there are great theologians in England who say that you have asked a silly question; those are not two things but one"? Or would you say, "Lord, I've been kidding myself for a long time." Or would you say, "Lord, I'm hungry for that power, can I start seeking?"

I know what the Lord's word to us would be on this subject: "If you, being evil, know how to give good gifts to your children, how much more will your heavenly Father give Holy Spirit to those who go on asking him?" (Luke 11:13).

Like Paul leaving Corinth, I can say to you, "I have told you of this, now it's your responsibility to ask Jesus." Ask him: "Am I living in full dimensions of Christian life? Am I a New Testament kind of Christian? Do I know God the Father, God the Son – my Saviour – and God the Holy Spirit, working in my life?"

Note

[1] Again, see my book: *The Normal Christian Birth*.

24

Riot in Ephesus
Read Acts 19:7–41

Have you ever seen a grain of mustard seed? It's about the size of a small pinhead, maybe even smaller. You can just see it in the palm of your hand. Yet a mustard tree is big enough for birds to come and nest in. You wonder how on earth that tree could possibly be packed inside such a tiny seed. Jesus said that the kingdom of God is like that. It started so small. A dozen men, one of whom was a dud anyway, so it was eleven men—just a little group wandering around the lanes of Galilee. That is how the kingdom of God broke in on earth. Now hundreds of millions of people profess to follow the Lord Jesus Christ.

That is how the work started in Ephesus. It took two years to move from twelve men to setting the whole city in an uproar for two hours, with twenty-five thousand people shouting their heads off. At least they had impact; at least they got through. That is what happens: small beginnings, just a few people starting something, and it blows up and up. It is thrilling to realise that we belong not to a dying cause, but to one of the fastest growing movements history has ever seen. It is thrilling to see the body of believers growing faster today than for two thousand years.

In Acts 19 you see a very small beginning. Twelve people who have tried to make a new start, who have tried to cleanse their life, trying to walk as Jesus would have them walk. Those twelve men were the beginning of it for Paul. When he came to Ephesus he told them that there was a power available; he told them that the Holy Spirit could fill them, setting them on fire. Just twelve people filled with the Holy Spirit can turn the world upside down or right way up, whichever way you look at it. That is where it usually starts, with those who not only believe in God, not only follow Jesus, but have the Holy Spirit fall on them. Things are going to happen after that. But what will happen? I can tell you that most disturbing things will happen. The kind of things that happen in this chapter will occur. When the Holy Spirit gets active in a place, evil spirits get active too. The battle we are in is not against people. Let it be widely known that we are not fighting flesh and blood. You will find that there is another supernatural world of evil spirits and they will do everything they can to bring the work to a standstill. Satan himself will try to stir up trouble, division and opposition.

It may be that we in this country are not making the impact we ought to make, not turning cities upside down, not causing unrest, precisely because we don't like trouble, because we want to keep out of the frontline of the battle. We have got to be honest with our own hearts, "Do I really want to see good and evil in open confrontation in my town? Do I really want to see the Holy Spirit so active that evil spirits fight him? Do I really want to be in the thick of it, or do I want a quiet, comfortable life in which I can go to church on Sunday undisturbed, and go through the week without too much bother?"

That is the message of Acts 19 to me: start with a few on fire in the Holy Spirit and you are heading straight for big trouble, but the kind of trouble in which people will see that Jesus Christ is alive and conqueror; the kind of trouble in which they will see that the kingdom of God is real, and that the real person on the throne is the Lord Jesus Christ, and that the events of this world are under his authority. He has the supreme power over this situation and therefore it is not hopeless and not lost. The Lord Jesus Christ is still in control and it is going to work out his way, not anybody else's.

Three kinds of trouble arose. The first was simply opposition to the preaching. The old story with which we are becoming familiar: Paul preaches to those who profess to believe in God, and the real opposition to the challenge of the Christian message comes from within the circles of those who have been regarded as religious, and it happens again here. Paul's preaching centres on just two words in this chapter: "kingdom" and "way". We need to remember these two words for they are the heart of the Christian message. When Jesus came preaching in Galilee, he preached the kingdom. Underline that word in his preaching, he uses it more than any other word: the kingdom of God has come upon you; the kingdom of God is among you; the kingdom of God is like.... The kingdom's breaking through. Now, you can't have a kingdom without a king. Human beings are not made to govern themselves in a democracy, nor are they made to be governed by each other in a dictatorship. Human nature needs a leader, a king, but not an earthly one. Human nature is so made that we need to be in the kingdom of God. We are never really happy until we have found Christ as our king, until *he* is reigning over us and that is why the kingdom is preached.

We are not made for the kind of freedom in which we do what we like. We are made for the kind of freedom in which we do what the King likes. That's the kingdom of God. When people accept the reign of God, the kingdom of God, things begin to happen that straighten out their lives.

Many believers have told me that when they asked Christ to reign over the situation and take it over, he began to straighten it out. As soon as you entered the kingdom (as the Bible would put it) and said, "I'm now subject to him; I am his subject," didn't life begin to be really free? Didn't it work out? Didn't it begin to get clean and pure? That is what the kingdom means. It is the power of God breaking through, reigning over a situation, ruling it, controlling it, and bringing it back under his control.

The other expression is "the Way". When I began my ministry I never heard that term used. Now it has come back into its own. It means that *Christianity is a way to life and a way of life*. It is both, not either/or. When the kingdom of God has broken in on my life, when God is King over me, when I am a subject of the royal throne of heaven, then I have found the way to life and I have found a new way of life. It is a new way, it is one way; it is *the* way through to life.

So Paul preached the kingdom and the way, but you preach that, and you will run into opposition very quickly. First, from those who say, "I don't want a king; I want to be free. I don't want God telling me what to do; I want to tell myself what to do. I am not going to accept this way to life; I've found the way. It's through this, that, and the other. It's through drugs; it's through sex; it's through thrills; it's through experience; it's through meditation. I'm not going to listen to those who say there's only *one* way. There are many ways." So you run into trouble! Paul ran into trouble just through preaching the kingdom and the way.

Let us look at the second trouble that came up in this chapter. When the kingdom and the way are spoken about, miracles can happen. I wonder if you really believe that. When the Holy Spirit really gets into even twelve men, miracles are going to happen. Unusual things occur that cannot be explained any other way. It says that even handkerchiefs did miracles when the Holy Spirit was around. Actually, the word in the Greek language is not "handkerchief" but "sweat rag". Do you know what that is? I used to use one out in Arabia. You put it around your head to stop the sweat pouring into your eyes. Paul, working at tent making, used to wear two garments: a sweat rag to stop the perspiration getting into his eyes and an apron just to keep his clothes reasonably clean while he worked with the black goat's hair cloth as a tent maker. It says that, "... such was the power of God that people were grabbing his sweat rag and were taking it to a sick person and the sick person was getting well." What do we make of that? It is not superstition, nor does the Bible ever say that the sweat rag had holy power or that there was magic in it. I will tell you what was doing it: not the sweat rag, but *faith that God could act*.

It is exactly the same order of miracle as was happening when a woman who had been suffering from a haemorrhage for many years, and had spent every penny on any doctor she could reach, said, "If I could only touch the tassel hanging from the hem of Jesus' garment I'd be okay." Pushing through the crowds one day, she touched just the tassel and Jesus immediately said, "Someone has been taking power from me. Who was it?" He turned around and there she was. It wasn't the tassel that did it; he told her that it was her faith. That is extremely important. Our faith can have the most peculiar things attached to it, but if it is faith in the power of God he honours that faith and then tells us better. He lets us have that faith even though we are ignorant of how his power comes to us. If it is faith in the divine power of the Holy Spirit, he is wonderfully patient with those who haven't thought it through. He honours that as long as they are seeking from him.

I remember a lad asking me if he could be baptised. He said, "When I'm baptised, if there are others who are going to be baptised, could I be done first?"

"Why?" I asked.

"Well," he said, "You know, it's to wash your sins away, isn't it? I don't want to pick up anybody else's sins. So will you do me first and then the others?

We would say that is a wrong understanding of baptism, but as you looked into that lad's face, you could see that he wanted to be clean. Even though he had a wrong idea about baptism, he was asking God to wash his sins away. Is that not the important thing? God is wonderfully patient with us. He does miracles sometimes in the most unexpected way. He doesn't tell us now all to rush around and grab everybody else's sweat rag or handkerchief and say that's the way that people are going to get healed.

Peter, as he walked along in the hot sun, cast a shadow and they brought sick people just to lay them on the road so that his shadow would go over them. We say "superstition" but they were saying: God is in that man so I am reaching after God – and they were healed. God is wonderfully patient with us.

Paul was doing miracles and not only casting out disease, (which is something that Jesus says can also come from Satan), but he was casting out demons. Early in my years in ministry, most of my friends disbelieved in demons. Most clergymen in this country never thought about them. Some, when they came to that kind of account of a demon-possessed person, said that this was an old-fashioned way of thinking of mental illness. Since then we have come to know better because we have seen more work of evil spirits in our country than for centuries. We never thought we would live to see the day in this modern, scientific era, where witches would hit the headlines, where occult powers would be freely talked about, where junior schools are asking teachers to give warnings to pupils about using Ouija boards and about trying to practise levitation. Suddenly, we are realising that we have been very silly indeed to laugh at demons. I almost tremble to speak of them, and I only dare to do so because Jesus is more powerful. But never laugh at the devil. He is not a joke; he is only too serious. When the power of the

Holy Spirit is present, people are set free from that, too.

The book entitled *From Witchcraft to Christ* by Doreen Irvine should be more widely read. It features one who was a prostitute, stripper, witch, Satanist's mistress — queen of Satanists in the southwest of England. She was possessed by over forty demons, which took seven months to get out. You read the story, but the last chapter is full of the power of the Lord Jesus Christ to deliver. That's what happens when the Holy Spirit gets busy and there is a confrontation.

There are going to be those who will try to jump on the bandwagon because there are always people with a morbid curiosity in the supernatural, and those who think it is easy to do these things. May I utter a warning to Christians? Don't think that any Christian can just go out and cast out demons. Don't start looking for demons under every bush, and don't think that you are called to go and exorcise everywhere. Tremble before you go; fast and pray before you go. Put on the whole armour of God before you go, because you are no match whatever for such evil powers. What happened in this chapter could happen to you too. There were some Jewish professional exorcists, and there was a great trade for such people in the world of those days when there was so much magic around. They thought that all they had to do was use the name of Jesus and then they would be able to do the things that Paul did. They tried it with a demon-possessed man and they said, "In the name of Jesus, come out." What did he do? He said, "I know Paul and I know Jesus, but I don't know you. I do not recognise you." One of the marks of being possessed is supernatural strength. It can take at least nine or ten men to hold a person who is possessed, and that one man was able to tear the clothes off the lot of them, fight them and send them packing. These are not areas to dabble in. Don't dabble in anything to do with the occult. Don't read your horoscope; don't play with it at school. Don't let it touch your life.

I have heard it said by a psychiatrist that 24% of the people who finished up permanently insane in this country have done so because they have first dabbled in such things and their integrity has disintegrated. But that is the kind of thing that was happening when Paul was preaching. When the Holy Spirit starts moving, the message is opposed and the miracles are imitated with disastrous results. But when Jesus Christ is there, and his power, his Spirit, is working, then he has the victory and there are those who have been delivered from these things and set free by the power of Jesus Christ in our day. Praise God for their release. If you want to see what God can do, then read that book unless you have a morbid curiosity – in which case don't.

When such things happen, who gets most scared? Christians! One of the signs of the Holy Spirit's moving is that Christians, when they see such things happening, realise that they themselves are not what they ought to be. It has been one of the marks of revivals that believers come and reveal what they have done – and in Acts they had a bonfire: books worth 50,000 pieces of silver, or many thousands of pounds. It was the best bonfire there had ever been.

I was reading the life of my great, great, great, great, great, great, great grandfather, a man called John Pawson. I am a bit embarrassed by what I'm going to tell you because he held a public bonfire in Leeds for all Christians to come and burn the works of William Shakespeare, and they did. They came and burnt those books, but at least they were getting something out of their system that they had found a temptation in those days. Is there a place for such a bonfire in your town? That would be a thing to have on November 5th, wouldn't it? Far more use than all the wasted fireworks! The lesson here is that when God is at work, Christians straight away feel that there are things they must get out of their life. When the Holy Spirit is moving, this is the result. It is one of the things we have got to face and be ready for. When God is going to move there are going to be things that need to go in the bonfire.

Paul was a man of ambition. Sometimes I am asked this question: "Should Christians have ambitions?" My answer is, "They should be the most ambitious people on earth." Paul was an ambitious man. What was his ambition? It was to go as far as he could with the gospel. Here we have a little glimpse of his ambitions. After these things happened, after the word of the Lord was growing powerful and strong (and no wonder, when Christians were having such bonfires), Paul realised there were other fields to conquer. He was a man whose eyes were always looking into the distance. He knew that he was to go to Rome. We know that he wanted to go to Spain. Paul was a man who wanted to move on with the Lord.

But before he could get away from Ephesus, the next kind of opposition came. It is something that had happened before, elsewhere. It was the opposition of those who were losing money because there were so many Christians. I believe this will happen in England in the foreseeable future. It is already happening. There are vested interests in evil. There is commercial exploitation of evil and they are going to be hurt and hit badly when the Holy Spirit moves. Commercial profits are not going to be made. It happened in Ephesus where, towering over that city, was a great temple in which you will recall was the goddess of Ephesus. In that city they had special priests who were eunuchs, looking after the goddess, and there were many priestesses who were nothing more than prostitutes in the temple, visited by the leading men of the town. That was Ephesus. Around this temple there were stores where you could buy little silver images of the temple and the goddess. It was a big trade because the objects were made of solid silver. A man called Demetrius, head of the chamber of commerce, dealt with the trade. I am sorry to have to tell you that we now preserve some of these items. You can go to museums and see these foul little solid silver things. In a London museum are copies of the very books that were burnt by the Christians in Acts 19. You need not bother to go and view them, but isn't it strange how we preserve the works of Satan in our museums?

It is such a mark of the Holy Spirit's work that the trade graph on Demetrius's wall went down and down and down. Business was bad, and I want you to notice that it was not because Paul preached against it. It was not because the Christians had a protest march against it. It was not because they attacked Demetrius. It was not because they preached against Diana of the Ephesians. The town clerk knew they hadn't done that. Shall I tell you why it was? It was simply because they were getting so many people converted – that's all. That's the way to tackle it!

However much you may feel like protesting against the state of Britain, however much you may feel like trying to stop the tide, I'll tell you the only thing that will do it is to get more and more people converted – there is no shortcut. The proportion of real believing Christians in the UK is probably no more than 1.5%, even if it looks more than that when we bunch together in large gatherings. But it has been said that you can change public opinion if you have 5% of the public with you in your convictions. Therefore, target number one for us in this country is to pray that we may treble the number of Christians. When we do that, you will find commerce changing. You will find the profits changing. You will find a total change will begin to appear in the scene. So this is what happened in Ephesus.

When people's pockets are hurt, they react angrily. The theatre of Ephesus was filled with a crowd and it could hold 25,000 people. It is a massive arena. They crowded in there and dragged two of Paul's friends in. Paul wanted to get in and at them. Doesn't that say something for him? They are rioting about Christianity – just let me get in there and preach to them! There is something about this, a holy boldness that is characteristic of those full of the Spirit. But his friends wisely told him to stay outside.

Into that riot there stepped the town clerk. Sometimes the Lord uses the most unlikely people. Have you ever read the life of John Wesley? You must read it. I know it is some three hundred years ago, but read how this little man, just over five feet tall, was dragged through the streets of Wolverhampton by his hair; how he went among the miners of Cornwall, how riots started because, when he preached, Cornish smugglers went out of business. In my home town, on the quayside in Newcastle upon Tyne, when Wesley got up to preach, a gang came with sticks and stones, intending to kill him. A great fisherwoman came and put her big, fat arm around little John Wesley and said, "Touch him if you dare." God can use the most unlikely people. John was safe in that fisherwoman's arms and he went on. God knows when to keep his servants safe and when to let them be martyred. It is always for his glory.

Paul was not caught up in the riot, but when Christianity is really getting a hold, there may be disturbances, not because the Christians cause them but because the anger of Satan's hosts wants to blame Christians for causing them. Christians have respect for authority. Christians pray for the police. Christians should not be at fault for civic disturbance, but they will be accused of it.

The town clerk stepped in and warned the people to be careful. He knew what a mob could do. They first found a slogan and down the street they went, chanting it. Mobs don't listen to reason. So the official stood up and calmly said, "If you have a grievance, this can be settled in the courts." How wise!

If we really let the Holy Spirit do with us what he wants, we are heading straight for trouble. Are you ready to face that? God wants people in England who are ready for anything, who are willing not only to let him work in them, but to let him put them in the frontline of the battle. Are you willing to face opposition to the message? Are you willing to see supernatural battles take place? Are you willing to be confronted with such activities of God that you are afraid of him? Do you want to get things put right and see those bonfires started? Do you realise that civic disturbances may result (though you will not start them)?

It is going to hurt people in their pockets. They are going to come back fighting hard. Are you ready for that? Paul was. For one reason: whatever trouble came, Jesus Christ would be victor; whatever confrontations took place, good is more powerful than evil and Christ is in authority over the devil.

All over the world, there are victories being won for the Lord Jesus Christ this day by people who are ready for trouble, who realise that this world is Satan's world and that he is the god of it and the ruler of it and the prince of it; and that, whether people know it or not, he is using them and gripping them. So we don't hate people. We don't fight people. No man is our enemy, but there is a battle on. So let us put on the whole armour of God.

25

Eutychus Raised; Farewell to Ephesus
Read Acts 20

Paul is on his way to Jerusalem and he is saying certain things because he knows that he will not pass this way again. Places are listed now, rather as if you are reading a tour itinerary. There seems to be little in it to hold the attention unless you are interested in taking out an atlas and pinpointing places and drawing dotted lines for Paul's journeys. When I was at school, in Religious Knowledge lessons that seemed to be all we ever did until I could almost draw Paul's missionary journeys in my sleep! It is as if putting the dotted line on a map of the Middle East did something for us. I am not sure it does a great deal, although it does show you how much Paul travelled. Incidentally, when you visit Israel, one of the things that hits you was how far Jesus walked. Mile after mile, up and down the country. When you draw dotted lines for Paul's missionary journeys, apart from the voyages in ships, the rest was on his own two feet. When you trace those dotted lines, you just bow in wonder that the Lord gave this little man the strength to walk all over the world carrying the gospel.

Not only did he walk, he preached. He founded churches, he organised, and he wrote letters. It was during this journey described in Acts 20 that he wrote the letter to the Romans and the second letter to the Corinthians, dashing off letters full of the word of God to people. Not only that, he was organising a collection, and wherever he went he had an appeal for the poor Christians in Jerusalem. This man was a marvel. I say it advisedly, but I don't think he could have done it with a family. I am certain he couldn't have done it without the Lord. This man, full of the Lord, went off and travelled the world collecting money, preaching the gospel, writing letters, organising churches, giving counsel, leading. How did he pack it all in? The first sixteen verses cover about twelve months in the life of Paul. Of all those travels, Luke only singles out one incident. I am not surprised as it is a pretty startling one.

It was in the very place where Paul had seen a vision of a man of Macedonia, and now he had been to Macedonia three times and was back in Troas where it had all started, and he is there for the last time. So Paul preached one Sunday evening, and he preached and he preached and he preached! Now I know it was the last time he would be there, but nevertheless all the records we have from the early church indicate that the average length of a church service in the New Testament days and for the next two hundred years was around two hours. I don't know where the English got the idea that one hour is quite long enough for God, but it seems that in the early church when they met together they wanted to spend the time between meals worshipping God.

This was a good deal longer than two hours. What a joy it is to preach to those who are hungry and just say, "Go on, I want to know more and more about the truth of God." There would be communion after the sermon and they must have been wondering when that was coming. The place was packed and hot. Luke must have been there because he describes even the oil lamps burning and making the atmosphere hot and stuffy. Some sat on the windowsills. God was moving in that service. Then, right at midnight, somebody just dropped out of a window, and it was a long drop. Poor Eutychus fell down three storeys and lay, a little huddled, lifeless corpse, in the street. So they came down and Luke was a doctor. I am glad that the book of Acts was written by a doctor, a scientific man who would not exaggerate but tell the truth. The doctor said he was dead.

So they told Paul and he came running down the stairs. He took that corpse and he did with it what Elijah had done with a corpse. He hugged the body and God brought the young man back to life. You would have thought after things like that they wouldn't continue the service. Hadn't they had enough excitement for one evening? No, Paul hadn't finished his sermon. Back upstairs, having taken the young man up alive, Paul went on with his next point! Then, having restored a broken body to life, they took a loaf and broke it to remember that Jesus' body was broken to death. They held a communion service, and then what did they do? Thankfully go home to their beds? No, they said, "Paul, will you please go on preaching." So he went on speaking until dawn. What a night! What a privilege to sit at Paul's feet. I would love to have done that, and just heard him preach all the night long, wouldn't you? The young man Eutychus would never forget that night, and I am sure he would have sat in a different seat at the next meeting! The order of the verses (10–13) suggest that he might have been at the shore to wave Paul off when he sailed.

It is interesting that this was the only occasion, as far as I am aware, on which Paul raised somebody from the dead. Just as there is one occasion recorded when Simon Peter raised someone from the dead. It is a superficial view of miracles to say, "Well if Christians can raise the dead, they ought to go around emptying all the cemeteries." Jesus didn't do that – there are three or four occasions when Jesus knew it was God's will that he should raise the dead. He also told his disciples that they would do the same – not that they could stop every funeral they saw in the streets, but there were occasions.

The early Christians did a lot of eating together and we

notice that they had a meal at Troas. Communion invariably came as part of a meal. It wasn't just a little bit of bread and a tiny little glass of wine. They had a full meal together, then they passed around the loaf and the cup. Christians love to eat together.

We move on with Paul to the second part of the chapter. He wanted to be in Jerusalem for Pentecost and he was already late. The believers at Ephesus had begged him to come back and preach to the church, and he knew he couldn't. He had to sail, and the ship was only in for twenty-four hours to load and unload at the Port of Miletus, just a few miles from Ephesus. What could he do? He sent a runner on ahead by land, who told the elders of the church to come to the quayside where Paul would like to meet them for the very last time. So the elders came, the shepherds of the flock. Paul spoke to these elders with words that are among the most moving in the New Testament. He speaks very poignantly, very personally about his relationship with them, about his past with them, and their future without him. Let us study these lovely words and see if we can get inside Paul's skin as he talks.

The first thing I notice about his last message to them is this: *Paul can talk about himself without appearing proud*. That is an extraordinary achievement. It comes from someone who is filled with the Spirit of the Lord Jesus. Jesus was constantly using the word "I" but nobody ever accused Jesus of being proud because they knew he was saying the simple truth, not to draw attention to himself but to help those to whom he spoke.

Some of us may start out self-centred but the Lord weans believers off that, helping them to talk about him. But you can reach a point where you are able to talk about yourself in such a way that it helps others and draws attention to Jesus. It is mature saints who can do that. Paul had now matured to the point where he could say, "I was humble when I spent time with you." Paul could say this without any pride or self-glorifying, just sheer honest goodness, stating the truth: "I".

He is talking about what he *did* among them and what he had *been* among them. He draws attention to some qualities in his own life which he wants to see in them. It takes a bold man to do this, to say: look at me and do the same. Paul said in one of his letters: imitate me. You have really got to have reached quite a height before you dare say such a thing. He draws attention first of all to his zeal in mission. With little couplets of words, he draws attention to aspects of his evangelistic approach. First a little couplet of phrases that tells us he never gave up: he never flagged from the first day for the whole time. He tells us where he did it: in public and from house to house. Again a little couplet that tells you of his zeal – public and private, helping the crowd, helping the individual. He tells us, thirdly, what he said to them, "Repent from your sins and believe in the Lord Jesus." Again a little couplet and both are desperately needed; they belong together. Belief without repentance leads to shallow conversion. Repentance without belief leads to despair. But the two together lead to the new birth. He tells us who he spoke to: Jew and Gentile. He had no favourites: he went to those who were near him and those who were different from him. He tells us how he spoke to them: with humility and tears. Aren't these little couplets interesting? They balance each other again and again, and they tell you of a man whose ambition was to get on with the job and do it for the glory of God.

Notice the word "tears". Some people are scared of emotion, feelings, but that is so unlike the New Testament. Paul says that he spoke with *tears*. Did they not feel his emotions as he spoke with humility? What does he mean? He means that he wasn't thinking that he knew everything, that he had the answer to every question. He just came to them as a channel of the truth, with God's truth, not his own; with God's ideas, not Paul's. Did you not sense that? So he speaks of his zeal in evangelism as much as to say: you know how I was among you, now do you think you could go on like that? Do you think you could be the same?

The second thing he drew attention to was his *courage*. I don't know of any man who has been as brave as Paul. He reminds them of the troubles he had been through. He had fought with wild beasts and he tells them now a secret that there is in his heart. He tells them he is facing certain imprisonment and afflictions. But he didn't count his life of any value to him. I want to underline this courage that says, "My life is not worth anything to me." The only value of my life is to God. We don't always behave like this. The slightest threat to our life, and we hang on to it so closely, as much as to say, "My life is precious to me. It's valuable to me. It's everything to me, and any threat to it is a threat to me because this is my most precious possession."

Could you say today that your life next week is of no value to you? That the only value that there is in you going on living is to complete the job that God has given you to do? You have really reached freedom when you have such courage. It is not a courage that many of us possess, but Paul did. He spoke about it quite simply, and this is what he communicated: you can see this, the way I behaved when I was among you, the way I am facing certain imprisonment now; you can see that I place no value on my life for me – the only value of my life is to go on doing the job until it is complete, and then God can take my life, I am not going to hang on to it beyond the life that he wants me to have.

John Wesley used to pray very earnestly all his life, "Lord, let me not live to be useless." He prayed this more and more as he got older, "Lord, let me not live to be useless."

You know he prayed it so earnestly in the Lord that the Lord answered his prayer. He was getting on for eighty when one Sunday morning he preached in Wesley Chapel, City Road, which you can still see today in east London. By Tuesday he had gone. In fact, the very last sermon he preached was at Leatherhead, and if you ever go there, look at the council offices and on the parapet in the car park in front of the building there is a little brass plate which tells you, "On this spot John Wesley preached his last sermon." He had only one ambition: not to hang on to his life but to complete the job. It is because he had that attitude when he was young and fit that I believe God answered his prayer later. But those who hang on to their life while they are still enjoying it and suddenly change their mind and ask God to take it when it's a misery to them, that's nothing to do with this attitude at all. Be ready to say: "Lord, I don't mind if I live to be twenty, forty, sixty or eighty, I just want to do the job you have given me to do." That takes very big courage. Only God knows how long it will take for you to complete that job. Sometimes he completes a person's job when they are still very young. Sometimes he lets them spread that job over many years. Praise God, it is in his hands – but what courage Paul has as he quietly tells them about his own courage in renouncing the value of his own life.

The next thing he talks about in himself is his *innocence*. He can now face God with a clear conscience about them, not because he had them all where they ought to be, but because he had told them everything he ought to tell them. That is the only thing that can give a clear conscience to you. Not whether a person has responded to what you have said or not. They are responsible to God for what they do with what you say. Our responsibility before God is to tell them all we ought to tell them. That is all that God holds us responsible for. I hope this will comfort you. You may have had a job telling somebody else and they have been hard and unresponsive, and you have felt guilty because maybe a loved one of yours to whom you have witnessed has not responded. Let me tell you on the authority of the Word of God: your job was to tell them all that God wanted them to hear. If you have done that, you are clear and it is their responsibility before God what they did with it. That doesn't give us an excuse for being offensive in what we say, of discharging our responsibility in a rude and discourteous manner to people and saying, "There we are, I've discharged my responsibility." I once heard a lady on a boat in the River Thames, shouting Bible texts at the top of her voice in the most abusive way. When she was done, she announced to the whole ship full of people that their blood was on their heads and that her conscience was clear before God. But that was not done in the manner of Christ. It wasn't done in humility and tears, but as she said it, my heart was convicted. All right, she may have been doing it in a wrong way but was I doing it in a right way?

The important thing is that my conscience is only clear before God if I have told people everything he wanted them to know. "I didn't shrink," says Paul, "from declaring the whole counsel of God." *You* can do that. It's so much easier to tell them the nice part of the counsel of God and not the other: to talk of God's mercy but not his justice; to talk of heaven but not of hell; to talk of justification but not sanctification; to talk of happiness in the Lord, but not holiness in the Lord. *A man or a woman is only clear in conscience if they have declared the whole counsel of God and told the whole truth to people, and given them everything God wanted them to hear.* So Paul declares his innocence. In talking about himself, he challenges them: do you feel that you ought to share my zeal in evangelism, my courage in renouncing life and my innocence in having told the whole truth about God?

Now, finally, we look to what Paul says about them and their future without him. He is concerned about what will happen when he has gone. They are his children. Paul, as far as we know, had no physical children but he had hundreds of spiritual children all over, and these children at Ephesus are his. So now he is leaving them and wondering how they will get on without him. We all do that, and the Lord has his way of showing us that he can look after our children.

Paul knew that he would never see their faces again on earth. Who will write letters to them? Who will watch over them and counsel them? Paul did not know at this stage but it was God's will to send the apostle John to look after that fellowship. John lived and died there as an old man at Ephesus. God always has somebody to take over, but Paul gives three things: a warning, a commendation and an example.

The warning is this: wherever there are sheep, there will be wolves. This is true of the flock of God. Think of God's part in the church. It is the church of God bought with Christ and ordered by the Holy Spirit. You are the church of God whom he made his own through the death of his Son. You were purchased by the blood of Christ, and the Holy Spirit made elders in it. The Trinity is involved in a church. Therefore it is very precious to God. It must be watched over and kept carefully. The amazing thing to me is that God, whose church it is and who paid for it with his own Son's life and who gives his Holy Spirit to it, nevertheless says to human beings: you are to look after my church. He gives us the privilege of doing so. Now the warning is that where there are sheep, wolves come in and often they come from within the congregation itself. They come with words that lead people away from the whole truth. It is through false teaching that wolves wreck a flock. Paul is absolutely sure that, after he has left, others will come in and teach false doctrine to destroy the flock. But watch over the people. Feed the flock and watch the wolves.

Secondly, there is a *commendation*. "Now I commend you to God and the word of his grace which is able to build you up and give you an inheritance among those who are sanctified." What a text! When a preacher goes, he doesn't commend his people to his successor, he commends his people to God. Preachers come and go, but there is one who always stays in the church, who can do things for you that no preacher can do. A preacher can't build you up, can't give you an inheritance among those who are sanctified. Only God, in the word of his grace, can. That is where your eyes should be, not on who will minister next, but on the Lord who is able to do for you all these things.

The last thing Paul gave them was an *example*. It is a very surprising one that I want to emphasise, though I do not feel I am totally qualified to emphasise it for an obvious reason – because I do not work for my living. I live by the gospel, which Paul did say in 1 Corinthians 9 was legitimate for a person to do. But the real blessing comes to those who work for their living. I want to emphasise it for this reason: that the emphasis today and maybe for too long a time has been on the blessing of *receiving*.

One evening I heard a powerful address from Loren Cunningham, the leader of Youth With a Mission (YWAM). For forty minutes he told us of the blessings YWAM had been receiving. He told us of castles that had been given by the Lord to YWAM. He told us they saw a vision of ships to take the gospel to islands in the Pacific, and how God gave them two ships in Amsterdam, and within three days, released the money to buy those boats. Then he saw a vision of a larger ship, 450 feet long, and he prayed for it, and God was releasing the money and the ship. The whole address was on that line and it was spectacular. It made you want to drop everything and get into this received blessing. But one thing he never mentioned, and my mind was thinking about it all through his address: who gave these things? They did not come down from heaven. The ship didn't float down through the clouds, nor did the castle. It was never in the air – somebody *gave*. Somebody released the money and we didn't hear a word about that. Now of course all giving should be anonymous, and there is a big reason for that, but the emphasis was such that my heart was saying, "If you want to be in the place of blessing, you need to be on the receiving end of these blessings, in a place where you are constantly receiving things by believing God."

Then on Friday night I went home with a Professor and we sat talking until about midnight. I heard a totally different thing. He said, "These forty-six young men (from YWAM) will have to go on working in their spare time for the next year to two years to pay for the privilege of coming to sing in England." He said, "They are selling their own blood, for in America it is not a voluntary transfusion service, you are paid for every pint of blood you give, and those men you heard singing sold their own blood to come and sing. What you gave for that concert didn't go halfway to cover the cost of them singing to you. They will have to go on working another eighteen months." But the blessing of that showed in those lads' faces. They were not coming with a shout, "The Lord gave us twenty thousand pounds" [that's what it cost them to do the tour]. "The Lord gave us twenty thousand pounds out of the blue, great!" No, they didn't say that. They were on the giving end and there is even more blessing there.

I mention this because we are being overwhelmed with stories of what God has given, but the real story that God is most interested in is not the lump sums that we receive but the blessing for those who quietly, behind the scenes, go out and do what Paul says he gave an example to do. He went out and worked and gave. Do you really believe that that is where the blessing lies? Jesus didn't say, "There's no blessing in receiving." Paul didn't say that in quoting him. But Paul did teach us that the greater blessing lies with those who work for their living and are in a position to give. That is why Jesus was not so much impressed with the collection given in the temple treasury one Sabbath except in the case of a widow who brought two mites and gave all she had.

Have you ever read stories of great people of faith who went to the distant parts of the earth and had all their needs provided, and envied them their blessing and wished that you could have that blessing? Well, maybe the Lord will grant it to you, but get this firm in your mind: the greater blessing belongs to those who go on working for their living and who give to help. That is what Paul is saying. Even as a missionary, he did not want to lose the blessing of working for his living, and giving, and being on that end of the blessing.

So praise God you can read the stories of faith. You can read the stories of gigantic blessings out of the blue for those who are on the receiving end, but when you have read all that, say, "Lord, thank you for the greater blessing of enabling me to have a job and to go and work at it that I might be able to be on the giving end too." That's a revolution in thinking, isn't it? We no longer think of Christians in two groups or two strata, some living by faith and some not.

Paul finishes his last sermon to the Ephesians with a quotation from Jesus, which we might never have had if he had not remembered it. There must be hundreds of things which Jesus said that we don't know. Thank God Paul just recalled this: "Now I leave you with this word to live by, this text, this beatitude [this beautiful attitude]: it is more blessed to give than to receive."

Then there comes a most emotional scene. They hugged him, they kissed him, they cried over him. I don't think we realise how much we mean to each other until we have to say goodbye. That seems to bring home to us how deep the relationship has been. Although Christians are going to meet in heaven, it is sad parting on earth. We are human, as well as being God's children. When the time comes to say goodbye, you realise how deeply God has welded you together in the mutual giving and receiving which is part of God's blessing.

Paul knew this to a great degree because he was such a great apostle. He didn't have that false kind of piety that says, "Christians should never weep at saying goodbye because we are all going to meet together in glory." It's true we are, and that's a deeper joy that girds you but in the immediate situation, we are human. He left because God had told him to go to Jerusalem and they brought him to the ship.

26

Riot in Jerusalem
Read Acts 21:1–22:29

Paul is going to Jerusalem for the last time. When I read a biography, I am far more interested in what a person *is* than in what he has *done*. One wants to know what makes him tick. Some biographies just give you the outside of a life, but you want to get behind that to feel and understand things as the person understood them.

You read the Gospels and at first you are simply interested in the man who stilled the storm, raised the dead and made the lame walk, the deaf hear and the blind see. You are interested in what Jesus *did*, but after a bit you find yourself saying, "But what was Jesus like *inside*? Who was he? What made him tick? Why did he react as he did?" It is true that with Paul at first you get a list of the places he went to and what he did and the miracles that happened, but after a while you find yourself wanting to know what Paul was really like inside.

Acts 21 tells us a very great deal about the man in his own heart. It is not a chapter I would have taken unless I was going through Acts. That is the great advantage or disadvantage for preachers who work their way through the Bible. They can't pick and choose the "nice" texts. You come to a chapter like this, look at it and say, "Why did you put that in the Bible, Lord? It is of historical interest. It has some very interesting, complicated situations about the Jews and the Gentiles, but what have you got to say to us today?"

Let me try to tell you what God has said to me through this chapter. There are three relationships which every Christian has to develop: his relationship with God, his relationship with his neighbour, and his relationship with his fellow Christians.

Without any hesitation I can say that the third is the hardest of the three. It is comparatively easy to love God – after all, he is so lovable. I hope you don't think that's irreverent, but he is. The more you know about God, the more you love him, and the more you feel how wonderful he is. So to love God with all your heart, mind, soul and strength is comparatively easy. What about your neighbour? Jesus taught that your neighbour is anyone at all who is in need of your help. It is comparatively easy for human nature, seeing someone in real need, to want to do something about it. But when it comes to other Christians, that is a different matter. You don't choose your brothers and sisters when you are born. (You don't even choose to be born.) I was born with two sisters. I didn't choose them but I had to learn to live with them. We didn't always manage it. When you are born again into God's family, you find you are in a family of brothers and sisters. You can't choose them. Some of those who belong to the body of Christ you will like immediately, some of them you will not. But God says that this will be the proof to all people that you belong to him – that you are rightly related to your fellow Christians; that you love one another. It is the one argument that no-one can deny for the proof of God's reconciling power. If they can come into a fellowship and see Christians who would otherwise never have met, who are now really related to each other, they have an answerable, logical argument for the gospel. That is why Satan puts fellowship between Christians higher on his list of priorities to demolish. He can do it so easily. He can either do it by forming cliques or clubs within a church of like-minded people at the same age and the same background and the same outlook, so that the church is divided into groups.

All the young people in this corner, all the older people in that corner, all the wealthy people in this corner, and all the poorer people in that corner, and so on. Or he can even take a group of people out of a church because they don't like others in the church or the way they behave.

One of the questions which we find most difficult to answer is this: how far should an individual Christian take the advice of other Christians? In this unusual chapter we have one situation in which Christians plead with Paul *not* to do something and he goes right ahead and does it. Then, a few days later, we find Christians begging him to *do* something and he goes right ahead and does it. On both occasions he got into trouble for the decision he made and things didn't seem to work out very well. Nor I am afraid does the Bible say in this chapter on either occasion whether he did right or wrong.

Someone said to me, "You know life is very like Acts 21: you don't always know whether you've done right or you've done wrong. Sometimes you listen to Christians, sometimes you don't." But life is this kind of muddle! On the other hand, the way we make those decisions and the way we react to the advice of other Christians reveals to us a far more important thing. In chapter 21 it is not so important to study what Paul decides to do as why he decided to do it – why in the one case he went against Christians pleading and in the other case he followed it.

Let us look at the two situations – you can trace the journey on a map if you want to, I am just going to highlight two towns. The ship called in at the ports Tyre and Caesarea. In both cases Christians pleaded with Paul not to go to Jerusalem and it did no good at all, he went straight on. Now why did he ignore what they said? In Tyre they met a few believers. By now there were little groups of Christians in every town and port. Wherever you went, you would find them, so they spent a short time there and met for worship. One of the things that can happen in Christian worship is this: there can be prophecy, which is not preaching. Preaching is explaining to people the meaning of what God has already said. Prophecy is a new word from God for the people in that place, at that time. The Spirit of God can use a person's mouth – and sometimes the most unlikely person – to give a word from God for that people at that time in that place.

In Tyre Paul was given such a word by the Spirit of God through one of the believers. It was not a word that there would be peace but a word that if he went up to Jerusalem, he was heading straight for danger and disaster – that there was trouble waiting for him. The next sentence says, "But we went on our way." Why did he ignore that word from the Spirit of God and go on?

The next place they called at was Caesarea and much the same thing happened. This church was full of prophets and prophetesses. There was one man there who had first been appointed a deacon of the church in Jerusalem, who developed the gift of an evangelist. Now living in Caesarea, he had four daughters who were prophetesses. The New Testament, while it does not have women teachers in the church, most certainly has women prophets. They proclaimed the word of God and they were mouthpieces for God but it wasn't one of the four women who spoke, it was a man called Agabus. We came across him earlier in Acts when by the Spirit of God he predicted a famine and told them to get a fund ready for when it came. That is unusual isn't it, for Christians to start collecting money for a disaster that hasn't happened yet? The world can only collect for a disaster after it has occurred, but in this case Agabus the prophet got the Christians ready beforehand.

Here he is again, and he takes Paul's belt from around his coat, binds his hands and feet, and says that the owner of the belt was going to be tied up in Jerusalem. Once again, a word from God through the Christians to Paul. When they heard this, all Paul's friends gathered around, including his personal friend Dr Luke who wrote all about this, and they pleaded with him, with tears in their eyes, "Paul, please don't go."

Now why did Paul ignore what they said? One very simple reason: it was a human concern for him that made them say it. You notice that what God said was that he would be tied up. It was man who is saying, "Then don't go." This is an instinctive reaction: when there is danger or trouble, avoid it. The assumption was being made by Christians that if God was going to tell us of trouble ahead, he was doing so in order that you could avoid it. Far from that, God was not telling this to Paul to discourage him from going but to encourage him, to fill him and prepare him. That is why the Bible tells you about great troubles coming on the earth. Building up to the end of history when the trouble will be worse than ever, it is called the big trouble – the Great Tribulation. I know many Christians who are hoping to get out of it before it happens, but when I read my Bible we are told about the big trouble not to get out of it but to prepare to go into it.

I notice that in Today's English Version, there is a verse in Revelation 7 which is translated, "These are they who have come safely through the great persecution." That is true to the Greek: come through it victorious. If God tells you trouble is coming, he is not telling you that in order for you to run away, he is telling you so that you may receive courage and strength, and prepare for it and seek his grace, to get the anchor down before the storm blows up, and that is what he was doing here. When Christians were concerned about his safety, health and welfare, Paul got going. We Christians can be over-protective because of our human concern for one another.

Paul said in Acts 20 that God had told him to go to Jerusalem. He was bound in the Spirit and had got to go. He would not be deflected. As I read this part of the story, I was seeing something that happened some years before in the north of Galilee when Jesus let his disciples know that he had got to go to Jerusalem, where he would be arrested, tried and killed. Peter, with all the love in his heart, with all the concern for the dearest friend he had ever known, tried to dissuade him. Jesus recognised this deep human concern as a point at which Satan could tempt by deflecting him from his course.

Paul arrived in Jerusalem, met the Christians there, and told them all that the Lord had done for him on his missionary tours. They were thrilled, they praised God, and then they told him about a bit of a problem. He was an embarrassment to them. People were going to talk now that he was there. The background is the familiar one: when you become a Christian, how much of your background do you have to give up? How much of your culture do you have to drop? For the Gentiles who came to Christ, the matter was simple – they had to drop all idolatry and immorality and anything connected with those two things. But when a Jew came to Jesus, how much should he drop, given that he was never guilty of idolatry, worshipped only the one true God, and his laws were laws of high morality? The answer, surprisingly, is nothing. If a Jew comes to Christ, he can go on being a Jew. The only thing that Paul said quite simply and utterly dogmatically in the letter to the Galatians was that a Jew becoming a Christian can stay a Jew but he mustn't ever tell a Gentile becoming a Christian that he must become a Jew. So there are messianic Jews today.

James knew that Paul's coming would upset some people because they had heard rumours that you not only tell Gentiles they needn't become Jews, you could tell Jews that they can stop being Jews. This is the thing Paul never did and never taught. So he was asked for the sake of the other Christians in Jerusalem to join in with a rite of purification that would put him right with their culture.

Now some people would say, "Paul hold on, you're going to be led straight into compromise. After writing the letter to the Galatians, you can't do it!" But Paul was a big man with a big heart. He listened to the Christians and did what they said. Why? Because for Paul the unity of Christians is a very important thing. If they told him to do something because of their concern for him, he didn't listen. But if they told him to do something because of their concern for other brothers in Christ, Paul would co-operate.

Sometimes we are called to do things that people might misunderstand, and some might accuse us of being inconsistent. Paul listened to the Christians and did something that he could have argued was unnecessary. In the light of the events it proved to be a disaster, but he did it because he loved them. He had been advised that this would remove rumours and set their hearts at rest. So he went into the temple, paid the expenses of the rite, bought the sacrifices for the others, shaved his head and entered into that thing which Christ had not told him to do, which was not part of the Christian life, but which would draw him closer to the brethren. No principle was involved, the gospel was not being denied, so he did it. Here is a man who would not do anything for his own sake, even on the advice of other Christians, but whose heart could always be touched by an appeal to their welfare. Paul is not contradicting himself, he is showing a divine consistency. Isn't that a lovely attitude and a model for us?

Of course it didn't work out. Those who say that if things go wrong it can't have been in the Lord have a bit of a problem with this chapter. I suppose none of us will ever get to know what was right or wrong in this situation until we get to glory. I am just looking forward to getting to Paul and saying, "Paul, I've got a number of questions I have had for many years.

Actually when I get to see Paul in glory I'm quite sure I won't bother with the questions! But I would love to just get Paul and say, "Paul do you regret doing that? What do you feel about those two decisions now, in the light of eternity?" I have the feeling Paul would still say this, "Well maybe I wasn't sure at the time but I was sure that if God had told me to do something, I mustn't let other Christians put me off for my safety." I'm sure that it is always good to bend over backwards to remove false rumours that are dividing Christians from one another.

God knows the heart, and God knows what is right for the heart to do. Now Paul did get into trouble. A riot started. He was seen in the temple and was accused of breaking the law. In 1871 and again in 1935, digging in the dust, archaeologists discovered blocks of stone in the ruins of Jerusalem. They found two stones which belonged to the wall around the inner temple, and carved on the stone are these words: *"No man of alien race is to enter within the balustrade fence that goes round the temple. If anyone is taken in the act, let him know that he has himself to blame for the penalty of death that follows."* That notice was all around the temple. The Gentiles could come into the outer court, but not through the middle wall of partition. Paul had preached that in Christ the middle wall of partition is down and gone, and there is no division now. Anybody can come right into the holy place of God's presence, but Paul did not violate that Jewish law. He had not taken a Gentile in, but he was being falsely accused of doing so. In spirit he had broken that wall down by preaching that Christianity was for all, but in practice he had respected this scruple of the

Jews, yet he was accused of not doing so. A riot started and they beat him and dragged him, and the soldiers just caught him in the nick of time. As we will see, he was saved by four things: his Greek language, Roman citizenship, Hebrew blood, and Christian experience. The crowd shouted, "Kill him, kill him" – and he was saved.

As I read that, my mind went a little further back into the New Testament. The irony of history is that in that very city, about twenty years or so earlier, Stephen had been the first Christian to die for his faith. He too was falsely accused of breaking down the Jewish law. They had dragged him out. The mob had taken him.

But let's go a little further back. It was in this same city that the Lord Jesus had likewise been caught by the crowd, and they had shouted for him to be crucified. I have the feeling that as Paul was carried he literally had to be held aloft by the soldiers taking him back to the Antonia fortress which looked out over the temple area. Paul maybe was thinking about Stephen and about Jesus. As a servant of Christ he was now in the same boat.

If you do what you believe to be right in the sight of the Lord, expect trouble, expect misunderstanding, expect people to say false things – but then you are called to share the sufferings of Jesus. Jesus called us to take up our cross and follow him. He never said that if you do what's right, everybody will understand and be thrilled. I say to people at their baptism: you are doing what is right but people will not understand; there will be those who say, "What did you do that for?" There may be those who accuse you of false actions and even false motives. Count yourself blessed because you are following the steps of Jesus. What is baptism but, having taken up the cross of Christ, being willing to be buried with him and raised with him, identified with him and his passion so that you may share the joy. As you experience misunderstanding, trouble, gossip and even anger on the part of people who don't understand what you are doing, then feel very close to Jesus Christ for he is right there.

27

Transfer to Caesarea
Read Acts 22:30–23:35

Why was Paul always getting into trouble? There are some who say because he was that kind of person, and that someone so single-minded and provocative was bound to rub people up the wrong way. But I don't think that is the answer, because the troubles in which Paul found himself were exactly the same kind of troubles that our Lord Jesus underwent. Are you going to say Jesus got into trouble because of his temperament? No, I believe the answer lies in the kind of world this is.

One of the most important questions you can ask is this: is our world basically a good world or a bad world? If it is a good world then good people should find life easier in it, but all the facts of our experience run in the opposite direction. The more you seek to live by God's will, the more trouble you will get into and the harder it will become. I am quoting Jesus here as well as Paul. Jesus was an honest person and he made no bones about it. He said, "In this world you're going to have trouble." He used the word "tribulation," which is a Latin word coming from the name *tribulum*, which was used of a threshing sledge, a heavy instrument of timbers crossed over each other with spikes underneath, pulled across the grain to separate it from the husk. Sometimes we feel just like that, as if we are going right through it, and there is a threshing sledge battering us. Jesus said that is how it has got to be. That is how it was for him. Because this world was once a good world when God had finished making it and had put people in it, and he had tremendous satisfaction. He said, "That's very good." But nobody in their senses could look at the world today and say it is very good. In fact, I believe that our Western civilization at least, if not the whole world, is going to become more and more difficult a place to live in as a Christian. The signs are there. In area after area in our social life in England, it is becoming almost impossible to be a Christian. I never thought that medicine, a high calling if ever there was one, would become a vocation from which Christians would shrink. But there is an increasing number of Christian doctors and nurses who wonder how long they can carry on in their professions, particularly in certain spheres in which they are having to make frightful decisions which they cannot relate to their moral principles.

There are Christian policeman who are saying that we are reaching the point where law and morality are so far apart that it is becoming almost impossible to be a Christian policeman. Did you think that day would come? I meet Christian businessmen in certain spheres of work who are saying, "I've just got to get out if I am to keep my moral integrity."

This world in which we live is increasingly a bad world, and the Bible tell us why. The Bible does not say that this world is as God made it or as he intended it to be. It says that Satan has got hold of it. The world as a system is not in God's hands – not immediately anyway. Maybe ultimately, but at the moment the god of this world, and the ruler of this world, and the prince of this world (those are big titles which Jesus gave) are in the hands of an evil intelligence called Satan. When I look at the spheres of our social life and see how he has got hold of them, one wonders just how much longer it is going to be possible to remain in society and be a Christian.

Take, for example, the area of science. Before I became a

preacher, I had a scientific training (if not a very extensive one) and I found it fascinating. I found the almost drug-like addiction to discovering something new. There is an urge in a scientist for knowledge. I for one am grateful for many of the benefits that science has brought into our lives, things which we often take for granted. But Satan has got hold of science. The tragedy is that not only is every discovery that we make capable of being used for evil (and indeed with many recent discoveries they have been used for evil before they have been used for good), but now science is unleashing such powers that we are living in a frightened age.

Genetic engineering is here, and mankind is going to be able to shape the kind of babies that are born and decide their intelligence, hair colour and gender. The thought appals us and it is like a Pandora's box. That fear would not be there unless Satan had got hold of this realm of human endeavour. So now we are saying, "Who will stop the scientist discovering these things? Who will call a halt until we are morally capable of using properly the discoveries that have been made?"

Since the Bible revealed to me what Satan's aim and object is, I can see how he is controlling the world of politics. His object is to have the whole world under one government, and to have that government in the hands of one of *his* servants – a puppet dictator. He once offered the job to Jesus and said, "If you'll bow down to me I'll give you all the kingdoms of the world." But he will one day offer the job to someone and there will be a man who will be a world dictator who will be given such power that the whole world will not only be in his hands, but in Satan's, because he will be in Satan's hands. Can you not see politics shaping up to that? Can you not see Satan destroying democracy by anarchy until people, in their fear and insecurity, will cry out for a dictator who will bring them back some law and order by his own arbitrary and totalitarian authority? *So the Bible teaches that this world is not God's world, that you can't be a friend of God and a friend of the system, that the two are incompatible, and that this world is like a ship that has already been holed below the waterline and is going down.* Many people on the ship are like those who on the night the Titanic went down, after it had struck the iceberg, did not realise what was happening and went on singing and dancing in the bars and ballrooms on board. But it was going down.

So Christians get into trouble. I know that sometimes they can be blamed for tactlessness and for temperamental weaknesses, which come out and spoil their witness, and we always have to remember that we may be the offence to someone else, and not the cross. But even allowing for that, the truer Christians are to Jesus Christ, the more they will get into hot water and go from one crisis to another and one trouble to another. The life of Paul tells us that it was not the kind of person he was that got him into trouble, it was the kind of world he lived in. It is a world that doesn't love God, it is a world that doesn't want God, and it is a world in the grip of Satan.

Having explained the troubles, we come now to the question of how a Christian copes with those troubles. What should he do about them? Should he run away from them? Should he fight as he is fought? Or should he resign himself to his fate and accept the troubles? Wouldn't it be lovely if there were one simple rule to apply to every situation – either that when trouble comes, a Christian must fight it, or must simply resign himself to it and accept it or try to avoid it. But there is no simple answer to this question, except one, which we will come to later.

Here in chapter 23 we have Paul in two different kinds of trouble: before the Council and under threat of a conspiracy. In the one situation he faces it and fights it. I must say that he gave as good as he got, and he finished up the winner. In the other situation he ran, or at least he made it possible for himself to be taken out of the trouble. Do these events help us with our question: should a Christian face it and fight it, and when should he go out of it? Let us look at the two situations and see if we can get any guidance from them.

The Sanhedrin was the council of the Jewish nation. Peter, James, John and Stephen had appeared before them and this council must have got fed up with being called together to deal with Christians. The Roman commander was trying desperately to get rid of his responsibility in Paul's case on the ground that he was not a criminal in the civil law, it was a religious matter. So Paul was before the Sanhedrin. Whether or not you think he was being wise, let's see what he did, because we can't alter the facts.

He opened the case himself. The best form of defence is attack and it is interesting that he opened the case and spoke before he was spoken to, and simply got up in the dock and said, "I am innocent and my conscience is absolutely clear before God to this very day." In other words: as touching the laws which that Council represented, he was blameless. He had made that claim in Philippians 3 – "As touching the law, blameless."

The High Priest said, "Hit that man on his mouth." It was to shut him up. Somebody nearby did that.

Paul said, "You whitewashed wall."

Should he have said that? Is that a Christian thing to do? Remember that Jesus said to people, "You whited sepulchre." There may well be a time and place to say this. From what we know of the High Priest at that time, a man called Ananias, nothing could have been said that was truer to that High Priest's character. Let me tell you a little about him. He was a glutton and everybody knew that the High Priest was an over eater – a sin condemned in the Bible quite frequently.

It is one of the seven deadly sins according to one Christian classification. He was such a glutton that when the people came to the Temple they would sing a perverted version of Psalm 24 about him. He was also a thief and robber. There were junior priests who had starved because this rapacious High Priest had taken the money and food that should have gone to them. Not only that, he was a murderer and an assassin. If anybody crossed this High Priest he arranged for their death. That is what lies behind the conspiracy the next day. This man had got his job from Herod, and he had wormed his way into it. Later this High Priest was to be sought by the crowd wanting to kill him. They found him hiding in a sewer under Jerusalem, and they took him out and lynched him.

That was the man before whom Paul stood, and who said, "Hit that man on his mouth," to whom Paul said, "You whitewashed wall." To strike a man before he had been proved guilty, to punish him, was illegal.

I don't think Paul knew all about this man because he said in a moment that he didn't know that he was the High Priest. But God can enable a person to say an appropriate word without their natural knowledge. Here was a man in the dock who, before God, had a clear conscience, and the judge on the bench was a man like this. God had enabled Paul to say something that was so true.

Somebody standing near Paul asked him whether he realised he had insulted the High Priest. At this stage Paul says, "I didn't know he was the High Priest." That is a puzzling thing. The High Priest would sit in the chief seat and he would have the High Priest's robes, and he would be the judge. Some think that Paul is being sarcastic: "I didn't know *he* was the High Priest." In other words, "He's an interloper" or, "He shouldn't be there." Yet Paul goes on, "I didn't know he was the High Priest for the scripture says, "You shall not speak badly of a ruler of your people."

It seems as if Paul's eyesight let him down again. He could see at a distance and he could see large writing close up, but one of the symptoms of trachoma is that you cannot see middle distance. You can't see a face across the room. Maybe that was the problem.

Whatever the explanation, Paul immediately articulates a profound Christian truth. However evil the authorities are, a Christian must always give them respect. One of the most astonishing things is that, in the days of Nero, Peter wrote a letter telling Christians to honour the emperor. We live in a day when people dishonour even relatively good leaders, tearing them to pieces with sarcasm, irony and satire.

Paul does seem to be apologising here as if his temperament did run away with him, and he hadn't realised what he was doing. That put him in a rather weak position. Did you think Paul would shut up? No! Did you think he would let the advantage go to the Council? Never.

What he did next was to make an astute observation that there were two denominations represented in the Council. He quickly lined himself up with one and said that he disagreed with the other – a brilliant move. If you want to get away from your enemies, divide them amongst themselves and get them fighting each other. The two denominations in the Judaism of those days were Pharisees and Sadducees. You will recall that the Pharisees were the conservatives, still believing in supernatural things: spirits, angels, and the resurrection from the dead. The Sadducees were the liberals—they didn't believe in the supernatural; religion was all in this life. So they didn't believe in a resurrection.

It is similar to one kind of division you can meet among Christians today. You find conservatives and liberals – those who still believe in the supernatural and those who don't. Now that doesn't mean that either Pharisees or Sadducees were all that God wanted them to be, but a person who believed in the supernatural was always an easier person to win for the Lord. Paul had been a Pharisee, and many of the early Christians were Pharisees first. At least they believed in the supernatural even if they got a bit tied up in their strict morality.

Paul said that he was on trial there because he was a Pharisee. He wasn't just using this as a gimmick to get out of the trouble. He was stating a sober truth that for him the resurrection from the dead was the key of his whole faith: Jesus had risen from the dead. So he wasn't pulling a fast one, he was stating a truth. Look what happened. Immediately the Pharisees thought: he was not such a bad fellow after all; he says he met Jesus, but it could have been a spirit or an angel speaking – you know, it's a supernatural experience. They got quite friendly towards him, the Sadducees got very upset, and the whole thing split down the middle. Paul got out of that trouble – just. The poor commander had to dash into the Council and take him back to prison in chains.

That was the first situation. Was Paul right to tackle it in that way? Was he right to fight back? Was he right to use worldly weapons – and they were – to cause disorder in the Council?

The next day he faces a very different thing. You can't stir up people like this without repercussions. The trouble is that if people can't win a verbal battle with you, they can resort to physical violence. But those who know they could not win the battle in the open, and those who know they could not verbally present a valid reason for what they do, go underground and seek to use conspiracy and force. That was what happened with Paul. Some of those Jews, I guess probably from the Sadducee side, went underground and conspired, vowing before God not to eat or drink until they had dealt with him. They devised a plot and said to the

Council, "Call him back and we will kill him on the way, and it will all be done secretly." That is what they did to Jesus. When they couldn't arrest him openly in the Temple, what did they do? They got hold of Judas and said, "Can you do it secretly with us? We will give you lots of money." When Jesus was on trial he had said that he was openly in the Temple. They could have arrested him then. Why had they done it in that underhand way? Someone rebuked Jesus at his own trial. "Don't speak to the High Priest like that." So much is being repeated – but the conspiracy was on.

The plot became known to Paul through his nephew, and we don't know how. But the nephew came and told Paul. What should Paul do now? Trouble is looming. Should he face it? Should he, like a courageous martyr, go right into the arena and face death? Or, should he fight it? Or should he escape from it? On this occasion he chose that last answer. He ensured that the Roman commander knew, and off he went with 470 soldiers around him. Should a Christian do that? Should a Christian ever ask the police for protection? Should a Christian go to a Roman commander and say, "Come and deal with this"? At any rate with that many soldiers he was fairly safe and off he set. Nine o'clock at night – can you see that little army setting out? Just to take one Jewish Christian sixty miles away to Caesarea. So Paul arrived there safely.

If you have been following the last few chapters you may see some humour in this. Listen to this sentence in the Roman commander's letter to the governor: "I learned that he is a Roman citizen so I went with my soldiers and rescued him." Do you remember what really happened? The mob was about to kill Paul and the Roman commander rescued him and tied him up to be tortured, and then learned that he was a Roman citizen. There is something very human about that commander's letter, just reversing two little facts and missing out the fact that he had been just about to torture

Paul to get the truth out of him. Anyway it shows they were still human, and that the Roman commander was just putting it nicely to the governor so that he could keep in with him.

So there were two situations, and in one Paul faced it and fought it hard, while in the other he claims the protection of unbelieving soldiers, and he goes. Which was right? Were both right? Or was neither right? How do you find out? Do you examine each situation? Do you say, "Well now, in the Council it was open and public and he had a chance of winning, whereas the conspiracy was in the dark and he had a chance of losing?" Do you weigh up the situations like that? I think there is one answer to this. It is a very simple and profound one. It applies to every trouble that every one of us may be facing right now. Should you face it and stay there, or should you run away? Should you do what Paul did in the first half of chapter 23 or the second?

Here is the answer: 23:11. Something happened between these two events. After that business in the Council, Paul was lying in his cell in chains, probably a bit discouraged because you know if you win a battle in the way that he won that battle in the Council I'll guarantee you will have a reaction afterwards. You'll say, "Was that too much of me? Was I really being a bit naughty to play them off against each other?" Suddenly there was someone else in the cell, and it was Jesus. Jesus didn't say, "Paul we rather messed that up, didn't we?" Jesus didn't say, "Paul there was a bit too much of Paul fighting there in the council."

Jesus said, "Take courage, Paul; as you have testified about the things concerning me in Jerusalem, thus it is necessary also in Rome to testify."

So Paul was willing to go and to run away from the trouble. Now we have our answer to the question, "When you're in trouble should you face it and fight it, or should you turn away from it?" The answer is: let Jesus decide that.

Be the kind of person Jesus can talk to and then you will know the answer. Sometimes he'll say, "Stay right there." Sometimes he'll say, "Go."

What kind of a person does Jesus talk to, and how does he talk to them? First of all, Jesus only speaks to people in crisis if they are the kind of people who speak to him when everything is going all right. That is a simple principle, but how do you recognise his voice if you don't often hear it? If you are not used to talking to Jesus normally, you may have difficulty hearing him when the crunch comes. Paul was a person who talked to Jesus normally, and therefore in that night Jesus could speak to him.

The second thing is this: Jesus can talk to people who are dead to self. The problem is that when we are quiet and thinking, self keeps talking, and self keeps looking at what will happen to self in such and such a course of action. But only a person who is dead to self will run away from trouble at the command of the Lord Jesus. Because it takes courage to run away and not be worried about what people will think about you. In other words, only if my self is totally dead am I free to stay and face trouble or free to run without thinking of what will happen to me if I do either. If I stay and fight might I be killed, or might I be hurt? Or if I run, will people think I am a coward? Both ways, self is still very much arguing in the picture. Only a person who is dead to self can hear the voice of Jesus clearly telling them what to do and then self-motives don't confuse the issue. It is those who are alive to God and whose only ambition is to do what *he* wants them to do – and who are not concerned with how long they live or where they live or how they live – who are open to hearing Jesus speak.

How does he speak? Here I can only, I suppose, speak within the limits and framework of one's own experience and of what one has shared with the experience of others. There is no single way in which Jesus speaks. Sometimes it comes almost visually. Sometimes there is such a clear picture in the mind that it is very difficult to draw the line between what these eyes see and what the eyes of the mind see. Paul had this problem – he said he was taken up to heaven, whether in the body or out of the body he didn't know. It was such a real thing that he couldn't tell whether it was his senses or his spirit telling him where he was. There is a narrow dividing line. Sometimes you see a thing so clearly in your mind that you can almost see it with your eyes. I remember almost getting to that point when it seemed to me that the word "Guildford" was written on the wallpaper of a bedroom in Chalfont St. Peter when the Lord was telling me to move.

There are other occasions when a sentence comes to you so clearly that you can't tell whether you heard it with your physical ears or not. On occasions when I have been preaching someone has come to me afterwards and said, "You know when you said so and so, that was just what I needed to hear from God." I am absolutely certain that I did not say what they "heard". What has happened? While they have been listening and quiet and open to the Lord, God spoke to them and they heard him speak, and it was so clear and so definite that they thought that I had said it. So you cannot just draw a dividing line.

Sometimes as you read your Bible he will take words almost out of their context and they leap out of the page and are as clear as if they had come in an envelope addressed to you. That word is so clear that Jesus has spoken. Sometimes if someone else is present it can be in a conversation with them, and some words come from them which stab you very deeply and go straight into your heart, and you know the Lord has said something to you. I am carefully guarding against suggesting there is only one way of Jesus speaking to you. That I believe is why the Bible so often does not tell us the *way* in which the Lord spoke to people. It simply says that Jesus said to Paul in the middle of the night....

The main thing is for you to be the kind of person Jesus can talk to. You will make mistakes in your early Christian life. Everyone does, because your own impulses and the leading of the Spirit are sometimes so like each other in your experience. Never believe that you are infallible. There are Christians who say, "The Lord has told me...." and the hotline to heaven has sent an "infallible message". There is nothing you can do. You can't discuss or pray with a Christian who says that to you.

Check your guidance. Check it again and again with God's Word, with circumstances, with the advice and opinions of mature believers – especially in the early days. As you grow and as you walk with the Lord, you will begin to recognise his voice more and more clearly, and distinguish it from your own impulses and the pressures of others. As you get to know a person, you get to know the kind of thing they say and the kind of tone they use. Sometimes it's not a spectacular voice but what Elijah heard in stillness.

There are things my wife can say to me without opening her mouth because we have lived together long enough now and I know what she's wanting me to know. Is that not true of a relationship that deepens?

Maybe the Lord has compassion on us in our early Christian life, and speaks so clearly, because he knows we are not mature enough to wrestle with the relationship. Sometimes, to help us grow up, he leaves us in a position of doubt and uncertainty about a course of action so that we may seek him the more.

28

Trial before Felix
Read Acts 24

Paul having been taken secretly to Caesarea by night, his accusers have come down to state their case before the governor Felix.

Consider something that everyone possesses. You have had it for many years. If you treat it well, it will last you a lifetime and even improve with age. If you treat it badly, it will let you down very quickly indeed. It is one of your most precious possessions and yet there have been times when you would have loved to get rid of it. It has given you some pleasure and a great deal of pain. It has saved you a lot of trouble, but it has also caused you a lot of trouble. Some people have killed for it and others have died for it. Some would count it a real blessing of life and others regard it as a curse. It is one of the few things that you can take with you when you die though many people have tried to kill it before they died. I refer to your *conscience*. It is one of the features that marks all human beings as distinct from all animals. It is something that we have to live with, and we become aware of it very early in life. It accuses us of doing wrong and sentences us to fear, shame and guilt. Though we share this thing in common with everybody else, it often separates us from other people and makes us want to run away from them. It is the proof that we have freewill, for it is God's voice within us holding us responsible for our own actions. Though I know that conscience can be conditioned by our upbringing, our society and people around us, the person who is most responsible for conditioning my conscience is myself.

Acts 24 is a study in conscience. It is an account of three men at a public investigation, and the representative of the Roman state is Felix. Paul is being investigated and is therefore being questioned in the dock. There is a lawyer called Tertullus who is in charge of the prosecution. These three men all have a conscience but in each case it is in a different condition. First, we have a man with a dead conscience – he has stifled it until it seems to work no more. Second, we have a man with a clear conscience, who is not afraid of the truth because his conscience is right. Thirdly, we see a man who shows all the signs of a guilty conscience.

As we study this chapter I want you to answer one simple question: which of these three more nearly represents your conscience at this time? Take first the man with the dead conscience: Tertullus. The scene is Caesarea, an audience chamber in the palace of Herod, which is now lived in by the Roman governor. There is Paul, sitting or standing in the dock before the governor perhaps, and the lawyer opens his speech for the prosecution. He is a clever lawyer who knows his job and he certainly knows how to put a speech together. His name indicates that they have hired this lawyer because he is a Greek-speaking Jew and familiar with the culture of the judge.

His speech is a masterpiece and it resembles speeches made today in courts of law. Confident, remarkable oratory, yet there is one fatal flaw – it is not true. I want you to notice two ways in which this lawyer is not speaking the truth, which, because he does it without any apparent hesitation or embarrassment, tell us that here we have got a lawyer who has killed his conscience and is only interested in his client and his fee. The two halves of the speech are devoted to what he says about Felix the governor and Paul the prisoner. The good things he says about Felix are not true, and the bad things he says about Paul the prisoner are not true. Here is a lawyer who has sold his soul. He has no conscience left and he is only a professional. He has identified himself with the perjury that is being committed.

Consider what he says about Felix. It is customary, even to this day, to begin a speech in court with a word of courtesy to the judge, but what is said here is not just courtesy, this is downright flattery. Do you notice that half the speech for the prosecution (if you count the words) is concerned with buttering up the judge? Most of it is totally untrue. Indeed, I couldn't find a word of truth in what he said about Felix. This nauseating flattery is just to try to get the judge on his side, and that is stooping to a very low trick. He says to Felix that he is noted for his clemency, for his reforms, for the good that he had done to the nation. Looking at the life of Felix, this is blatantly untrue. He was governor of Samaria for two years followed by five years as governor of Judea. During that time the weaknesses in his character came out abundantly. This man began life as a slave. He would never have got any higher in society than that, had his brother not become one of the favourite slaves of the emperor Nero. His brother started pulling strings for him. First he was free, then he got a job in the civil service. Gradually he climbed up the social ladder until he became the first slave ever to become a Roman governor. The tragedy was that he never left behind his slave mentality and he had a chip on his shoulder about the brutality that he had received as a slave. The result was that when he came into power, he was ruthless. For example, when there was rebellion, and there was a great outburst of terrorism under Felix, he hired thugs to go and murder the terrorists. This was his method of controlling the situation. The result was that terrorism accelerated during the five years of his governorship, and here Tertullus was thanking Felix for bringing peace, reform of the land, and controlling the situation, declaring what a wonderful governor he was! Far from it, Felix had made things worse. The Roman historian Tacitus was much more truthful when he said about Felix that he exercised the power of a king with the mind of a slave.

Now look at the bad things Tertullus says about Paul, which are equally untrue. The second half of the speech is as far from reality as the first. He accuses Paul of three criminal acts: sedition, he says he's a perfect pest – that is a literal translation of the Greek – always stirring up trouble, civil disorder. Secondly, the crime of sectarianism. Every religion in those days had to be registered and become what was called a *religio licita*. If you were not registered you were a *religio ilicita* and you could not meet. So they accused him of starting a new religion and of being a leader of a new sect called the Nazarenes, which was not registered. The third crime of which he charges Paul is sacrilege, though he does have the grace to say Paul only attempted to defile the temple – even that was not true. As if this was not enough, he said, "I accuse your representative Lysias of obstructing justice. We arrested Paul and we were going to try him and your man Lysias interrupted and used great violence to take him from us," and so obstructed justice.

Here is a lawyer who is committing perjury with every sentence he utters. It shows that you can sell your conscience and you can stifle it. You can kill it. In our world, not only in law but in medicine, in industry, in so many other spheres, people are now under pressure to kill their conscience and to stifle it until they no longer know what is true and what is untrue. Tertullus, a man with a dead conscience, doesn't even betray any twinges whatever the lies he is telling.

Now let us look at Paul, the man with a clear conscience. It is a remarkable speech. There is no trace of bitterness, no trace of self-pity, no trace of rancour. Nor does Paul appeal to the feelings of those to whom he speaks. He simply states the facts. Only a man who has a clear conscience can make a speech like this. Only a man who knows he is in the right can speak so openly, so frankly, and just declare the truth. With particulars, not the kind of generalities that the lawyer used, he demolishes those charges one by one.

He says, "Am I accused of constantly causing disorder? I have only been in this city twelve days, and you never found me with a crowd, and you never found me arguing anywhere in the city." Fact! "Am I propounding a new religion? Have I started a new sect? I admit that I worship the God of our ancestors and I believe everything in the Law and the Prophets. Does that sound like a new religion to you? Am I accused of sacrilege? What was I doing in the temple when they caught me? I was offering sacrifices and going through one of the Temple ceremonies of purification." Fact, fact, fact; truth, truth, truth—if you have a clear conscience that is all you need say.

But Paul says that he has admitted some things. He admits freely that he believes this new faith in Jesus is the completion of the old religion. He has not ceased to be a Jew; he has become a complete Jew. The only dispute between those Jewish leaders and Paul was that they believe the resurrection will come in the future, but he believed that it had already happened to one person. He is encouraging Felix to use his brain, to think about this. There is no criminal charge here whatever. No one can pin any crime on him. The New Testament makes it clear that a Christian should be careful to see that no crime can ever be pinned on him. Again and again you find that in the epistles. Paul is someone who can stand there, and no-one could pin a criminal charge on him. He had done his best to have a clear conscience before God and before men. A man with a clear conscience, he can state the truth as simply and as soberly as that, because he has nothing to lose by the facts.

Now we come to Felix, the man with a guilty conscience. Everything he does shows that deep down he is troubled, worried, anxious – he can't live with himself. He knows perfectly well now that there is no case and that he ought to let Paul go. As we read this record of the events, do you not get echoes of something else? Of course you do. Twenty-two years earlier, Jesus stood before a Roman governor accused by Jewish leaders of stirring up the people, setting himself up as king, forbidding taxes to Caesar, and it was all untrue. Jesus simply spoke of the truth, and the Roman governor in that case said, "What is truth?" Here is another Roman governor, and Felix, if not careful, could drop into the same trap that Pontius Pilate dropped into. Wherever in the world the account of Jesus has gone, Christians have said: "Suffered under Pontius Pilate". That man became infamous because at the critical point in his career he did not do what was right.

But Felix saw a loophole. His representative Claudius Lysias had been mentioned, so Felix would finish the case when he went to Caesarea and he could hear his side of the story. Now that was a legitimate thing for him to do, but it was a way out. At this critical point, because he didn't listen to his conscience, he put a good man in prison for at least two years and he never got him out. There is a point in every situation where if you do not follow conscience, you find yourself in a net of circumstances that you cannot escape from later. Let that point pass and it is too late. Felix let it pass. He had a guilty conscience from then on and he had to live with himself. He suffered from insomnia over this. He was troubled over this matter and two things reveal this. The first thing is that he held Paul so lightly. He knew that man should not be in his cell while he was in the palace. So he allowed Paul considerable freedom. He could take a walk down to the next cell and along the corridor and back again. I am afraid that in those days the practice if you were put in prison was that nobody met your needs, not even food was given to you. Did you know that? You were entirely dependent on your friends bringing help, and on that help being taken in. So Felix said that Paul could have visitors and receive help. Why did he do this? Can you see a man who knows he shouldn't keep Paul in prison, and yet he's trying to keep him there and yet wants to set him free? He is torn – he knows what's right and he just can't bring himself to go the whole way and let Paul go. So he gives him a bit of freedom and then puts him back in the cell. He gives him visitors but won't let him go home with them. He is torn between the two.

Why did Felix keep him there? For two reasons. One is that he thought Paul was rich, and he thought Paul might say, "Look I was in Jerusalem giving money away to the poor and I've got a lot of rich friends, and I could get some money if you could let me out of here." Felix kept Paul in prison because of cash. The other reason is this: it says that he wanted to favour the Jews. He was frightened of public opinion. I think that one of the greatest weaknesses of democracy as a system of government is that it pressurises politicians to consider public opinion. When they go in and out every four or five years, at least the last two years of their time of power is spent thinking of the next election and what is going to please public opinion, and what the opinion polls are saying. In those days they were not elected democratically but they still needed the goodwill of the people, and the political leaders were under this same pressure, "What are the public going to think? I must keep in with the public." So promises are made.

Here is a man under pressure from public opinion, who wants to keep in with the people, so he keeps an innocent man in jail. No wonder Felix had problems with his conscience. The other way in which it shows is in the fact that he kept sending for Paul, asking about Christianity, and as soon as he got to the last point in his sermon, packing him back into the cell. Felix loved to hear about Jesus but in two whole years he never became a Christian. Why? I'll tell you in a sentence: because he wouldn't listen to his conscience. He loved to hear Christian sermons, but when those sermons reached a personal level and spoke of changes that would be necessary in his life, and spoke of judgement to come for Felix, then he would send Paul back to his cell until another time.

Do you notice where Felix stopped listening? It was when Paul talked about three things: righteousness, self-control and the coming judgement. These are the three things that people do not want to hear about today. Faith in Jesus? Yes, that's lovely, that's good news, that's great. Go on, talk to us about Jesus. Let's have stage shows and films about Jesus. He's a superstar, let's all go and be entertained, but as long as those films, shows and songs keep off righteousness, self-control and judgement to come, we are interested. So we have a demand for religion without repentance, for God without goodness, for truth without tears, and that is the sort of Christianity that Felix was interested in.

Do you know why he listened to Paul? One of the early texts of the New Testament tells us, it just slips in this little phrase which is only in one or two manuscripts of Acts: "Felix sent frequently for Paul because Drusilla wanted to hear him." Let's look at this girl Drusilla sitting there by Felix's side – the governor's wife. Who is she? Well she is very young for one thing. Only twenty, and she has already been married twice. She is a princess and the daughter of the Herod who died of worms (in Acts 12). She is now Felix's third wife, and he has already got rid of two. The first one he married was the granddaughter of Antony and Cleopatra. The second was another royal princess and then he got rid of her. Then one day he met a king who had just married and his bride was a very attractive sixteen-year-old girl. Felix looked and said, "I'm going to have that girl." He went home and he got hold of a magician, believe it or not, who went and put that girl under a spell and took her away from the king and brought her to Caesarea. This girl of twenty is now sitting at the side of Felix. We are told it was she who wanted to hear Paul. Something was stirring in that young girl's heart. Something was saying, "I'm searching, I've been kicked around, I've been pushed around, I've been mistreated, but this man seems to have something to say to me." It was she who said, "Felix let's listen to this man," and frequently they did, but as soon as Paul got on to Felix's personal life, Felix wouldn't listen any more. How many proud husbands are in exactly the same boat? Their wives are interested and want to know, but what about the husband? Well he's interested in Christianity – but if it means *me*, if it means I am up for judgement, and if it means I have got to be righteous, that is a different thing. You see, righteousness is more than respectability. Husbands don't mind being respectable – but righteousness? It is saying this: you can't have faith in Jesus until you have faced up to the facts that you are not righteous, that you are not self-controlled, and that you are going to come to a Day of Judgement, and there is bound to be a day of reckoning.

That is the side of the gospel that is played down. I have seen a church's mission statement that only had in it that "God loves and God cares". That is not the gospel. The gospel includes righteousness, self-control and the Day of Judgement. Unless we preach on the God of judgement there is no point in the cross; unless the gospel is first bad news it cannot be good news. Unless you are to face people with God's absolute standards, there is no point in preaching forgiveness. There is no good news in telling someone, "I've found a doctor who can cure cancer" if that person does not believe they have cancer. This is the gospel that Paul preached—it's not just going out and telling people, "Believe in Jesus." *It is a gospel of holiness rather than happiness. It's a gospel of righteousness and self-control and judgment to come. That has got to be in the gospel or it isn't mission, and that's got to be there or people aren't going to get converted.*

Felix went a whole two years with Paul there in a cell, hearing him frequently, but he never became a Christian. He was interested in Jesus. Felix was left as a man with a guilty conscience who knew his life was not right, but would not listen to his conscience and face up to what it was saying. Therefore, he was a man who was not in a position to accept Christ.

Well now, which of these three men represents your position? Do you come as a person with a conscience that has been stifled until it's dead? That no longer warns as it should? Or do you come as a person with a clear conscience before God and men? Or do you come as a person with a guilty conscience, uneasy as soon as judgement is mentioned? Let me put it this way: supposing tonight your soul was required of you and you had to face your Maker, would you feel ready? That is what Paul is putting to Felix. Are you ready?

Look again at these three men. What about Tertullus? What was his future with a dead conscience? He would have a comparatively successful career. He would have a certain peace because when your conscience is dead you can be at peace. But one day Tertullus would be on trial himself. One day his conscience would be resurrected, whether in a trial on earth or not I do not know. One day Tertullus would have that whole dead conscience revived and have to face up to what he did with it for the sake of his career as a lawyer.

What is the prospect before Felix? Well I know this: that a man who has got an uneasy conscience will sooner or later make some bad decisions and wreck his career. That was exactly what happened to Felix. Just two years after this trial there was a riot in Caesarea and Felix was so ruthless in putting it down that he was dismissed from the governorship, had all his possessions confiscated, and became a wanderer on the face of the earth. His wife Drusilla and his son left him, going to live in a little village called Pompei where, in AD 79 they were buried in the flowing lava of Mount Vesuvius. Felix played around with his conscience too long, wrecked his career, and lost everything.

What about Paul? Paul standing there with a courage not born of brazenness or stubbornness but of innocence. Paul could stand there and know that he had nothing to fear from the truth. What was his prospect? One day he would stand before his Maker with the same courage. He was able to say, "My conscience is clear before God as well as before men." How did he get that way? How do you get a clear conscience? You will never get one by your own efforts. Some people try to get a clear conscience by forgetting what they have done and hoping that time will heal their conscience, but it doesn't. Some older folk know that memories of your sins can come back in later years, that you have forgotten about for twenty or thirty years, and they can come back with all their force. Then there are others who try to clear their conscience by saying, "Well everybody's doing it. So, we're all in the same boat and no-one is perfect." But that doesn't help you to have a clear conscience. What does?

Paul had made two discoveries that every true Christian has made. He had discovered what to do with his failures – that is the first thing. What do I do when I've done wrong? What do I do when I've gone against my conscience? What do I do with it? Do I live with it? Do I try and bury it? Do I try and forget it? The psychiatrist will tell you if you try to bury it you are really doing something very dangerous to yourself. You are going to repress something, and like digging couch grass into your garden it will come up worse than ever later. What do you do? Well, there's just one way of dealing with it and that is to go to the cross and to realise that because Jesus died on that cross and shed his blood, your sin can not only be forgiven but forgotten. God has promised to forget what is forgiven, and that means it need not be on your conscience any more. It will stay in your memory – one of the reasons you can't forgive yourself is that you can't forget. So you will never be able to forgive yourself. But what does it matter if it's on your memory if it's not in God's memory? Paul never forgot that he had persecuted the church of Christ and led Christians to death. He never forgot it, but it was not on his conscience – not now. It had been forgiven and forgotten by God, and all because of the cross.

That is why we remember the death of Jesus and we are so thrilled that he died for us. That is why we don't want to get away from the body and the blood. That is why it is at the heart of our gospel. For our gospel is not that Jesus lived a good life and if we try to do the same we'll leave the world a better place than we find it. Our gospel is that Jesus' body was broken and Jesus' blood was shed that we might stand before God with a clear conscience. We now know what to do with our failures, "If we confess our sins, he is just and can be trusted to forgive and cleanse us from every kind of wrong." That is good news. That is the first step to getting a clean conscience: to take a dirty one to the Lord. That is why baptism is so meaningful. That is why it is so expressive to have a washing from head to foot. We are told that baptism is not a cleansing of dirt from the body, but it is an appeal to God for a clear conscience. Baptism expresses that so simply and so superbly. But then, yes, we will sin again.

The second secret Paul had discovered was that the living Lord Jesus Christ will help you to reduce those failures. It is not just the forgiveness of the failures, it is the reduction of them that is the full gospel. It is not only a cross to forgive the past, it is a living Lord to deal with the future. So God has done everything that is needed to give you a clean conscience.

Paul was able to stand that day, not claiming to be a perfect saint, not claiming never to have sinned, but saying this: "My conscience is clear before God and men." He could say it because he had been to the cross and he knew the living Jesus. He could say it because not only had the past sins been forgiven, but the future ones were being reduced, and he looked forward to the day when they would go altogether and he pressed on to that.

If, as you read God's Word there is a stab of conscience about something, I beg you don't be disobedient to the heavenly vision. Don't go away and stifle it. Don't go away and bury it. Do something about it or you will finish up like Felix – interested in Christianity but no better.

Paul never got away from the cross, he knew that the secret of dealing with his conscience was not to try and be good but to let the life of Christ live in him. Jesus had a clear conscience. He could say, "Which of you convicts me of sin", and nobody could say a word. The privilege of the Christian is to stand before God and men with a clear conscience. Nobody else has that privilege.

29

Trial before Festus and Agrippa
Read Acts 25–26

Do you think you know what it is to take up a cross? For
Paul it was to go to prison for two years, at least in the part
of Acts that we are reading now. Can you imagine what it
would be like for a man like Paul to be confined to a prison
cell for that length of time? A man who walked all over the
world is pacing up and down a cell that was probably no
more than about ten feet square. Can you imagine what it
would be like for a man whose heart was bursting to tell the
world about Jesus?

So here is Paul, cooped up. Yet the amazing thing to me
is this: there are two years between chapters 24 and 25, yet
the Paul who speaks in those chapters is exactly the same
Paul. There is no bitterness, no turning in on himself, no
abject indulging in self-pity, but he is still bursting to give
his testimony. He is still more concerned about the welfare
of those who keep him in prison than about himself. What
a miracle! He was taking up his cross, and certainly he was
looking forward to a crown.

As we know, Felix blotted his copybook and was thrown
out of the governorship. When he went, he left Paul in that
cell. So when the new governor Festus came, he had a two-
year old problem on his hands. You can sympathise if you
have ever had that experience of taking over from somebody
else at the office. There was this pending file – Paul. No
doubt Festus would have read it through and was puzzled
by it and wondered what to do about it.

We know that Festus was an upright, honest man who

wanted to do what was right. He had an unblemished record in public service. Surely there would now be hope that Paul will get justice? I have no doubt that when Paul heard it was Festus who had come, his heart gave just a little leap! At last now he could get a fair trial, get out of that place and get on with his job. He wanted to take the gospel to Rome and to Spain. Paul had world ambitions for the gospel. But there were others who welcomed Festus too. The Jewish leaders saw their chance to get Paul out of prison in Caesarea and transferred to Jerusalem. On the way they could kill him. There was a plot.

So Festus found himself thrown right in at the deep end, into this horrible mess, confronted by Jews demanding a retrial of Paul back in Jerusalem. He realised that there was something fishy, and he said that Paul should remain in Caesarea and be tried before his court. If they wanted to charge him with anything, the Jewish accusers would have to come down to Caesarea.

Probably he thought they wouldn't bother, but when they came he realised they hated Paul. When he listened to their charges and then listened to Paul, it is like history repeating itself. Festus heard it through, as Felix had heard it through. Festus knew Paul was innocent. The new governor had reached the critical point in his own unblemished career. There was nothing against him up until this point and now it had come to this, was he going to stand by his conscience? Was he going to be a good man in this situation?

The tragedy is that at the crucial moment he began to wobble. The Jewish leaders knew that he was essentially a weak man and they knew they had got him.

He wobbled by seeking agreement with Paul. Would he be willing to do what they said and go back to Jerusalem? Would Paul do it for him, a new governor who wanted to keep everybody happy? He is asking the prisoner for a favour to save his own face, and he knows in his heart that is wrong. At this point Paul saw through Festus too, and realised that, good man though he was, when it came to the crunch he would save his own face.

Paul was in an impossible situation. He certainly would not get justice in Jerusalem. He now realised he wouldn't get it in Caesarea, so what was he to do? In his heart I think he would have prayed: "Now God, what do I do?" God told him what to do.

Paul was now given astonishing boldness. We might paraphrase something like this: Festus, I thought I was before a Roman court and I thought Roman courts gave justice. You know perfectly well what is the just thing to do in this situation, but I can see that I'm not going to get justice from you. I appeal to the emperor.

Every Roman citizen had the right to go to a higher court. Paul had been born one, which means that his father had been one before him, so he had the right to take his case to the very top court and, under the emperor himself, have his case heard. Do you know who was emperor at that time? A very fine young man who was doing a lot of good for the empire, who was being guided by elderly, wise statesmen, and who was already much loved of the people – a man called Nero. By the time Paul got to Rome however, Nero's wise elderly advisors would be dead. Nero would be turning in a totally different direction, and would become the evil monster we know now by that the name. But when Paul appealed to the emperor, Nero was behaving himself.

Paul was appealing for justice. Alas, Festus found himself eagerly seizing the easy way out of the situation. We can imagine him rubbing his hands and thinking: good, I can get rid of Paul and the Jews can't blame me for doing so because it is Roman law that has led him away. Paul would have been rather glad about the decision because he must have been thinking about going to Rome, where he wanted to take the gospel. The only people who were really cross about it were the Jewish leaders, heading back to Jerusalem in a rather disgruntled state.

We can think of Festus really feeling so relieved until suddenly it hit him: what on earth am I going to write to the emperor? A man who appealed to a higher court did so because he had been found guilty in a lower court, and this man had not been found guilty. He realises he is going to look awfully silly in the eyes of the emperor if he sends a prisoner and can't say what he's done wrong. Poor old Festus is out of the frying pan and into the fire. We must learn a profound lesson from Festus here: if you waver in your moral decisions because you want to keep popularity and favour with people, sooner or later you will find yourself in some very difficult situations not knowing what to say.

Festus was like so many political leaders who are under constant pressure to give the people what they want. Like many politicians before and since, he did what he thought the crowd would like. He wobbled at the crucial point. May God grant us political leaders who have a conscience and who will follow it when the crunch comes, regardless of popular opinion. He saw a way out of the dilemma because he looked in his diary and there was a state visit of King Agrippa who had been in the country for many years. Although Agrippa wasn't born a Jew he now said he was, and he was interested in the Jewish religion. There was the man to help! Festus would consult him during that state visit. Festus could ask the king for his opinion. Great idea! So King Agrippa came on his visit to the new governor.

What a family this was. Agrippa came from the blood-stained race of Herod. His great-grandfather was Herod the Great, the man who rebuilt the temple of Jerusalem and who slaughtered all those innocent babies because he couldn't bear the thought of a rival to his throne. The grandfather of this man was the Herod who mocked Jesus at his trial and said, "Perform some miracles for us." To his grandfather, Jesus had nothing to say. His father Herod had chopped off the head of James (the brother of John, one of Jesus' favourite three disciples) and was the one who had died of worms in front of the crowd in this very town of Caesarea.

So here was the great-grandson, Herod Agrippa. Like all his forbears, he got his throne by playing up to the Romans. They had installed him as a puppet king over part of the region. He brought with him a woman who was his sister and his mistress. She had already been the wife of his uncle. Later she was to become the mistress of the Roman emperor Titus, who destroyed Jerusalem. So Agrippa and his sister who incidentally was also a sister of Drusilla, the wife of Felix, were all tied up in it together, and there came the state visit to Festus.

Festus told them about his problem. Could Agrippa tell him what he could do with Paul? He had to write that letter to the emperor. Agrippa was fascinated. Jesus was the man whom his great-grandfather had tried to kill, whom his grandfather had met and despised, whom his father had also mentioned because his followers were such a nuisance, and Agrippa said, "I'd like to hear this man."

So one day, to the sound of trumpets and the rattle of drums, with all the pomp and ceremony of a petty little puppet king, Agrippa and Bernice came into the courtroom. The governor Festus entered, the leading civic leaders and the military leaders came in too. It was a great occasion and everybody was excited, and into the middle of the room, there came a little Jewish tent maker in chains. They all looked at Paul. They had no idea that but for that little man they would be forgotten; they had no idea they were writing history that day. Their only claim to fame is that they were present to hear that little man on that day. What a dramatic scene!

Agrippa said, "You can speak." Paul extended his hand and saluted the king, and said, "I'm glad to be able to tell you, King Agrippa, about my story." He didn't say that because Agrippa was a good man – he wasn't. But Agrippa did know more than Festus about Jewish religion, so Paul was glad to be able to explain, and he gave his testimony.

There were two things that Jesus promised in Matthew 10:18–19. In v. 18 Jesus promised his followers: you will be led before governors and kings. That promise was fulfilled this day. Matthew 10:19 tells us not to worry about what to say – the Holy Spirit will tell you. I am quite sure that Paul claimed those two promises at that moment.

Paul is not a man complaining about his lot, he is a man bursting with Jesus! Look at the opportunity: a governor, a king, the leaders of the city, the military officers, everybody. What was Paul going to say?

The fact that his testimony appears three times in Acts shows us that God must think it is extremely important. It is the only testimony in the New Testament that we have in such detail. I ask this question: what was the real change in Paul's life before and after he met Jesus? That is a good question to ask of yourself. Write it down honestly: what was the biggest change in your life after you met Jesus?

Look again at Paul. I do not discern that there was any change in Paul's temperament. I don't believe there is a change in temperament after you have met Jesus. Paul was a man with ambition and drive, single-mindedness; whatever he did, he went hard after it, and that was just as true before as after. So there was no change in his temperament nor will there be any change in your temperament. But I hope that you will find that the weaknesses of your temperament are overcome in the Holy Spirit and the strength of your temperament is brought out. God doesn't want robots; he doesn't want a computer. He wants people, and he has made us different, and I notice all the apostles had the same temperaments after they had met Jesus as they had before. It was simply dedicated and sanctified.

Nor do I think there was any great change about Paul's moral life. He wasn't a bad man before – as touching the law, blameless. He lived right, devoting his whole life to that. He had a very high standard of morality and he did his level best to live up to it, so that he didn't get up and say, "You know, I was a terrible chap before and I did dreadful things before, and now I'm living at this standard."

Nor again was it a *religious* change in Paul's life. He wasn't an atheist or an agnostic before. He had loved God before, or at least he thought he did. He had certainly wanted to devote his whole life to God. He was prepared to be a missionary for God. He was absolutely dedicated to God. He spent his whole life trying to keep the law of God.

So he didn't change his religion, he didn't change his God. He is claiming here that there was continuity. He just followed his religion through to its conclusion. He didn't change his belief in the resurrection. He believed in the resurrection of the dead before he became a Christian. He believed that Jesus had risen from the dead, but he didn't change his basic belief in resurrection of the dead.

Then what changed? As I read this testimony, something exciting hit me. The biggest change in Paul's life was this: from an exclusive religion to an inclusive religion. That is the change he talks about here. The religion he used to have cut him off from people. He was always shutting people out of it. It was a religion that got tighter and narrower. That is true of many forms of religion today. He had been worshipping the right God but in the wrong way. Therefore his religion was a shrinking religion. For one thing, he had no room for

Gentiles – no hope for them, they were seen as being beyond redemption. More than that, he had no room for many of his fellow Jews. He was a Pharisee who thought Pharisees were the only true Jews and the others were playing at it. As for these Christian Jews, he certainly had no room for them in his religion so he did everything he could to get rid of them. The tragedy was that he had no room for Jesus in his religion, that was what was wrong.

Take this as a very solemn warning from me in the name of the Lord Jesus: a religion that has no room for Jesus is no good. There is something terribly wrong with it.

Then one day he met Jesus. Paul, it is yourself you're hurting! In a vivid word picture, this proves to me this was the Lord Jesus speaking, because he used to pick little pictures from domestic life, and here is Jesus picking a picture out of agricultural life and speaking of Paul as one would of an animal who was kicking against the goads like an ox. When they used to plough in those days they used to have a pointed stick, and as long as the ox went along in the right way, it was alright, it didn't hurt itself, but if it got rebellious and lashed out with its back leg (as I have seen cows do – they have kicked me when I've been milking them, as they lash out with their back legs) then they only hurt themselves, because there was the pointed stick, the goad.

Jesus's message to Paul was that Paul's religion was hurting him. Paul was hurting himself. It's hard to kick against the goads. Paul had seen a Christian die. If you have seen a Christian die, you know that it is jolly hard to live with that if you are not a Christian. Saul, why are you kicking?

Paul had seen Stephen die with the face of an angel. He had seen Stephen die committing himself into the hands of the Lord Jesus. He had seen Stephen die with an inclusive religion that said, "Father, forgive them." That hurt because it was a prayer that Saul could not have prayed.

In his heart, Saul knew that his exclusive religion was wrong, and so he kicked. When he had looked out at people before, he had thought, "You're no good for my religion," and he wrote them off, but now he was going to see them as blind people whose eyes he could open; as bound people whom he could set free; as guilty people to whom he could bring the good news of forgiveness, and as alienated people to whom he could bring the good news that God had chosen them to be part of his family. Can you see the absolute transformation? How you look at people depends on whether you have met Jesus. Whether you write them off and say they are beyond redemption or whether you say, "God has sent me to help them," will depend on whether you have had an encounter with the Lord Jesus. This was the change, and so Paul not only had a heavenly vision of Jesus, but saw the world through Jesus' eyes. That is the vision that came to him.

Then comes the vital thing. When God gives you a vision, he is not necessarily telling you that this is what *must* happen, he is often saying this is what *may* happen. He is waiting for you to say, "I'll help you, Lord, to bring that vision to come to pass."

One can have visions. You can have a vision of your home town transformed by the Holy Spirit. You can have a vision of people crowding to hear about Jesus Christ. God shows you the vision, and waits for something. Paul gave Jesus what was needed to make that vision come about. Paul said, "I was not disobedient to the heavenly vision." When Isaiah saw the Lord high and lifted up, what was Isaiah's response? "Here am I, send me" – and the vision came to pass. Do you catch the vision? Do you see? Does God give you a picture of revival? Why doesn't it come? Maybe God is waiting for someone to say, "I'll be obedient to that vision; whatever time it takes, whatever it costs me or my family, if I have to meet with Christians every day to pray, I will not be disobedient to that vision." When somebody is not disobedient, then God can work wonders. Many ignore what Paul *did* to obey the vision: he told the Gentiles to repent (of their sins), turn to God (of Israel) and *prove their repentance by their deeds*.

So Paul was able to tell the governor and the king what he had been doing since he had seen the heavenly vision. He went out to Jews and Gentiles, small and great. He had gone everywhere, telling them that the Messiah has been and that he was raised from the dead and is alive, and that salvation is now available.

He didn't make faith cheap, superficial or shallow. He wanted to include everybody in it, but that didn't mean he went around telling everybody they were alright and that there was nothing they need do. He went around with a firm message: you must repent and show that you have repented by outward acts. You must believe in Jesus. Paul had gone to Jew and Gentile and had said: repent and believe.

I can see this scene in the courtroom in Caesarea, and Paul is in a pulpit now. I know it looks like a dock but a dock and a pulpit usually look much the same. Paul is preaching and he has a wonderful congregation, and he is getting very near the bone. He is saying: I'm offering you salvation, small and great. The governor, the king, the centurion at the door, Paul was preaching salvation to them.

Festus can't take any more and he says, "Paul, you're mad. You've gone off your head." Literally, in the Greek he says, "You've got mania." As soon as you get excited about the Lord, somebody will think you have got a mania. If you are prepared to wreck your career as Paul was, somebody will say, "You're mad." If you are on trial for your life and all you can think of doing is giving a testimony, then no wonder they will say, "You really are mad."

Festus was a practical Roman man of the world. He had been out of his depth for the last twenty minutes. He was telling Paul that he just had this religious bug. The Romans liked religion but they kept it strictly in its place, as most people do. It's all right to go once on Sunday. That is rational. It is British, it is Roman. But really you've got it bad Paul. Festus represents those people for whom talk of an encounter with a person two thousand years dead is madness. Talk of heavenly visions is seen as madness. So Festus thought it was religious mania but Paul said that he was not mad but speaking words of truth and reason. Paul was never more sober than that moment. He realised that he would get nowhere with Festus, so he turned to Agrippa and said, "King Agrippa do you believe the prophets? I know you do believe." What Paul had been proclaiming had not been done in a corner.

Poor Agrippa, every eye is on him. Is he going to get converted? Is the prisoner going to lead the king to Christ? They are all watching with bated breath and Agrippa looks around and laughs it off. I know that there are many commentators who say that his words were spoken sincerely: "You've almost persuaded me to be a Christian." But I am afraid that is neither true to the Greek nor to Agrippa, nor to what happened afterwards. Agrippa's words were spoken sarcastically. Did Paul think that in a short period like that, one sermon, he could make Agrippa a Christian? There are people today who say: no, it's not as simple as that, life is more complicated. They hear a testimony about Christ and they say, "No you're not going to convert me. Life's much too complex. It's not as simple as you're making out." They laugh it off and say, "No, you can't make me a Christian as quickly as that." Paul, with the last sentence, realising that his time had gone, that he couldn't say any more than one more, came out with the most moving and sincere statement:

"I would to God that every one of you could be just what I am except these chains." In other words, my total concern is for you. What a man! What a love he must have had. What a passion for souls. Knowing that it looked as if he was going to go on in those chains for maybe another two years, perhaps longer, he nevertheless uttered those words.

Festus got up, Agrippa got up, they all got up; they walked out and left Paul standing there with the centurion. We can think of Festus and Agrippa shaking their heads as Agrippa said, "This man might have been set free if he had not appealed to Caesar." They didn't say, "Let's set him free." They could have done. They knew he had done nothing to deserve death or chains.

They pitied Paul, but the pitiable ones were Festus and Agrippa. What happened to them? Nothing. Festus hung on without another event of excitement or importance happening in his governorship. Two years later, he was dead.

What happened to Agrippa? Same thing—the Romans retired him from kingship and he spent the following years digging his back garden somewhere in Israel, doing absolutely nothing, and in the year AD 100, Agrippa also died, the last of that bloodstained family of Herod.

What do I deduce from that? When someone comes near to becoming a Christian and hears the gospel, and thinks it is either madness or misguided enthusiasm and does nothing about it, then frankly the rest of his life is quite meaningless in God's sight and that person will just die.

But that is not the end of the matter. One day Festus and Agrippa will come out of their graves – the Bible says that everybody, good or bad, will. Festus and Agrippa will stand before the Lord Jesus Christ. He will say, "Festus, is this madness?" He will say, "Agrippa, is this misguided enthusiasm? You had your opportunity to believe in me and now it is too late. Here is my servant Paul. He has not got chains now. He has got a crown."

30

Voyage to Rome, Shipwreck on Malta
Read Acts 27:1–28:10

"How do we know that the Bible is true?" I am often asked this question, especially by people who don't want it to be true. The proof we need is two-fold. First we must have a reliable record of what happened, and that record must have been passed down to us intact so it has not been altered or embellished over the centuries. The second thing we need to be sure of is that the person who first wrote down the record was in a position to know what happened, and indeed was an honest and reliable person.

How do we know that the events recorded in Acts 27 happened? Firstly, do we have a reliable copy today of what was originally written? I am thankful that this question is settled. We have many copies of the ancient documents of the New Testament. But that takes us back only to the original record that was written. How do we know that that is true? Well the answer lies in this: check everything you can check in the record, and if everything that can be checked proves to be accurate, that gives you tremendous confidence that the writer was stating the truth. You can't check it all but at least you can check many of the facts. Now in this chapter 27, there are three kinds of fact we can check today.

The first kind of fact is *geographical*. There are descriptions of islands, ports and other places, quicksands and harbours. The fascinating thing is that you can actually take Acts 27 and a modern map of the eastern Mediterranean and check the details, charting the voyage in every particular. So accurate is the account that they have been able to identify the very bay on Malta, now called St. Paul's Bay, where they swam ashore. They did it by the sandbar at the mouth of the bay as described in Acts 27. Now at one of the two islands at the mouth of that bay there stands a big statue of St Paul. Geographically, every detail in Acts 27 stands up to checking.

A second kind of fact that we can check is *nautical*. This is a wonderful record of sea travel, and if you are a sailor or interested in ships, you will find some fascinating details in this account. But are they true? Do they fit? For example, were there ships that could hold 276 people? How were they steered? How were they navigated? What was done in a storm? We now have many records of sailing in the Mediterranean. We know from drawings what the ships were like. We know, for example, about great grain ships which went from Alexandria in Egypt to Rome, taking from the granary of the empire, the Nile Delta, grain to feed the population of the capital. We know that these ships were 130 feet long, 30 feet wide, and 30 feet draught, and that they could embark as many as 500 people. We know, too, that they were not steered with a rudder but by two oars, either side of the hull. Luke mentions those in Acts 27. He gives us a perfect description of what the crew did when they found themselves in a storm, how they coped with it, even to the description of a dinghy being towed along behind. If you go to the British Museum and look at some of the ancient carvings of sea scenes, you can see this.

So we can check the nautical facts. I tell you now that every detail Luke records in Acts 27 is absolutely accurate to the nautical knowledge we have of those days. But there is something even more interesting and that is the *meteorological* facts he records. The meteorology of this chapter is fascinating. Luke gives a very careful description of the time of year. He gives us the exact date: October 5th.

He tells us what the prevailing winds were. He tells us how the ship drifted at 1.5 miles an hour for 14 days and where it landed. The amazing thing is that if you take a yacht into the eastern Mediterranean today, you can use Acts 27 to tell you what the winds are going to be at that time of year and where you will be going. It is a perfect description and can still be used by a sailor to make the same voyage if he wishes to risk his life. The description of the Northeasters and the Westerlies and the soft south wind all happen, to this very day. Now in the light of the fact that geographical details are absolutely correct, that the nautical details are accurate, that the meteorological details are so good that you can use them to navigate a ship even now, I am prepared to accept the rest on trust. I am prepared to go along with Abraham Lincoln who said, "Accept as much of the Bible as you can on the basis of reason, take the rest on faith and you'll live and die a happy man." Chapter after chapter of the Bible is opening up to this kind of examination: if God is truth, then he doesn't mind us submitting the Bible to checking, because it will hold up under such examination. Check everything that can be checked by archeology, by meteorology, by geography, you study the books.[1] Read Adolf Keller's book *The Bible as History* and see just how much has been checked by archeologists. You can't prove that the events took place but the reliability of the record stands. If someone says, "I can't believe this, it's full of myth and legend," then he can only say it by refusing the facts and refusing to be open-minded.

Now let us approach the truth of this chapter because it isn't written to give us a geography lesson. It isn't written to teach us how to sail a ship in a storm. It isn't written so that we might study the weather and give us British people something more to talk about! It is given as part of the Word of God. Therefore, the primary truth is personal. It is truth about people, it is truth about God, and it is truth about certain men of God and these are the three truths that we want to get out of this chapter.

What does this tell us about people? It tells us a lot because under the stress and strain of danger, human beings reveal their real feelings and attitudes. In such circumstances, human nature is laid bare and you see what stuff we are made of – and we see superstition, panic and obstinacy. In this account we are shown something of the character of God and what he does, because when people cry out to God and are in touch with him in a crisis, then he reveals himself as he is. We shall see some lovely things about God.

But I think the focus of this chapter is on a man of God. What happens to a man of God in a crisis? His attitude and bearing in this situation is so different from the other people. I have divided it into four parts, entitled: *sailing*; *storm-tossed*; *shipwrecked*; *safe*. In each one I am going to draw a contrast between the man of God and the others. Then we are going to consider God as God.

SAILING

Paul is in custody, he has appealed to the emperor, he has got to be shipped to Rome, and he is put in the care of a very fine officer who belongs to the emperor's own regiment as it was called in those days. It is his job to take prisoners from the far corners of the empire back to Rome for trial before the emperor. If a prisoner escapes, he, the soldier on guard, will have to stand in for the prisoner and will be punished with the exact punishment that was due to the prisoner. A responsible job!

A very kindly and considerate man he is, who immediately respects Paul for what he is and gives him considerable liberty in the ports where they call, allowing Paul to go and see his friends. The first stage of the journey is very ordinary. They take a coastal vessel from Caesarea to Sidon. It manages to cut across on the leeward side of Cyprus because the easterly winds are blowing. The ship manages to make the coast of Asia (now Turkey) then creeps along the coast.

Then they reach a large harbour, and from the little coastal vessel the officer transfers the prisoners to a very large grain ship, full of wheat from Egypt, trying to make Rome before winter sets in. Between mid-September and mid-November, sailing in the eastern Mediterranean is very difficult. After early November it is impossible. We are told that they reached this main harbour by 5th October. Right in the middle of the dangerous period, when the wind is veering around but steadily becoming more and more the dreaded Northeaster, which prevails through the winter in the eastern Mediterranean.

Paul is an experienced sailor. He has been shipwrecked three times and has had the experience of being adrift in the open sea for a whole night and a day. They call him in and hold a council, "Should we go?" You notice that Paul says no. He is not speaking by revelation but by experience and intuition. It is a human message. Everything in him says, "No, don't go. If you go you will lose the ship, lose the cargo, lose life." Paul cried out against this voyage and he shared his concern with the owner, the captain, and the officer in charge. He knew what he was talking about. Why did they not take any notice of him? Well I suppose they could have said, "You are not a member of the crew." But there was one profound reason why they ignored Paul: money. It is a sad fact that once people have got their hands on potential profit they are very reluctant to let that go. Here were men who valued the cargo more than the crew. Here were men who knew that if they didn't get this cargo to Rome, a lot of it could go bad, it could get wet and rot. They could lose the whole lot and so the captain was influenced by the owner of the ship. Here you have a situation in which caution is opposed to vested interest. Human safety is in one scale, and in the other pan of the scale is profit, and it was decided to go.

Paul had a concern for human life and every Christian should have that. When human life is being treated as expendable, Christians have to speak out. There are many situations in our day in which this is happening. Paul spoke out and warned about the loss of life and cargo. He was virtually saying: if you sail, you will be murderers. But the captain listened to the owner and the officer listened to the captain. They sailed, setting off in the big cargo vessel, and it managed to go a little way along the coast but could then go no further against the wind. So they decided to try and get around the leeward side of Crete and they came south, round that island. They just managed to make a little harbour at the eastern end of Crete – Fair Havens – where they held up for a number of weeks.

It was a bad harbour to winter in, and the water was getting into the grain and rotting it. They wanted to get to a safer harbour to save the grain. Again, you notice, the grain! They decided to leave Fair Havens and try to cross a big bay to the south of Crete, making for a harbour called Phoenix where they would be sheltered for the winter. At this point, a soft south wind began to blow, which they thought could take them northwest across the bay. I want to say a word of warning here to those who seek guidance, and that means all of us: when we want to do a thing, we will seize on the slightest favourable circumstances as proof that we ought to do it, thinking it is God's guidance, and we may be utterly wrong. A little breeze from the south and they thought they ought to go because it favoured their plans.

They set off and were halfway across the bay when the Northeaster came. If you trace the line of that Northeaster and draw the line from Crete, it goes straight for the Syrtis Sands off the coast of Libya.

STORM-TOSSED

So we come to the second part of this account. For fourteen days that great lumbering cargo ship, which couldn't be kept head into the wind, wallowed around, drifting sideways, tossed around, making about a mile and a half every hour. Those onboard were so seasick they couldn't eat.

Can you see the scene? The steps they took to counter the storm were all good sailors' routine. First: run before the wind in a ship that size. If you can't keep the head into the wind, let her go. Second: get the dinghy aboard. They had to wait some days to do that. They got in the shelter of an island, passing it. They couldn't get to the island but they did manage to get the dinghy aboard – Luke said with difficulty, remembering his own blisters no doubt, and they got the dinghy up on deck. Then they drifted on again. Thirdly: take great ropes and loop them over the bow and back under the ship, then tie them across the top in a knot. Then take a great piece of wood and wind the rope round, tightening it because in a storm like that and a big, long cargo ship, it was twisting. The timbers were springing open and always the thing to do is to tie ropes round and round the ship, winding them tighter and tighter so that the timbers are held together. So they tried that. Fourth: they lowered the sail, which had by now become just a complication, causing them to be blown in all directions. Fifth: they threw their cargo overboard. What the owner must have felt at this point! At least he realised now it was his life at stake. Sixth: they jettisoned all the spare equipment (and ships carried a duplicate of every important part of the ship). But no matter what the crew did, they could not save themselves.

They realised after fourteen days that there was no hope and the ship was breaking up underneath them. Despair set in. That is the human reaction in a situation like this, when you have done everything you can. What does the man of

God do? When man has done everything he can, that is just the point at which God can step in. It is the point now at which God steps in. Paul said his prayers on that fourteenth night and God sent him a personal message. There was an angel in the boat with him. The angel assured him that it was going to be alright. God wanted Paul in Rome and he was going to get there. There is some lovely news, "For your sake, God is going to give you every life on this ship." What a message to have to take to them! Can you imagine? Paul couldn't resist saying, "I told you so." Do you notice that it began like that? He called them all together and he said, "Now you should have listened to me." He wasn't just getting a kick out of being right when all the others were wrong. He was saying that if only they had listened, he would have given them the truth. Now they should have seen that he knew what he was talking about.

Paul told them to take heart. There would be no loss of life, only of the ship. He could tell them that the God he worshipped had granted him all who sailed with him. I sometimes wonder how many people in this world have been saved from death because they have been with a Christian. I believe there are many situations in which unbelievers, though they don't know it, have been safe because God had a servant of his nearby. That does not mean that the way to avoid accidents is to take a Christian with you wherever you go. I will come back to the problems and the questions this raises, and the fact that Christians have been killed in car crashes and in plane crashes. But where God speaks, you are safe. I think of John Hunt again, that Lincolnshire ploughboy who went as the first missionary to Fiji and Tonga. After the long voyage with all its hazards, the ship arrived within sight of Fiji and was caught on the coral reef outside the bay and wrecked. The ship was breaking up and John Hunt prayed: "Oh God, you didn't bring me all this way to let me drown." When he opened his eyes, bearing down on them was a gigantic tidal wave that seemed to be coming to drown them, but instead it picked up what remained of the ship and carried it one whole mile, and it set it down upright on the shore before retreating. John Hunt and everybody on board climbed onto the sand. God wanted him in Fiji. All the coral reefs in the world can't stop God's will being done. What a contrast between men of despair and men of God.

SHIPWRECKED

The sailors knew they were getting near land. Maybe it was sailors' instinct or the colour of the sea, or maybe they could hear breakers. They threw a leadline, took soundings and the water was getting shallower. It was dark and they did a very wise thing throwing out four sea anchors, which would go down below the shifting waves and hold the ship, slowly drifting, until dawn. Then Paul saw panic. Panic does extraordinary things. Have you ever been in a situation where people have panicked? Have you ever seen how selfish people can get? It can happen when there is a crowd and there is danger. Panic produces selfishness. The sailors knew there was only one dinghy, they were near land, the ship was going to break up. They wanted to get the dinghy overboard and get out while they could. So they lowered the dinghy, pretending they were going to put an anchor at the bows. But they weren't. They were off, and Paul saw it. Paul warned that unless those men stayed on board the ship, others could not be saved. The soldiers cut the ropes and the dinghy floated off.

Why did Paul do that? Where a group of people have been spoken to by God, any of those people who act as if it is not true put the whole group in jeopardy. This is an important principle, which I want to apply to the church. If God speaks to a fellowship and assures them of something, it would only require a few people in the fellowship to undo that word, to wreck the fellowship by not believing God and not acting together on God's word. It is a dangerous situation when a few think they know better than God. Had those sailors got into that dinghy, they were dead men and so were their compatriots and companions onboard.

If God has assured us we are all safe, then we must trust him, not try to save ourselves. The panic of those crew members had led to an utter concern for themselves at the cost of leaving everybody else. Against that panic there is the man of God who is only concerned about others. Look at what he does now. He encourages them to eat some food. Isn't that practical? I love it when I read of the saints who are practical. So he organised a meal in the middle of the night. He did say grace for them, and he made sure that they realised it was because of the goodness of God that they were going to have that meal. They needed food for energy because they were going into the water.

Then when daylight came they saw the bay which you can now see in Malta, a lovely little bay with a beach and a horseshoe-shaped cove, which has two islands guarding the entrance. They were just outside it and the sailors still believed they could save the ship, and they said, "If we put the sail at the bows, the Northeaster will take us straight in," and God had said, "The ship will be lost." Who was going to be right? They did not know that there was a sandbar, which is there to this day, across the mouth. The bow stuck in it, the stern was battered by the waves and the ship broke up. At that point there was great danger from the soldiers panicking and killing the prisoners. So the officer at this stage came to the rescue of Paul, ordering those soldiers who could do so to swim for the shore. That dawn, in the rain, wind and cold, you could look into that bay and see the heads of people who were clinging to planks and bits of barrel, spars and anything that floats, and so they all came ashore.

When God speaks, what he predicts will come true to the last letter. That is why the Bible is such a wonderful book about the future. For God has revealed so many things in the Bible about what is going to happen in our human race. When God says he will save people and get them safely to shore, they can absolutely rely on that – he will bring them to the haven.

SAFE

Cold in the wind and rain, you could see them all huddled on the beach in their wet clothes, miserable – safe, yes, but not yet happy. The natives on the island are friendly, building a bonfire for them. Here again is Paul, the great man of God who has saved the whole ship and brought them through, because a man who is led by God is fit to lead others – having led them all to safety, you might have thought that he could say: "Now you build a fire for me and get me warm as a reward for saving you." No – what is Paul doing? Gathering firewood! Isn't that great? The man of God, the preacher, the greatest missionary perhaps there has ever been, gathering firewood. That is Christianity! Then comes the moment where he suddenly pulls his hand back and there's a viper hanging from his hand. It was among the brushwood he had been collecting. There are no poisonous snakes in Malta today, they have got rid of them, but there were snakes in the biblical days and there it was, fastened on his hand. How superstitious people can be! They immediately jumped to two wrong conclusions. The first was that they believed *fate* must be fastening on to this man Paul, and that he must be a murderer – after all, he had chains on. Had he escaped? And had "fate" overtaken him? The Bible never says there is such a thing as fate or luck or chance, and I hope you never use those words. They watched Paul to see if he would swell up or die, but he shook the snake off into the fire.

Jesus had said of disciples that they would take up snakes and come to no harm. That doesn't mean we are to tempt the Lord our God, as some American worshippers do, bringing rattlesnakes to church with them and handing them around the congregation. I have spoken to a missionary who was bitten by a poisonous snake, and who said, "God, I believe you still have more work for me to do in this place and I claim that promise." God kept his word in that missionary's life when there was no help or serum available. He claimed that promise and God kept his word.

Paul shook the snake off. Then they said, "He is a god." Human superstition! What crazy ideas superstition leads you to – they changed from thinking of Paul as a murderer to being a god! The real truth was he was an ordinary man with an extraordinary God. Those hands that could shake off a snake could also ward off sickness. Publius, the chief of the island, gave them hospitality, and they had no money. They had thrown their cargo overboard. They only had the wet clothes they stood up in. How could they ever repay?

But God blesses those who help Jesus' brethren, disciples, like Paul in this case. Jesus said, "Inasmuch as you have done it to the least of these my *brethren...*" (so often mistakenly taken as meaning whatever you do for your *neighbour*). Blessings certainly followed in Malta. Publius, who had given the welcome, had a father sick with a very common disease in Malta – fever, dysentery due to a microbe in the goat's milk there. Paul laid his hands on the sick man. He was healed, and soon all the sick people in the island were there. How they must have blessed God for that shipwreck! Paul left an island of healthy people.

When they continue on their way to Rome they take gifts from the islanders, and there is goodwill and love left behind. It is a lovely finish, a happy ending.

What does this tell us about God? It tells us firstly about his *knowledge*, that he knows every detail. Imagine it – the God who put the stars in the sky, by which the ancient mariners navigated, knew what was happening on one tiny ship in the middle of the Mediterranean. He knows. You need never fear that God is surprised by what happens.

Secondly, it speaks to me of his *power*. God had that situation under control. One commentator said that it was nothing less than a miracle that, of the whole Mediterranean, they got into that bay. God's power has the situation completely under control.

How do I apply Acts 27 to myself? Can I claim on the grounds of this chapter that a Christian is always utterly safe from danger and disaster? It would be wonderful if I could. It would make Christian faith the best insurance policy there is, but I can't claim that. A few years ago I heard of two people, two great Christians. One was a friend of mine, a minister in this country, and he was due to fly from Edinburgh to London. As he prayed that morning, God said, "Go by train," so he did, even though he had already bought his air ticket. That plane crashed at Heathrow. At about the same time I heard of Fred Mitchell of the China Inland Mission, leaving the Far East to come home on furlough, and taking off from India in a Comet plane that exploded shortly after leaving the airport. It is a mystery, isn't it? Why? I do not believe that the Christian faith offers us a guarantee of safety in all danger. Is there any principle? Is there some guideline here? There is: If you are in the centre of God's will and God has promised that he will get you somewhere, then you can claim his safety.

Note

[1] The two most exciting and convincing volumes I have read are: *A Test of Time – Pharaohs and Kings* and *Legend – the Genesis of Civilisation* by David Rohl, a non-Christian Egyptologist in London University who has confirmed the historical accuracy of the Old Testament.

31

House Arrest in Rome
Read Acts 28:11–30

This passage is very quiet by comparison with what had just taken place but I have found great benefit in studying this last chapter. There are no shipwrecks, no miracles, nothing sensational, nothing spectacular, but God is in this and it is a word of encouragement to those who may not see many spectacular or sensational things.

It is an account of someone who is confined to one house, yet though the messenger is confined, the message ripples out and reaches a variety of people, from runaway slaves to imperial staff. There are readers who have to spend their lives in constricted circumstances, and for some that can be in a bedroom. Never mind – God is in the ordinary and he can speak to anyone, anywhere.

We can divide this into: *the way to Rome* and *the witness in Rome*. Under these two headings, I want you to notice under each of them three unusual features. First of all, we take the *way to Rome*. We left Paul on Malta, healing people. I have no doubt he preached to them as well, though that is not mentioned, and he spent three months there waiting for the winter to end and the spring westerly winds to blow. By the middle of February they were ready to sail, and they did, on a granary ship called, "The Castor and Pollux," or "The Heavenly Twins." Many sailors are superstitious and this is the first point of interest I want you to notice.

When I began my ministry in the Shetland Islands, I found that many seafarers lived very close to superstition. When you are battling with powers greater than yourself and go down to the sea in ships and do your business in great waters, there is a sense of being at the mercy of the elements. Some sailors I met were so superstitious they would not take a pig or a parson on board when they sailed. I know why the pig is regarded as an unclean animal, but I could never figure out the other! There were mascots, omens, and though they navigate by the stars some also looked into the stars for their fortunes.

Castor and Pollux were two of those stars, the "heavenly twins" particularly appealed to by those shipwrecked sailors in Acts. These mariners were in for a good voyage, not because they had a Castor and Pollux figurehead on the bows but because they had Paul in the bunks of that ship, and God was with Paul. Somebody has said that Christianity is the only religion in the world which believes in a God who promises to live within his people. That is an astonishing truth if you just let it sink in. With Paul on board they had his guard on board, and that was all they needed because God had said to Paul, "You will witness for me in Rome." To my mind this probably explains the second unusual feature of this part of the story – the favourable weather. They covered 180 nautical miles in less than two days. If you chart this on a map, the wind always seemed to be just right. It was wrong for a week while Paul stayed with the Christians in Syracuse, and then it was just right the day he sailed. God was going to get Paul to Rome, and we believe in a God who controls the weather, who has everything in the hollow of his hand. But what strikes me most in this journey to Rome is this: the widespread presence of Christians. Here is Paul who is usually accustomed to going to places where he is the first Christian they have seen. Yet now, as he sails up the western coast of Italy, everywhere he goes there are already Christians and it is only thirty years since Jesus died on the cross. Remember that they had no transport faster than a horse. Remember that they had no mass media, no printed word, no radio, no television, and already there are Christians everywhere in that ancient world. It is quite remarkable but as soon as the ship puts in at the Bay of Naples, the first thing Paul did was to find believers.

There were already believers in Rome. Paul had written to them three years earlier in his letter to the Romans. What an encouragement! I have had this encouragement now on a much wider geographical scale than Paul ever experienced. Everywhere I have been, I have found believers. Maybe just a handful, maybe just one, but what an encouragement it is to know that God has planted his witnesses all over the world, to the uttermost parts of the earth. Wherever you go, if you look for them, you will find brothers and sisters you have never met but within five minutes you feel you've got everything in common with them, and you have.

So Paul took courage. What a hero's welcome he got. When it says that Paul took courage, I think it means, reading between the lines, that he had been a little bit down. Why should he be? He is achieving a lifelong ambition and so came to Rome. But look how he was coming – chained, walking between Roman soldiers through the Pontine Marshes towards the capital of the then known world.

What picked him up? The fact that Christians walked forty-three miles to meet him. Some of them only managed thirty-three, I've checked this on a map. Some of them got as far as Appia which was thirty-three miles, but some of them got to the Three Inns which was forty-three. Think of it—what a welcome for this little man in chains. I don't think any Roman emperor ever had such a welcome from that city as this great missionary had that morning.

I remember one Easter Sunday morning when it was my privilege to walk along the Appian Way. The very stones from Paul's day were still there, and I was walking all alone. Sun shining, those tall cypress trees by the road, and the ancient tombs of the Romans were on either side. As I walked, I thought: what was Paul thinking as his feet trod these stones? What was passing through his mind and heart as he came within sight of this magnificent city on seven hills? There was one text that went through my mind: "I am not ashamed...." —of what? Chains? Coming as a prisoner; being laughed at by the people who saw him—no, "I am not ashamed of the gospel." Why? Because it is power, and he was coming to the centre of an empire whose "god" was military power. The armour of Rome's soldiers glinted in the sunlight. The size of its buildings and walls spoke to the world of power, but Paul said, "I'm not ashamed of the gospel." Little did he know that within the foreseeable future the Roman emperor himself would bow the knee to Jesus Christ.

So Paul came to Rome. It's all in that little phrase: "so we came to Rome." The gospel came to the capital of Europe. We still benefit from that coming of the gospel to the West.

Let us look at what happened in Rome. In England we have only two ways of dealing with those who have been charged with a crime between that moment and their trial, we either remand them in custody or we release them on bail. Now the Romans had a kind of compromise between those two, a combination. They could be released in custody and that is what happened to Paul. He was chained to a Roman soldier but allowed to go and live in his own rented accommodation. So in a sense he was free and in another sense he was not.

He was not free to go to people but he was free to have people come to him, as would not have been true in jail. Here, within these limited circumstances, Paul saw not a handicap but an opportunity. It is marvellous through the book of Acts how the things we would count as handicaps and disasters turn out for the furtherance of the gospel. That is the Christian way to look at things. In Acts 8, for example, when the church is scattered abroad through persecution, how did the Christians regard that, having lost their homes and possessions and roots? They went everywhere gossiping the word, we are told. They regarded it as an export of the entire church—what an outlook!

So when Paul found himself chained to a centurion, he didn't sit down and have a good old moan and indulge in that awful sin of self-pity which is one of the more common sins that afflicts the human heart. Instead, he saw it as an opportunity. I wouldn't give anything for the chances of that soldier remaining an unbeliever – chained to this missionary! We know that through those centuries the Word of God got into Caesar's household. But if Paul couldn't get to people, he could issue invitations to come to him. Has that ever occurred to you? If you find yourself housebound, does that mean your testimony stops? Does that mean you can't work for the Lord? Nothing of the kind.

I remember hearing of a dear old lady who lived in Cambridge who led as many people to Christ as anyone I know, and she never left the house. How did she do it? Asked for her secret, she said, "A cup of tea and an hour's prayer beforehand, that's all." If you can't go to people, then invite them to come to you. Share your table; share your Sunday lunch. Have them come to you if you can. You can't go to Africa or China maybe, but you can invite a person to come and have a meal with you or come and see you. It took Paul three days to get his strategy settled. Just three days to get settled in, and then he was off. He invited the Jewish leaders to come to him.

Why did he invite the Jews? There are many reasons. First of all he was beginning with those he understood best, those who were like himself, of his own background, and that is a good principle of evangelism. Secondly, he was starting with those who already believed in some way in God, and we have seen in these studies that everywhere Paul went he made straight for those who had some kind of a faith in God, the god-fearers, so that he could build on what they already had—that is strategy. He also called the Jewish leaders because he needed to know how he stood with them in Rome and whether they would testify against him at his trial. So he called them to explain why he was there as a prisoner.

But there is a fourth and fundamental reason why Paul went to the Jew first: that this was God's pattern. Paul was indebted to all men, but to the Jew first and then to the others. For God in his wisdom (and if you question this wisdom, you must question God not anyone else) chose the Jew first, to speak to first, to bless first, to share his grace with first. That is what Paul did whenever he found them. This is a priority that Christians should have. I hope you pray for the Jews and have a burden for them. They are God's first choice, God's first people.

So he explained to them the circumstances of his arrival. He explained to them his trial, claiming innocence from any political charge. He pointed out that he was there purely on a religious issue. In fact, he was there for one reason and one only: that whereas the Jews of the world hope for things in the future, Paul believed those hopes had already come true in the past. That was the only difference.

So the first thing I want you to notice about the witness in Rome was the eager apostle. Paul was not saying: "Well I'm going to retire now and leave the younger folk to get on with witnessing. I'm more confined now. I'm on the shelf now and I'm going to sit and watch." Not a bit of it! Paul knew that there is no discharge in this war, and that even though he was confined, he could still go on witnessing.

I recall the testimony of a woman who spoke of months

in hospital, flat on her back, before the Lord healed her later. But she said, "What a wonderful opportunity I had to witness to the Lord, because when people came to see me they were so sorry for me that they couldn't get away from me. They had to listen. While they ate my grapes, I told them about Jesus Christ."

She couldn't travel but she had people come to her. It doesn't matter what your circumstances are, if you are as keen on spreading the gospel as Paul was, you will find a way to do it. The messenger may be bound, but the message is not bound.

The second thing I want you to notice and this is very serious, is the *active word*. Whenever the Word of God is being preached, three things will happen. They don't happen when the politician speaks or when the scientist speaks or when the teacher in the classroom speaks, but when the Word of God is being preached, for the Word of God is living and active. It has power in itself; it is sharper than any two-edged sword. The Roman soldier had different kinds of sword for different kinds of battle but one sword was broad and short, shaped exactly like a tongue. Swung by two hands from side to side, one man could keep many at bay, for it could cut flesh and bone, piercing to the marrow. That's why the Bible so often likens the tongue to a sword – a sword in the mouth. But it is two-edged, it cuts both ways. The Word of God is living and active, sharper than any two-edged sword. There are three kinds of cut it makes. Paul, as he talked to these Jewish leaders about the kingdom of God, about their own scriptures, the Law and the Prophets, about Jesus, everything pointing up to Jesus, he saw three things happen and every preacher sees them happen.

The first thing that the Word of God does because it is active is to cut a congregation in two. There will be those who believe it and who are saying, "That's true and I accept it and I'm going to live by it," and those who say, "I don't believe it, I reject it. I argue against it."

Paul saw his audience in that crowded room with the centurion and the Jewish leaders packed in—he saw the sword of God's Word cut between believers and unbelievers.

The second cut that the Word of God makes is between the believer and his sin. It is a glorious cut. It is the healing of a surgeon's knife, cutting out the cancer of sin that is going to bring us to death unless it is dealt with. It is something that happens to those who believe, and the Word of God separates the sinner from his sin so that he is free for God.

There is a third cut to which Paul now refers, a very serious cut which we don't like to think of, and that's why when we translate the words of Isaiah that refer to it we get all puzzled by it and we twist the translation. The third cut is this: to those who do not believe the Bible, the Word of God, the sword of the Spirit, the sharp edge, cuts the unbeliever off from God. Now that is an extraordinary truth but it is written right through the Bible. We cannot ignore or deny the fact that if you hear the Word of God and reject it, you cannot remain in the same condition in which you were before. You are worse off than you were before, you are further from God if you are not nearer. You can't go on listening to sermons and remain the same.

I have seen this happen over and over again. People have come, they have been interested. They have listened and said, "Well, yes there seems to be quite a lot there." Then they come to the point where they realise there is a fork in the road. Some of them accept and believe, and you see that the sword of God's Word cuts them from their sins and sets them free. But others who do not believe cannot go on coming because they become harder and harder and harder, they become blinder and blinder, they become more and more deaf, and the prophet Isaiah said that. Time and again when

I have heard Isaiah 6 read in the pulpit, people have stopped at the wrong point. Preachers have read those magnificent words, "In the year that King Uzziah died I saw the Lord high and lifted up and his train filled the temple." Going right through that experience of personal conviction, "Woe is me for I am undone," and then the cleansing, the purging, the burning away that left (I believe) a scar on Isaiah's lips for life; a burning coal can't touch your lips without something being there but it purged his sin. Then God said, "Who will go for us?" Isaiah said, "Here am I. Send me." That's where preachers stop, that's where readings stop, but listen to what God said. He said, "Go tell this people...." What? He had to go and tell them a word that was going to blind their eyes and stop their ears, "...lest they should turn to me," says God.

Isaiah trembled before that mission and said, "Lord, how long have I got to preach that way?" He said, "Until the cities are desolate." You see, every preacher knows that when he preaches the Word of God some are going to believe, and those who will believe, the sword of God's Word will separate them from their sins, but some are not going to believe – and those who are not going to believe, the preacher is pushing further from God and they will be more deaf and more blind and less able to see and less able to hear, yet God sends us to preach.

As Paul preached that day, he saw this happen. The Lord Jesus saw it happen when he preached. You will find it in Matthew 12; you find it in Mark 4; you find it in Luke 9. You find it in John 12. Jesus himself quotes Isaiah. Now Paul does the same as he does in Romans 11. Now Paul quotes Isaiah 6:9, 10. Preaching the Word of God was driving some further from God.

The greatest tragedy of the last two thousand years has been that the hardest people to win for Jesus have been Jews. Why? Because having received so much of the Word of God and refusing it, it blinded them and deafened them even more.

I tremble for some people who listen Sunday after Sunday to the Word of God. If you do not believe, what is the Word doing to you? So we must remember that those who refuse God's Word are not left neutral, not left in the same condition so that a year later they can come back and listen. Something has happened – they become calloused, harder, more difficult to persuade.

Finally, notice the unhindered gospel. What happens when people refuse the gospel when God gives them a chance at being saved, when he offers them a place in heaven forever and they refuse it? Does God take the gospel and put it into the cupboard unused? No, God will give it to someone else.

One of the loveliest parables that Jesus ever told was the parable of the king's banquet. He sent invitations to people and said, "Come to my banquet, everything's ready." Somebody said, "Well I can't come up. I've just got married." Somebody else said, "Well I'm tied up in business. I'd love to come but...." Seats were left empty. Do you think the king would leave them empty? Never! Jesus said, "The king said to his servants, "Go out to the highways and byways. Get hold of anybody. My house shall be full." That is one of my favourite texts, "My house shall be full." If you don't accept the gospel, God will give it to someone else.

Sometimes the most surprising people will come and take it. Jesus spoke to the religious leaders brought up from their youth, right in religion, in the worship of God. He said, "You'll see publicans and prostitutes sitting down in the kingdom and yourselves thrust out." I have seen that happen. I have seen good churchgoing people, brought up in Sunday School, living a decent life, but who have never known the Saviour. I have seen God take away their place in church, even their office in church, and give it to those who have no such background but come thankfully and receive the grace of God.

So Paul was declaring to the Jews what God was going to do. The gospel of salvation they were saying no to was going to the Gentiles.

The gospel has come to the Gentiles. What a solemn thought it is that if I don't take my place in heaven that is offered me in Christ, somebody else will have it. One thing you can be quite sure of – heaven is going to be crammed full. There won't be an empty seat at the King's banquet in his kingdom, but your seat might be taken by someone else. That is what Jesus said.

So Paul stayed for two years. That was the maximum time he could be kept in custody without trial. Two years was the period that they could keep a man chained to a soldier. Clearly, his accusers wouldn't come from Jerusalem. Clearly, there was no trial to hold. Clearly, Paul had to sit kicking his heels in that house for that period, but what happened?

I don't know of a single miracle happening in that time. Maybe they did, maybe they didn't. I know that a runaway slave came. I know that Paul took the chained hand and wrote letters to Christians: Colossae, Philippi; and I know that the message went out. Paul preached the gospel it says with freedom, without any hindrance.

The last word in this book is "freedom". I think of Martin Niemoller, Hitler's personal prisoner put into concentration camp in solitary confinement because he preached the truth about God and about men. There he was, shut off in his cell, but there was a little grating high up in that room, and outside that grating was a little yard, and round that yard the prisoners were walked, three yards apart, having their exercise. Through that grating every day Martin Niemoller would shout a text as each pair of footsteps passed by. The Word of God is not bound.

So for two years the gospel was unhindered, and the message of Acts is this: "Nothing can stop the gospel." That is why it has been preached all over the world. That is why no matter what laws men may make, no matter what prisons they may throw preachers into, no matter what barriers and discouragements they may put in the way of believers, nothing can stop the gospel.

So we come to the end of the book of Acts. But why does Acts finish here? It is called the Acts of the Apostles, but what about all the other apostles? What about John? Why didn't Luke go on recording what they did? Why did he not go on to Paul's trial and probable release, his further travels and his further arrest, imprisonment and death?

Some say that Luke perhaps died or went away at this point and was unable to go on keeping his diary. Some people say that his object was accomplished. He had set out as he tells us at the beginning of his two volumes, at the beginning of the Gospel of Luke, to convince an intelligent Roman that Rome had nothing to fear from Christianity. You can see how all that he has said about Paul in these latter years has underlined that the Romans had no quarrel with Christians.

Some have said that there is a sense in which Acts is an unfinished book and could never be rounded off. But I believe the book of Acts stops here because God didn't want any more to be written. Of all the two thousand years of church history, the first thirty years are to be our standard, our model, the norm by which we judge our own church life. We have got enough in this, the Acts of the Apostles, to tell us what kind of mission God wants us to exercise, so I believe God stopped it here.

I meet some Christians who talk about the Puritans with bated breath as if only we could get back to the Puritan era and Puritan preaching that would somehow recover what we have lost. Others talk about the Methodist Revival and John

Wesley's great movement that spread through England like a prairie fire, and others go back to the Reformation, but God wants us to be a church like this. While there have been great eras in the story of the gospel spreading through the world through the last two thousand years, the first generation of Christians were nearer to what God wants *us* to be and to do than I believe any other has ever been, so we go back.

The theme of the book of Acts is now complete. What is it? It is: How they brought the good news from Jerusalem to Rome.

What is the significance of that? It is how they brought the good news of Jesus from the *religious* capital of the world to the *secular* capital of the world. That is what God wants us to do with the gospel. He wants us to take it from the religious centre, from the spiritual centre, from God's people, and he wants us to take it all the way to Rome, to the centre of secular life.

He doesn't just want the gospel preached among God's people, he wants it taken to the very centre of the communities of people around us.

So we came to Rome....

CONCLUSION

This study of Acts left certain burdens that are very much on my heart, because studying the Bible is not just an academic thing that we do, then leave and say, "Well, we've done that book." It is God speaking, and God's Word needs not only to be heard, it needs to be obeyed. It is what we do about what we hear that is going to count in the last analysis.

I want to look back over the whole of Acts and draw from it some of the lessons I can on the theme of mission, evangelism, outreach, fishing for people. These words of Peter pinpoint my burden: "I will give you what I have." Of course, you cannot give anybody what you don't have, but what you do have you can't keep to yourself.

We have woken up to the fact that England is not a Christian country – if it ever really was. We are in a missionary situation and the vast majority of our fellow countrymen do not know Christ and are heading for hell.

Thinking about this some decades ago, I estimated that only some 1.5% of the population knew and loved Christ as Saviour and Lord, which meant that 98.5% were lost. So we have heard in the years since then many calls to "mission". What is mission? What are we going out to do? Who is lost and who needs saving? We have to wrestle with these questions. Churches have woken up to the fact that they are not geared to mission. For a long time we have been geared to maintaining the *status quo* in our churches. We have been geared to "keeping things going" in dwindling congregations.

We have been studying Acts to try to learn more about mission, to ask, "What's it all about? What are we sent to do? What is this mission that God wants us to complete so that one day we can stand before him and say, 'Lord, mission accomplished'"?

Acts covers the first thirty years of Christianity. That was the period in which God set the pattern for the church for all ages until the Lord Jesus Christ returns. It is to that period that we look to learn about mission. I am going to offer some of the thoughts that have been running through my mind as I have studied the whole of Acts. Then I must ask four devastating questions, for the Lord has told me to do so.

The first thing I noticed was this: *God uses people to do his purpose. There is not a single thing in the book of Acts that God does without people*. He wants us to co-operate; he wants us to be his co-workers, the channels of his blessing. So he uses individuals. They are not great, outstanding people in education or background, just ordinary people he uses, and that is exciting. You could not have a greater contrast than Peter and Paul – a rough fisherman and a university-educated lawyer, but they dominate the book of Acts and show you the range of people that God can use. You are not a person whom God cannot use; *everybody* could be used by God.

Second, not only does God use individuals, but he uses individuals who are not *individualists*. Do you know the difference? An individual is a person; an individual*ist* is a person who wants to act alone. We have all met those who work best as a committee of one. But in the book of Acts they do not act as individualists. Individuals, yes—Peter, Paul, Stephen, Philip – outstanding people in God's grace, yet they all always act as part of a team, a family. They often go out in twos. They are sent out by the fellowship; they are welcomed back by the fellowship. It is always the community of love reaching out through its members, a lovely combination of the individual and the family co-operating together to do God's will.

But the question that was in my mind was this: what had they got? What was the secret behind their evangelism? Because, judged by any standard, this first thirty years was the most successful period the church has ever seen in proportion to its numbers. They started with eleven men; then there was a prayer meeting of 120, then with the first public preaching: 3,000; a few months later, 5,000 men which meant that the church was already over ten thousand people, counting the women and young people.

Not only did they grow numerically, they grew socially. From slaves and beggars to governors and a Chancellor of the Exchequer. Not only numerically and socially, but geographically. Within that single generation they had jumped into two new continents — Europe and Africa. What did they have that we don't have? For it is patently obvious that we are not up to their standards of mission. As I pondered that question, the Lord gave me a most surprising answer. He said, "You've got the question the wrong way round. You should start by asking, 'What did they *not* have that we have?'" As soon as I asked that, light dawned. They didn't have money. "Silver and gold have I none" – they had to make that confession. So the size of the collection was not a factor in their mission, nor is it a factor in ours. They didn't have any buildings. If we rely on a building to do our work, it will never be done. They had no denominational headquarters. They had no think tank, no group up at the top organising the strategy. They were completely lacking in the kind of facilities we seem to think are necessary to modern church life. They had no schools, no hospitals and they were remarkably free of philanthropic organisations.

In fact, the more I read, the more I am convinced they

were free from the things that make us trust in ourselves, and that the first secret of their successful mission was that they lacked the things that make us self-sufficient. Therefore, they were driven back to God. Lacking human resources, they were thrown back on divine, and therefore they were richer than we are. That's the first thing that hit me square between the eyes.

Then I went deeper into it and asked, "Is there something in their method of evangelism that provides the secret? How did they set about winning people for Christ?" Again, I noticed sharp contrast to the way in which we approach the task. For example, I notice that they made straight for adults rather than children, on the very sound principle that if you get the parents, you will get the children. It does not follow, alas, as we have discovered in this country, that if you get the children you will get the adults. It doesn't even follow that you will keep the children.

They went for men rather than women. Again, it is easier to win women for Christ than men, but it does not follow that if you win the wife you will get the husband. However, if you win the husband, the head of the home and the family, then look at what will follow. Look what happens when a Philippian jailor is converted. Here was a strategy from which we could learn: our top priority, I believe, is to win men for Jesus Christ.

Then I looked at their strategy a little more deeply and I saw that they did not cheapen the gospel. They did not say, "All you've got to do is accept Jesus." They preached a full gospel. They included repentance from sin, which is a vital part of the offer of Jesus Christ.

It did include believing in Jesus, but that was a deep, personal trust not just a mental assent to certain doctrinal statements.

They said, "Be baptised in water." The idea that that was

an optional extra never occurred to them. It was part of the Great Commission. They went on to say, "Be filled with the Spirit." They went on to guide the converts into church fellowships under elders. The idea of leading someone to Christ and not integrating them into a church would not have occurred to them. So they preached a full gospel. Was this their secret?

Then I looked at something else. Here, I began to feel very challenged myself. I realised that one of the secrets of their success was that they reached people through two of their senses and not just one. We have, as you know, five senses: sight, hearing, taste, touch, smell. *From the very beginning, the gospel could be seen as well as heard.* Have you noticed how often those two verbs come together?

On the very day of Pentecost, Peter said, "He poured out this which you now see and hear..." (Acts 2:33b). Later, when he was on trial for what he had done for a lame beggar in the temple, as he stood in the dock, he said, "For we cannot but speak the things we have seen and heard." So if we just preach the gospel to people's ears, that is only half an apostolic gospel.

Paul again and again says that when he came, he did so with speech – trembling speech, yes, weakness and fear – and yet, there was a *demonstration*. The word he uses means a "visible demonstration of power". Here are the two great avenues into a person's soul: what he *hears* and what he *sees*. The apostles used both. People not only *heard* the gospel of Jesus Christ, they *saw* things happen which have no human explanation. I believe here is one of the deepest of their secrets. We are getting very near to the heart of the reason for their success. The gospel came in signs as well as word. Jesus had promised that it would. He told them to go and preach the gospel to every creature, and he promised to be with them. The result was, as we read, that they went everywhere preaching the Word, the Lord working with them, confirming that Word with signs following. They not only heard, they saw. When people can see as well as hear the gospel they are going to sit up and take notice – they cannot help but do so. You can't ignore things which happen that have no human explanation.

Why did those things happen? What did these Christians have? Why were they able to *do* as well as to speak? Was it that they had a strategy? Was it that they were specially organised? No, it was what I am going to call "overspill evangelism". These were not people digging down into their souls and scraping the bottom of the barrel for some little word to pass on to other people because they felt a compelling duty to go out and witness! These were people who were bursting! They were spilling over. They didn't sit down and ask, "How can we start mission?" These were people who couldn't stop it. It's the difference between *organised* and *organic* evangelism.

People meet to discuss mission, to train for mission, to prepare for mission. They are given techniques and strategy and tactics – but something needs to happen that will cause an *overspill*. When do you spill over? The answer is: when you are full up. If you are only a half-full Christian, evangelism is a duty – sheer drudgery. Though you may plug away at it with dogged loyalty, God isn't going to use or bless that. The evangelism of the New Testament was not a group of Christians saying, "We have got to evangelise. How can we do it?" It was a group of Christians who were so full they spilled over. If you are full to the brim, it just needs a little movement for you to spill over, and that is what was happening.

Let me look at these early Christians and say two things about them, which seem to me to get right to the point. Number one: they were all born again Christians because there is no other sort, but I want to say it because many of us who call ourselves "Christians" may not have been born again. To put it another way, this was the first generation of the Christian church, therefore it was made up of first generation Christians. Oh what a joy it is to meet a first generation Christian! Again, there's really no such thing as a second generation Christian. That is the snare and the danger. God has no grandsons, he only has sons, but what I mean by it is this: I suffer, as maybe you do, from having been brought up in a Christian home. Don't misunderstand me. I thank God for all the blessings that that now brings to me, for all that I was saved from – by the standards I was given, by the pressures of family opinion, and all the rest, but there are profound dangers in being brought up in a Christian home, two in particular.

Firstly, at that point where you become a teenager and want to be yourself and want to strike out and be an adult and make your own decisions, the awful danger is that you will identify that independence with freedom from your parents' faith. Many have done that, but the other danger is more subtle. This is, secondly, not that you will react against your parents' faith, but that you will submit to it without being born again – those of us who have been brought up in church and brought up in Sunday school, second and third generation. I am about a seventeenth generation Christian.

Those of us who have had all that can lack the fire and the enthusiasm of discovering Christ for ourselves. We can lack that deep sense of grace that comes to those who have known what the far country is like; who have known what despair is like; who have been right away from God. So I am writing now to second and third and fourth generation Christians, and say that we will never be able to mission, to evangelise as the early church did, until we become first generation Christians and discover Christ as Saviour and

Lord for ourselves.

Now I have said the first thing about the early Christians was that they were all born again Christians; they all had the degree of "B.A."! That's the degree that every Christian needs, the qualification before they can set out on mission. But there was a second thing about these Christians: not only were they all born again, they were all Spirit-filled. There are other sorts of Christian. One day I took my Bible and I read the book of Acts and I deliberately missed out chapter two. I started at 1:1 and I just read on to the end of chapter 1, then skipped a couple of pages and read on from 3:1. You know, it just didn't make sense. But how many of us are trying to have the rest of Acts without chapter two?

You notice that it comes not at the *end* of their mission as some reward for service, but at the beginning. That is when they needed it, and it was this that explained what happened. These people were full of God's Spirit and therefore they over-spilled. Their evangelism was spontaneous, nobody organised it. They went wherever they were scattered, they preached the Word.

When Christians are full to overflowing, you don't hear of any conferences on evangelism, you don't hear of any committees meeting for strategy. You don't even hear of training conferences. What you hear of is a burst of life that is reaching out in love and burning fire. Wind and fire came in Acts 2, and those are nature's two most destructive elements. They are the two most powerful things we know in nature. They produce fear, but these early Christians were "blown" and "burning". Here we have discovered the secret. Just think if we hadn't got Acts 2!

One of the most challenging comments I have heard is this: "If God withdrew his Holy Spirit from our churches, 95% of what we do could carry on as usual." If you forget everything else in this book, remember that. You could still have your refreshments, you could still have your talks on all kinds of subjects to the men and the ladies. We could still have services, and I daresay you could be kept entertained for an hour. We could still have the choir practice. So much could go on, but do you know that the only things that happen in your church that will last for eternity are the things that God does?

The only things that really constitute mission are the things that the power of the Holy Spirit does. This is the message of Acts.

As I look at the early church, a group of Christians that had far fewer things than we have, how much simpler was their love for the Lord? They didn't have a television to watch and an interesting programme just at the time of the prayer meeting. They didn't have cars to wash on Saturday morning. They didn't have Yorkshire pudding in the oven on Sunday. They gave themselves to the Lord; they got their priorities right.

I am coming now to four questions which the book of Acts has left me with. I don't know how you feel after studying Acts; some people feel very depressed – they feel that the gap between the early church and our churches today is so wide that they say, "We'll never make it."

Many times I have told the parable of the pessimistic plumber, and it is so appropriate. A plumber was sitting in his fireside chair one morning looking down in the mouth and reading the papers. His wife said, "Why don't you go to work?"

He said, "I'm too depressed."

"Why? What's the matter?"

"Well, look. In the papers it says that last night sharp frost means that there are 10,000 burst pipes in the London area alone. I just can't face it."

But his wife pulled him up out of the chair, put his coat on

him, pushed him out of the door said, "Off you go to work."
He came back at lunchtime, smiling, happy and whistling.

"What's got into you then?"

He said, "Now there are only 9,998 burst pipes in London!"

Though the gap is great between the book of Acts and ourselves, it is not unbridgeable. The thing to do is not to get depressed about that gap. Nor is the thing to do to criticise churches or Christians and tell them how far they are from what they ought to be. That doesn't do anything either. The thing is to get up, roll your sleeves up and take the first steps.

Other people read the book of Acts and get over-excited and this is the opposite extreme. They want to drop everything and rush out, shouting "Hallelujah!" straightaway. They are looking for an instant revival in these days when we have instant everything else. Is there any such thing? I have read accounts of many revivals and I don't think any of them was instant.

I feel neither depressed nor over-excited when I read Acts, I feel deeply challenged by four basic questions, and I want to leave them with you.

QUESTION 1

Do you honestly believe that these things of which we read in the book of Acts can happen today?

I come across two sorts of unbelief. One says that miracles never happen at all and you can explain away all the things in the Bible in terms of coincidence and natural events. That is the unbeliever's attitude to miracles and the power of God, but I meet a more subtle kind of unbelief among Christians and it is this: miracles happen within the covers of the Bible but not today. That is an unbelief that is due to one simple thing: the fact that you accept the power of God with your head, but not with your heart.

We say, "The apostles have died." Yes, but we say, "We now have the scripture. Does that mean we don't need the Spirit?" A world that doesn't read the Bible has got to see something else. So do you believe that these things can happen today? The simple truth is they *are* happening today to those who believe. We hear a lot of such things happening in some other countries. But in our sophisticated, materialist society, do we believe? That is the first challenge and question. Is the God of Peter and Paul my God too?

QUESTION 2

The next question Acts has left me with is an even more disturbing one: Do you want these things to happen today? All right, you believe in your heart, that they *can*, do you *want* them to? The honest answer, for many, is: "No, we'd rather not, thank you." For to live in the "Acts of the Apostles" was a very disturbing experience. Things happened that were unexpected. Church members dropped dead after the collection. Great fear came on them all. Do you want these things to happen today?

I'm not sure that I do – because it is going to disturb. It means that the church is no longer under the control of a trusted pastor. It is under the control of the Holy Spirit who can do anything. You will never quite know what he is going to do. It is always good, but you are constantly surprised. Do I want these things to happen today, with all my heart? Would I love to see God moving in and moving out? Because it is going to shake an established church to its roots; it is like new wine in old wineskins, and it will crack. Well, Lord, all right. I'll try to want it. I don't want to play safe; I want to see you working.

QUESTION 3

Are you prepared to meet the cost of these things?

Revival is not cheap, it is costly in terms of sacrifice and suffering. Revival is *so* costly – you will have to let your pet sins go as soon as revival comes. Are you prepared for the cost? Let's just think in terms of one thing only among many – *time*. How much time does it cost to have revival? You look back to the revivals that have come when the power of God has been poured out. You will find Christians who meet daily for prayer. Here is a letter from someone who went to India:

It's now 9:30 p.m., Sunday. The day's work is ended. We were around 700 gathered this morning, a good cross-section of Indian society – young and old, rich and poor. About twelve young people were baptised, that started the morning off. From then, the service ran through from 9:30 am to 1:30 p.m. About 600, including children, stayed for the midday love feast, which is customary here – plenty of opportunity for fellowship. Then the young men and young women had separate classes. Later, the former went with the older men for open-air witness before the evening service at 6.30 p.m. A full and happy day, praise the Lord. Tomorrow, a public holiday and so the church is going out, about 130 of them, brothers and sisters, for evangelism in a distant suburb of Madras. It is wonderful to see them using their holidays like this. They come back rejoicing.

In the UK we get grumbles if a service goes over an hour and a quarter. When a public holiday comes, seaside is the first thought. Am I prepared for the cost of revival? The cost in terms of time, giving God the priority, not what I can spare, not what's left over after I've done everything I want? Or will I turn up if I have nothing else to do, or there's nothing else interesting to do or see, or not if I want to work overtime to get a bit more money. Does God have first call? Am I prepared to meet the cost?

QUESTION 4

Do you really feel we need these things today? Can't we do without them?

The sad answer is that a lot of our activities could, but in God's sight the need is desperate, for when we stand before our Lord, he will not ask us how many meetings we held nor how big the congregation or the collection was. The barometer of a church is always its prayer meetings. For the quantity and quality of prayer reveals how needy that church feels. If the prayer is poor, then the church is saying louder than words: "We don't need God's help. Thank you, we can manage very well on our own." But a church that sees in the light of eternity what divine power does among us will last. That church will be a church that will pray and pray and pray until God sends the blessing – until people are full to overflowing and the Holy Spirit is moving in power amongst them.

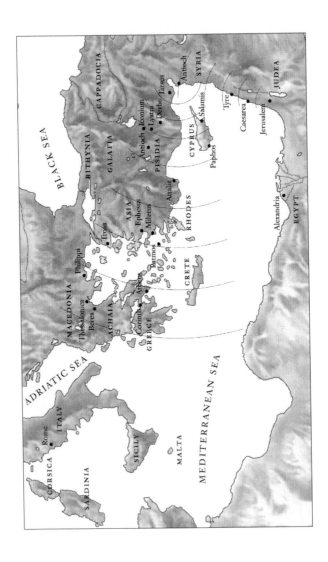

Map reprinted by permission of HarperCollins Publishers Ltd ©2003